THE
STOMACH
& DIGESTIVE
SYSTEM

THE
STOMACH
& DIGESTIVE
SYSTEM

Reader's Digest

The Reader's Digest Association Limited
London New York Sydney Montreal

The Stomach and Digestive System

was created and produced by
Carroll & Brown Limited
20 Lonsdale Road
London NW6 6RD
for Reader's Digest, London

ISBN 0 276 42482 4

Reproduced by Colourscan, Singapore
Printed and bound by Printer Industria
Gráfica S. A., Barcelona

We are committed to both the quality of our
products and the service we provide to our
customers. We value your comments, so please
feel free to contact us on 08705 11336, or via
our Web site at www.readersdigest.co.uk
If you have any comments about the content
of our books, you can contact us at:
gbeditorial@readersdigest.co.uk

The information in this book is for
reference only; it is not intended as a
substitute for a doctor's diagnosis and
care. The editors urge anyone with
continuing medical problems or
symptoms to consult a doctor.

Managing editor
Nikki Sims

Managing art editor
Justina Leitão

Editors
Jane de Burgh, Janet Mohun

Art editors
Sandra Brooke, Gilda Pacitti, Vimit Punater

Design assistant
Shahid Mahmood

Series medical consultant
Dr Douglas Carnall, MRCGP, MB ChB, Associate Editor *BMJ* and GP, London

Gastroenterology specialist consultant
Dr Elspeth M Alstead, MD, FRCP, Digestive Diseases Research Centre,
St Bartholomews, London

CONTRIBUTORS
Dr Elspeth M Alstead

Dr Saul Berkowitz, MRCP, Department of Gastroenterology, Whittington Hospital, London

Dr Harriet Gordon, MB BS, MRCP, MD, Department of Gastroenterology,
Whittington Hospital, London

Delilah Hassanally, MSc, MB BS, FRCS, Department of Surgery,
Whittington Hospital, London

Fiona Hunter, BSc, Dip, Dietitian

Joel Levy, BSc, MA, Medical Writer

Dr Geoff Smith, BSc, MB BS, MRCP, Digestive Diseases Research Centre,
St. Bartholomews, London

Karan Thomas, BSc, Physical Activity and Health Specialist

Dr Voi Shim Wong, BSc, MB, ChB, MRCP, MD, Department of Gastroenterology,
Whittington Hospital, London

For Reader's Digest
Series Editor Christine Noble
Art Editor Julie Bennett
Editorial Assistant Caroline Boucher
Reader's Digest General Books
Editorial Director Cortina Butler
Art Director Nick Clark

The Stomach and Digestive System

Awareness of health issues and expectations of medicine are greater today than ever before. A long and healthy life has come to be looked on as not so much a matter of luck but as almost a right. However, as our knowledge of health and the causes of disease has grown, it has become increasingly clear that health is something that we can all influence, for better or worse, through choices we make in our lives. *Your Body Your Health* is designed to help you make the right choices to make the most of your health potential. Each volume in the series focuses on a different physiological system of the body, explaining what it does and how it works. There is a wealth of advice and health tips on diet, exercise and lifestyle factors, as well as the health checks you can expect throughout life. You will find out what can go wrong and what can be done about it, and learn from people's real-life experiences of diagnosis and treatment. Finally, there is a detailed A to Z index of the major conditions which can affect the system. The series builds into a complete user's manual for the care and maintenance of the entire body.

In this volume we look at the pipeline and refinery behind your body's energy supply – the stomach and digestive system. Explore why the proper functioning of the digestive system is at the very centre of your everyday health and well-being. Discover the amazing subtleties of your ability to taste, the role performed by the vast numbers of hungry bacteria lining your digestive tract and the astonishing strength of the hydrochloric acid bath otherwise known as your stomach. Why does an aperitif seem to stimulate the appetite, while smoking suppresses it? Learn what you can do to safeguard your finely tuned digestive system, why fibre has such profound effects on the functioning and efficiency of the gut and which are the superfoods that can give you a real appetite for life. We meet the digestive system experts and reveal how they find out what is wrong, from physical examinations to sophisticated imaging techniques, as well as the wide range of treatments available, from drug therapy to advanced 'keyhole' surgery.

Contents

3

What happens when things go wrong

The life story of the stomach

Developing a relationship with your internal organs is difficult. It's hard to feel personally involved with your liver or warm towards your kidneys. Your digestive system, however, can seem almost human: it can gurgle contentedly, rumble plaintively or churn angrily. The emotional nature of the system is celebrated by common terms like 'gut feelings', 'butterflies in the stomach' or simply 'gutted'.

Writers and psychologists alike refer to the basic passions like fear, anger and joy as visceral emotions, meaning literally, the 'emotions of the gut'. But how did we get so personal about what is essentially an 8 metre (26 foot) long tube running from the mouth to the anus, encompassing the stomach and the small and large intestines on the way? What is so special about the digestive system?

GUT INSTINCT

First and foremost, hunger is one of the fundamental human drives. The urge to eat is hard-wired into the brain, and overrides more intellectual concerns with ease. In fact the spheres of the brain that generate feelings of hunger and appetite are closely linked to the areas responsible for thirst, sex drive and the impulse to violence or terror

(the fight-or-flight response). This means that the functioning of the digestive system is bound up with a number of primitive desires and drives.

Secondly, the production, preparation and consumption of food are a central feature of all human cultures. Quite apart from the sensual enjoyment we gain from a delicious meal, the rituals that surround the act have far-reaching social consequences, not least for family bonding and other personal relationships. In other words, the operation of your digestive system has a significance that reaches far beyond the purely biological.

Furthermore, the biological properties of the digestive system are so remarkable that it is a lot more special than you probably imagine. In the complex collaborative process of your body the digestive system is both supply pipeline and refinery. It channels raw material (food) from

Millions of glands in your stomach produce highly corrosive hydrochloric acid that is so powerful it can burn skin and dissolve razor blades.

the source (the mouth) through a series of stages of intense processing as fierce as any chemical factory (in the stomach and upper parts of the small intestine) and then extracts the nutrition with an efficiency unparalleled by human engineering (in the small intestine), leaving only waste that is neatly packaged for disposal (in the large intestine) and piped away.

INSTRUMENTS OF MASS DIGESTION

Each step in this vital process involves amazing biological tools. In your stomach, for instance, millions of glands produce highly corrosive hydrochloric acid, which is 1600 times more acidic than vinegar. Strong stuff, but your digestive system can handle it. The stomach lining is shielded by a layer of mucus secreted by cells in its wall and when the stomach contents reach your small intestine they are bathed in a flood of bicarbonate, which neutralises the otherwise lethal acid.

Also inhabiting your digestive fluids are billions of enzymes – special molecules produced by your cells, that act like tiny machines. These nanoscale biomachines go to work on the molecules that make up food – for instance, the starch in a potato or the protein in an egg – chopping them up into smaller bits. Scientists are envious of the amazing processing power of your body's enzymes, and occasionally use their secrets in factory and laboratory processes. Many biological washing powders, for instance, use enzymes to 'eat' the dirt off clothes.

Many of these bacteria are deadly killers if they stray from their usual homes. In your large intestine, for example, the most common bacterial resident is *Escherichia coli*, certain strains of which are the bane of

Digesting the dirt
The amazing abilities of your digestive enzymes, such as the pepsin shown left in crystallised form, are mimicked in biological washing detergents in order to break down dirt.

unhygienic food establishments and people with reduced resistance to infection. Not all bacteria deserve such bad reputations, many of the species living throughout your digestive system have a vital role to play, undertaking some digestive tasks that your own body cannot perform.

TUBE JOURNEY

It should already be obvious that there is a great deal more to your guts than a rumbling stomach or painful trapped wind. Your digestive tract is part of an extensive and convoluted system that includes the structures of the mouth and accessory organs such as the liver and pancreas. How did so much tissue get packed into your body?

The story begins in the womb where just three weeks after conception the tiny embryo has already organised itself into a number of distinct tissue layers. One of these is known as endoderm, and the tissues and organs that

BITES OF PASSAGE

As you journey through life, your nutritional needs will change and develop with you. From your specially formulated first feed through to the complex flavours and textures we enjoy as adults, food is the vital ingredient that can promote a healthy and lasting appetite for life.

NEWBORN

Keeping it in the family
In the womb, babies have sterile guts. At birth, bacteria (right) that they pick up from their mothers colonise their intestines.

arise from this layer will form the digestive system. Along the front of the embryo, the endoderm curls into a tube – the embryonic gut – on either side of which two cavities appear. These grow and join up to give the abdominal space in which your intestines will sit. Meanwhile the primitive gut is suspended between the front and back of the embryo by two sheets of tissue called mesenteries.

By week 6, two pockets of tissue have grown off the sides of the digestive tube and embedded themselves in the mesenteries. These will become the liver and pancreas. Simultaneously, the tube itself is getting longer, outgrowing the tiny space inside the embryo as it turns into intestine. It pushes out into the stalk of what will become the umbilical cord, coiling as it does so. Next to the liver the tube has expanded to form the stomach. By week 10, the

stomach, liver and pancreas are all in position and the coiled intestines start to move back into the body of what is now called the fetus. The digestive tract stretches all the way from the mouth to the anus of the fetus and can now begin to function in a rudimentary fashion.

In week 11, tiny movements start to pulse along the small intestine. Just over halfway through pregnancy, the baby starts to swallow amniotic fluid from the womb – up to 500ml (18floz) daily – and process it through the developing digestive system. The nutritional value of the fluid is negligible, but experts think that simply going through the motions of digestion helps to stimulate the further development of the system. Therefore, although the baby's main source of nutrition in the womb is via the umbilical cord, when the time comes for the baby to be

The energy of youth
Kids need a high-energy diet with proportionally less fibre, so eating starchy white bread instead of wholemeal is actually often better for them.

Keep your gut in good shape
The efficient functioning of your intestines are directly linked with your overall well-being.

ADULT

TEENAGE

Healthy habits for life
Teenagers have little time to devote to food preparation but it is vital they adopt a healthy diet to give them the energy they need and to protect them from problems in adult life.

A ripe old age
Looking after your body does not mean cutting out the enjoyment of food. Older adults need far less food than they did, but should aim to eat more fibre.

born, the digestive system is prepared to receive food via the mouth. Indeed, the newborn's stomach and intestines already contain the necessary acid and enzymes.

MOTHER'S MILK

As mammals, human babies feed on milk for the first few months of life. Ideally, the milk comes from the mother, but this is where human culture starts to get involved with biology. Different cultural groups have widely differing rules about how long a baby nurses at the breast, when to introduce solid meals and, of course, the type of food given as the child grows into adulthood. Interestingly, cultural practices may have actually caused genetic changes in some populations around the world. Caucasians traditionally consume large amounts of dairy products in

their diet even after weaning and most adults will retain the special enzyme (lactase) that they need to break down the sugar found in milk (lactose). There are many other ethnic groups, including Indians and Orientals, however, who do not generally drink milk after infancy and consequently they can very often lose the capacity to make lactase after they have been weaned.

The ability to tolerate lactose is just one example of how digestive systems vary between individuals. Your unique genetic and cultural inheritance means that your digestive system is unlike anyone else's. Its response to different foods and drinks is particular to you – for instance, you may be able to eat very spicy food without getting an upset stomach, while bran flakes or Brussels sprouts may cause you all sorts of embarrassing problems.

All along your digestive pathway, but most notably in your large intestine, lurks a secret population of alien invaders – bacteria, more than 750 trillion of them.

GUT HOUSEKEEPING

While each of us is unique, certain factors affect everyone's digestive system. As you age, your senses of taste and smell slowly decline. The muscles that keep food moving through your gut lose tone and your stomach and intestines gradually lose efficiency. These changes can make you more vulnerable to disease and other problems such as ulcers or constipation. Apart from a handful of conditions that can go unnoticed, many digestive illnesses make themselves felt immediately as niggling symptoms – from stomachache to constipation. Although digestive problems are not always serious, the digestive system does seem to have a disproportionate influence on your overall sense of well-being.

In fact, the gut can be called the key to good health. A fit and fully functional digestive system promotes a positive sense of well-being. It supplies nutrients that keep the rest of your body in top form. Enthusiasm for the digestive system as the instrument of healthy living reached a peak in the 19th century, when dietary zealots preached that good digestion was the cure for all ills. Sylvester Graham touted wholegrain bread as a modern-day panacea and John Harvey Kellogg warned that indigestion caused every disease from typhoid to 'mental derangement'.

GOOD HEALTH IS GUT HEALTH

While these dietary radicals were perhaps a little over-zealous, taking good care of your digestive system does undoubtedly pay big dividends for your general health. This need not involve a diet of prune juice and routine colonic irrigation. Common-sense steps are all you need to take: don't eat to excess, maintain a balanced diet rich in fibre, drink alcohol only in moderation, exercise regularly and practise good food hygiene. The benefits of such simple lifestyle rules include extra energy and vitality, easier and more regular bowel habits, the means to reach and maintain a sensible weight, better-looking skin, hair and nails, and improved health all round.

Unfortunately, few of us treat our guts with the care they deserve and illness related to the digestive system is one of the fastest growing health problems in the developed world. Poor diet, pollution and stress are making digestive problems such as irritable bowel syndrome increasingly common. Outside the Western world the problem is even worse. Digestive illnesses are the globe's biggest killers – diarrhoea and dysentery killed

The best medicine
A balanced diet that includes plenty of water and fresh produce will help to promote good gut health.

Foods of the future
*In years to come we may eat 'superfoods'
designed to promote particular aspects of
gut health and general well-being.*

more than 3 million people in 1998 alone. Medical science and epidemiology have made advances against some of these problems. Notable successes in the developed world include the virtual eradication of cholera along with a radical reduction of serious diarrhoeal disease, mainly due to improvements in sewer systems and water hygiene. More recently, the identification of the *Helicobacter pylori* bacterium as the agent responsible for stomach ulcers has opened up new avenues of treatment, while advanced diagnostic technologies are enabling doctors to cut colon cancer mortality rates.

WHAT DOES THE FUTURE HOLD?

In the future, genetic engineering promises to go beyond the battle against disease and transform the very fabric of our digestive systems. Most current genetic research is performed on bacteria, particularly the common human gut bacterium *E. coli*. The enormous population of bacteria that live in your intestines is an obvious target for genetic engineers. These industrious organisms are already helping your digestive system with tasks it cannot perform by itself. A relatively simple bit of genetic tinkering could transform your gut flora into a trillion microscopic factories, producing nutrients and pharmaceuticals from within. For instance, suppose that some of the bacteria that live in your small intestine could be encouraged to make vitamin C. You would then be guaranteed a lifetime supply of this important health-giving, anticancer nutrient. Fed up with excess wind? Simply engineer bacteria in your large intestine to produce enzymes that can break down the gas into a form that is easily absorbed.

The next step would be to engineer the digestive system itself, to create a genetically enhanced 'superhuman'. By adding the genes to produce new enzymes, your digestion could become more efficient. By altering the genes that control processes such as fat breakdown and absorption, genetic engineers could reduce the number of calories you absorb and even limit the amount of cholesterol working its way into your bloodstream, combating cardiovascular disease. Improbable though it may seem, the way to a superhuman's heart might be through the stomach.

1

How your digestion works

Your amazing stomach and digestive system

Your digestive system is your body's equivalent of an oil refinery. It processes the raw materials of food to produce the fuel that powers every cell in your body and keeps all of your other systems running.

LINES OF SUPPLY

Your digestive system is essentially a tube leading from your mouth to your anus. This tube has several names, including alimentary canal, gastrointestinal tract and digestive tract, and is roughly 8 metres (26 feet) long. It is divided into a number of sections: at the top end are the mouth, throat and oesophagus, which leads to the stomach. The stomach feeds into the small intestine, which in turn feeds into the large intestine, which ends at the anus. In addition, three other organs – the liver, pancreas and gallbladder – supply fluids vital to the digestive process.

The good, the bad and the ugly

The digestive system has three basic functions. Its primary purpose is digestion – to break down food into its constituent nutrients and to absorb these nutrients into the bloodstream. Secondly, it has a defensive role, protecting your body by destroying germs or making conditions too harsh for them to survive. Lastly, your digestive system disposes of waste, getting rid not just of the indigestible parts of food but also toxic substances and the waste products of normal bodily processes, such as breakdown products of old blood, by excreting them in stools.

▲ **Your friendly gut flora**
Bacteria are normally considered harmful, so it may be a surprise to learn that your large intestine could not function without them; see pages 32–33.

▼ **Biochemistry basics**
Discover how special proteins called enzymes break food down into its component molecules so they can be absorbed; see pages 30–31.

▲ **24-hour control**
Each part of the digestive system helps to control the activity of the others. On pages 34–35 we follow the journey of one meal for a day to see how they all work together.

The liver, gallbladder and pancreas are known as accessory organs. Although food does not travel through these organs, they supply essential digestive fluids to the intestines; see pages 28–29.

The oesophagus provides a pathway for food from the mouth to the stomach; see pages 20–21.

Food is moved along the digestive tract by a type of muscular activity called peristalsis, described on pages 20–21.

The stomach
Gastric glands in the stomach produce about 1.5 litres (2⅔ pints) of gastric juices every day. These fluids are vital to the stomach's churning and food-processing work; for more information, see pages 22–23.

The small intestine is the workhorse of the digestive system: 80 per cent of digestion takes place here. Find out what it looks like on the inside on pages 24–25.

The large intestine encircles the small intestine and ends in the rectum. For more on what it does, see pages 32–33.

The lining of the small intestine is specialised to enhance its ability to absorb food. Turn to pages 26–27 to find out how it does this at the microscopic level.

You will spend five whole years eating and drinking during your lifetime.

The mouth

As well as being the gateway to your digestive system, the mouth is where the first steps in food breakdown occur. The efforts of your teeth, tongue and salivary glands combine to turn solid food into a digestible mash.

MAKING AN ENTRANCE

The mouth is more than simply the entrance to the gut – vital steps in the process of digestion are performed here. The teeth break up food into manageable lumps, ready for mixing with saliva to produce a semi-liquid pulp. Saliva also lubricates the movement of this pulp down the throat, and flushes away oral bacteria, helping to prevent dental cavities and gum damage.

The salivary glands *exist in three pairs – one pair in the floor of your mouth, underneath your tongue; another pair nearer the back of the jaw; and the third just in front of your ears. Small connecting tubes deliver 1–1.5 litres (1¾–2⅔ pints) of saliva to the mouth every day.*

The teeth *perform the mechanical break-up of food.*

The palate *forms the roof of your mouth. At the front it is bony and immobile (the hard palate), while at the back it is soft and flexible (the soft palate). The palate prevents food from going up your nose rather than down your throat.*

As well as taste buds, your tongue has receptors for pressure, pain and temperature.

The tongue *is a muscular organ used to manipulate food in the mouth. It coordinates the movement of food between the different types of teeth, and then rolls the resulting pulp into a ball, or bolus, and pushes it towards the throat. The tongue's surface is packed with receptors called taste buds, which (together with your nose's 'smell' receptors) provide your sense of taste. Tasting food is vital for stimulating appetite as well as increasing secretions lower down in your digestive tract.*

Say 'Cheese!'

Your teeth are set into sockets in the jaw bone. Each tooth has an outer shell of enamel – the hardest substance that your body makes. This tough layer surrounds another hard substance called dentine (similar to bone) and a soft central pulp cavity. Depending on their position within your mouth, each type of tooth has a particular function. Your front teeth (incisors and canines) cut and tear food into bite-sized chunks. Then your back teeth (premolars and molars) grind it into a pulp, ready for swallowing.

The tingling sensation that you get from a fizzy drink is actually pain. The carbon dioxide gas, which makes the drink fizz, turns to acid in your mouth, stimulating the pain receptors on your tongue.

What is saliva?

The vast majority – 99.4 per cent – of your saliva is water; other components include enzymes, salts and molecules that maintain a constant pH of 6.8. This slightly acidic environment provides the perfect conditions for the initial stages of digestion. Saliva is essential for tasting: it dissolves chemicals from the food or drink, which your taste buds perceive as flavours.

The taste sensation

The sensation of flavour produced, in part, by your taste buds allows you to distinguish between foods. A typical adult has about 10,000 taste buds – the bulk of them on the tongue, with a few scattered around the back of the mouth. Each bud is specialised to detect one of four primary taste sensations: salt, sweet, sour or bitter. Your sensitivity to tastes varies: for example, your taste buds are 1000 times more sensitive to sour tastes than to sweet or salty ones, and 100 times more sensitive to bitter tastes than to sour ones.

The throat and oesophagus

The throat is a thoroughfare for several different substances, including food and drink. These have to be directed to the oesophagus, which carries them to the stomach at a rate of up to 4cm (1½in) per second.

A PASSAGE TO YOUR STOMACH

Your oesophagus is a 25cm (10in) long muscular tube, stretching from your throat to your stomach. Once you have chewed a mouthful of food, a precise sequence of swallowing manoeuvres directs the ball of mush, or bolus, first to the throat and then into the oesophagus. Food moves along your oesophagus by a muscular activity called peristalsis – a rhythmic sequence of contraction and relaxation by bands of muscle. The oesophagus empties into the stomach at an opening called the cardiac orifice. On average, food plops into your stomach about 6–8 seconds after you swallowed it, while liquids whiz through in 1 second flat. Rings of muscle called sphincters constrict the top and bottom of the oesophagus to prevent stomach contents going backwards into the throat or mouth. They are called simply the upper and lower oesophageal sphincters.

Travelling in reverse

Unfortunately the oesophagus does not always experience a one-way downwards flow of traffic. The stomach contents are sometimes forcefully ejected by vomiting – an involuntary reflex that, although unpleasant, can serve a protective function. Vomiting helps to get rid of potentially dangerous substances very rapidly, ejecting poisons before they can get into the bloodstream.

The epiglottis – keeping food on the right track

Imagine that you are a piece of food that has just been swallowed en route to the stomach. Take a false turn in the throat, and you could end up going down the wrong tube. Two passages lead off the throat – the trachea and the oesophagus. When you swallow a mouthful of food, the epiglottis closes over the end of the trachea until the food has passed by – a bit like railway points directing a train down a particular track. If a morsel does go down the wrong way, you choke and cough sharply to bring it back up to the throat to be re-swallowed.

The epiglottis *is a flap of tissue that directs food and drink down the oesophagus. Here it is in its normal position, allowing air into the trachea.*

The trachea, *or windpipe, channels air to the lungs.*

The oesophagus *is a thin muscular tube, which is normally squashed flat by its position between the trachea and the spine.*

The oesophagus in section
This micrograph shows the various layers in the oesophagus wall. Its highly folded interior allows it to stretch around mouthfuls of food.

The cardiac orifice is *where the oesophagus empties into the stomach.*

1   2   3

Down the hatch – the three phases of swallowing

1 Buccal phase The swallowing sequence starts voluntarily – in other words, it is under your control. When you are ready to swallow a bolus of food, your tongue pushes it up against the roof of your mouth and towards your throat. The combined mass of tongue and food raises your soft palate, shutting off the nasal space from your throat, so that food or drink doesn't go up the back of your nose. The bolus is then pushed into your throat, and the rest of the sequence proceeds involuntarily.

2 Pharyngeal phase As the bolus travels down your throat (the pharynx), your epiglottis folds over the opening of the trachea to prevent food going down the wrong way. Between 0.2 and 0.3 seconds after you began to swallow, your upper oesophageal sphincter relaxes to admit the bolus into the oesophagus.

3 Oesophageal phase Peristaltic waves of contraction and relaxation within the oesophagus walls carry the bolus down towards the stomach. Once it arrives at the cardiac orifice, the lower sphincter opens to allow it to enter the stomach.

During swallowing, you actually stop breathing for a fraction of a second, as food travels past the closed entrance to the trachea.

The diaphragm *bounds the top of the abdominal cavity; all the other digestive organs are located below here.*

Peristalsis – muscular movement

Your digestive tract moves food along using muscles within its walls. Some muscles run lengthways along the tract (longitudinal muscles) while others encircle it (circular muscles). In order to move food along, both muscle types work together in a mechanism called peristalsis. A wave of contraction passes along the tract and this pushes a mass of food ahead of it. At the same time, a wave of relaxation moves along in front, lessening resistance to the food's passage. Peristalsis is not only a human mechanism, it is well illustrated by the way snakes swallow prey whole. This X-ray shows a frog en route from the snake's mouth along its digestive tract.

The stomach

The real business of digestion gets underway in the stomach, an inflatable bag that shrinks and grows according to how much you eat and drink, and which operates like a combination of food processor and acid bath.

Gastric glands
This coloured scanning electron micrograph shows a highly magnified view of the surface of the stomach lining. Here, globules of protective mucus (yellow) surround the mucus-secreting cells (red-brown).

TURNING YOUR STOMACH

Your stomach is a muscular J-shaped bag that has a smooth outer surface and a heavily folded lining, rich in gastric glands that produce digestive fluids and mucus. At the top of the stomach are the cardia, where food enters from the oesophagus, and the fundus, which is heavily endowed with secreting glands. The outer curve of the 'J' makes up the bulk of the stomach, known as the body, and at the bottom of the stomach is the antrum. The pylorus connects the stomach to the duodenum (the first part of the small intestine).

Flexing its muscles

Your stomach completes the mechanical breakdown of food, which was started off by your teeth. Within the walls of the stomach are three bands of muscle, each orientated in a different direction, which enables your stomach wall to flex in three dimensions at once. This gives it the ability to churn, kneading and mixing food and gastric juices together into a thick, soupy substance called chyme. Your stomach also acts as a 'storage tank' for food: an entire meal can be taken on board, churned into chyme and then dispensed into the small intestine a little at a time. This slowing down of the chyme is vital as the intestines work best on relatively small loads; if a meal were to flood through at the same rate at which you ate it, your intestine would not have time to process it properly.

The acid house

Glands in your stomach lining secrete hydrochloric acid, a powerful acid that helps to break down all but the toughest components of food. It also provides a valuable line of defence against germs – few can survive this hostile environment for long. Many people will be familiar with the sensation of heartburn – this is when stomach acid leaks back into the oesophagus. To prevent the corrosive fluid eating away at the stomach, the stomach lining is protected by a mucus layer, which contains a neutralising agent (bicarbonate). If the mucus layer is damaged, however, say by bacterial invasion or by excessive alcohol an ulcer may form.

The pyloric sphincter
opens and closes to control the flow of chyme, letting it through in small squirts.

The ring masters

Movement of food through the pyloric outlet is controlled by a band of muscle – a sphincter. Normally this muscle is contracted, preventing material from passing through. When the sphincter relaxes the outlet opens to allow some chyme to flow out of the stomach and into the duodenum. Other sphincters of the digestive system are located at the top and bottom of the oesophagus; where the secretions of the liver, gallbladder and pancreas feed into the duodenum; at the junction of the small and large intestines; at the end of the large intestine; and two (internal and external) in the anus. All except the last are involuntary: you have no conscious control over their opening and closing.

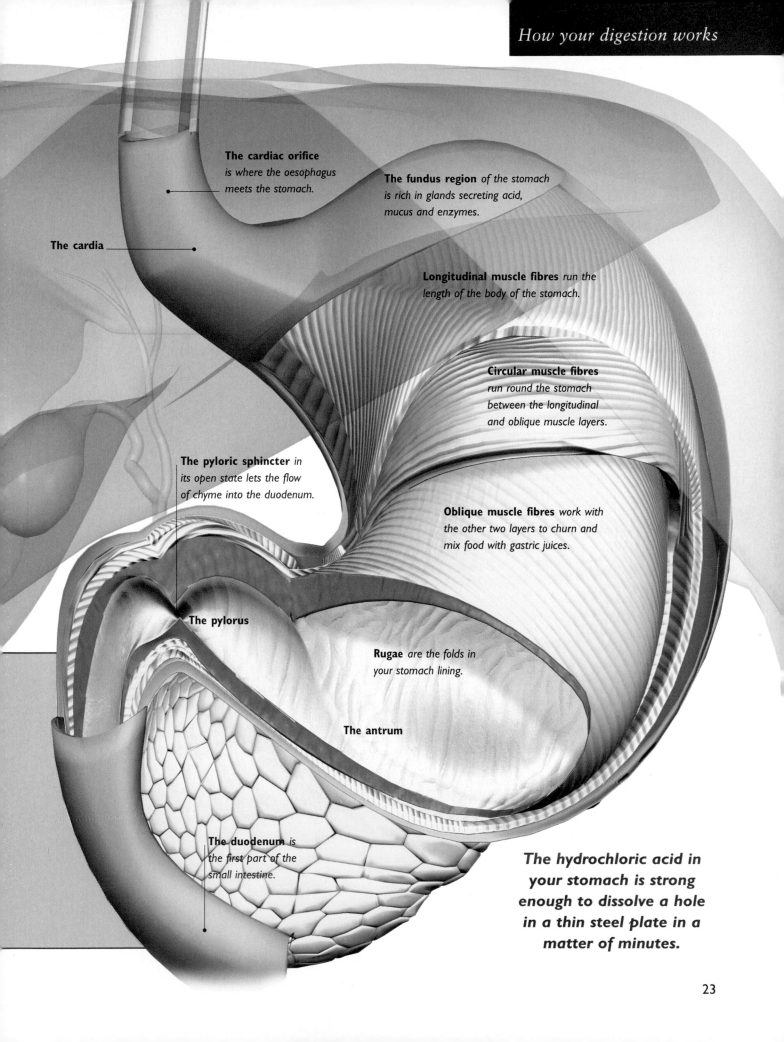

The cardiac orifice *is where the oesophagus meets the stomach.*

The fundus region *of the stomach is rich in glands secreting acid, mucus and enzymes.*

The cardia

Longitudinal muscle fibres *run the length of the body of the stomach.*

Circular muscle fibres *run round the stomach between the longitudinal and oblique muscle layers.*

The pyloric sphincter *in its open state lets the flow of chyme into the duodenum.*

Oblique muscle fibres *work with the other two layers to churn and mix food with gastric juices.*

The pylorus

Rugae *are the folds in your stomach lining.*

The antrum

The duodenum *is the first part of the small intestine.*

The hydrochloric acid in your stomach is strong enough to dissolve a hole in a thin steel plate in a matter of minutes.

The small intestine

Packed into your abdomen is the small intestine, the workhorse of the digestive system. This stretch of tubing, several metres long, is where the vast majority of digestion and nutrient absorption takes place.

THE LONG AND WINDING GUT

Some 80 per cent of nutrient absorption occurs in your small intestine, together with most of the chemical (as opposed to mechanical) digestion of food. The small intestine is a tube about 6m (20ft) long and 2.5–4cm (1–1½in) wide. In order to squeeze all of its length into your abdomen, the tube is folded repeatedly, winding back on itself several times. It is divided into three sections.

- **The duodenum** This is the first and shortest section of the small intestine, averaging about 25cm (10in). It acts a bit like a mixing bowl, blending the digestive juices from the liver, gallbladder and pancreas with the soupy chyme from the stomach.
- **The jejunum** A sharp bend marks the beginning of this 2.25m (7ft 6in) long section, where the bulk of the digestive and absorptive action happens.
- **The ileum** More digestion and absorption happens in this longest section – at 3.5m (11ft 8in); it ends in a sphincter that leads to the large intestine.

RIDING THE WAVES

A cross-section of the small intestine reveals a structure highly adapted for its role. Within the intestinal walls are both circular and longitudinal layers of muscle. Interleaved with these are networks of nerves, called plexi, which stimulate the muscles into three types of movement.

- **Segmentation** Rippling waves of contraction of the circular muscle churn the chyme on a stretch of intestine, ensuring that it mixes evenly with the digestive juices that are working on it.
- **Local peristalsis** Weak waves of peristalsis, limited to just a few centimetres at a time, keep chyme moving slowly along the intestine.
- **Coordinated movements** Occasionally, larger-scale peristalsis shifts chyme in bulk, moving it several feet at a time, encouraging the release of more chyme from the small into the large intestine.

The membrane that lines your abdominal cavity, the peritoneum, secretes 7 litres (12 pints) of lubricating fluid every day to prevent your intestines chafing against other organs as you move around.

The serosa *is the outermost layer of the intestine.*

Mesentery

Peritoneum

What's holding your gut in?

Your digestive tract and its associated organs are supported and held in place in your abdomen by the muscles of your back, abdominal wall and diaphragm, and also by a set of membranes called mesenteries. These are sheets of connective tissue that anchor the tubes, bags and organs of the digestive system to one another and also to the peritoneum – the membrane that lines the inside of the abdominal wall. Mesenteries also carry vital blood vessels and nerve fibres.

Longitudinal muscle fibres *surround the layers of circular muscle.*

Circular muscle fibres *wrap around within the intestinal wall, either side of the submucosa.*

Nerve fibres *run within the muscular layers in networks called plexi; they coordinate contraction and relaxation of muscle fibres to move the contents through the intestine.*

Finger-like projections *line the intestine; see pages 26–27.*

Blood vessels *run within the submucosal layer.*

A mucosal surface *lines the intestinal cavity.*

The mesentery *runs the length of the digestive tract and carries a vast network of blood vessels, which supply the many layers of the intestinal wall.*

The intestinal lining

To maximise the absorption of nutrients from the food and liquids that enter your digestive tract every day, the lining of your intestine is a highly specialised environment of fluid-spewing crypts and towering nutrient-hungry columns.

AN ABSORBING TALE

Imagine that you are a particle of food, drifting through the small intestine. On all sides gigantic columns, the villi, rear above you, their surfaces coated with a rippling carpet of hairs. At the feet of the villi are strange holes, the intestinal crypts, which produce 1.8 litres (3⅛ pints) of fluid in the intestine every day. The surface of both the villi and crypts are composed of two types of cell, enterocytes and goblet cells. Wherever they are, the goblet cells have one purpose: to secrete a layer of protective mucus that also lubricates the passage of the chyme. The enterocytes, however, have two roles. In the crypts, they secrete a watery fluid that helps to dissolve the nutritious products of enzyme digestion in the chyme; the enterocytes on the villi actively absorb the nutrient-rich fluid. Enterocytes are highly active cells that 'burn out' and die in just five days.

Wall-to-wall carpet in your gut
The velvety lining of the small intestine has many folds, each covered in millions of tiny, finger-like projections called villi (seen here from above magnified 85 times). The surface of each cell on the villi is studded with up to 1000 tiny hairs called microvilli. In a 3cm² (½sqin) area of lining, there would be about 10,000 villi and 5000 million microvilli.

Down in the crypts
This micrograph shows a longitudinal section through an intestinal crypt, also known as a crypt of Lieberkühn. Towards the top, the crypt's entrance into the intestinal lumen is visible, bounded by the bases of two villi.

An enterocyte *manufactures and secretes the watery fluid vital to the absorptive functions of the villi.*

A goblet cell *makes protective mucus.*

A Paneth cell *may secrete an enzyme called lysozyme, but researchers are still not clear on all of its functions.*

The story at the surface
The outer cell layer of the villi is perfectly designed to maximise the body's ability to absorb nutrients.

Enterocyte cells cover the villi, and absorb digested nutrients from the passing chyme.

A goblet cell sits in the layer at intervals, and secretes a protective, lubricating mucus.

Microvilli are tiny hairs on the surface of the enterocytes. Also called a 'brush border', these increase the surface area for absorption.

Inside the villi
Beneath the outside layer is a network of vessels and nerves carrying vital supplies to the enterocytes and goblet cells, and transporting the absorbed nutrients to the rest of the body.

The lacteal vessel picks up and transports digested fats and fatty substances.

Oxygen-rich blood (red) is supplied to the cells by microscopic blood vessels called capillaries.

A nerve transmits nerve signals to the capillaries, instructing them to dilate or constrict, according to how much blood is needed by the digestive system.

Deoxygenated blood (blue) is carried away to the liver, having exchanged its load of oxygen for nutrients absorbed from the gut.

The liver, gallbladder and pancreas

Although not part of the digestive tract that food passes through, the help of the accessory organs – the liver, gallbladder and pancreas – is essential to digest the large and complex molecules that make up food.

THE LIVER

Digestion is only one of the liver's areas of responsibility – it is the most versatile organ in the body, with over 200 different functions. In digestion it controls the manufacture of bile, the collection and processing of nutrients, and vital metabolic functions.

- **Manufacture of bile** Bile is a green liquid made in the liver and stored in the gallbladder. It is mostly water but also contains buffers and bile salts. Buffers help to counteract stomach acid to keep the conditions in the small intestine at the right pH for enzymes to work on the chyme. Bile salts come into play on foods that are too much for enzymes alone, helping to break up large droplets of fat in the chyme into tiny ones. This process, known as emulsification, allows the digestive enzymes to break down the fats into molecules small enough to be absorbed in the small intestine.
- **Collection and processing of nutrients** The nutrients absorbed by your stomach and intestines have to be treated by the liver before they can be used by the rest of your body. A large blood vessel called the portal vein collects all nutrient-rich blood returning from the intestinal lining and takes it directly to the liver. Once processed, nutrients are fed back into the bloodstream to be circulated to the rest of the body.
- **Metabolic functions** The liver performs an array of life-supporting functions via complex metabolic pathways, including manufacturing enzymes, breaking down toxins, removing alcohol from the blood and storing energy in the form of a quickly accessible carbohydrate reserve called glycogen.

THE PANCREAS

Lying behind the stomach is the 15cm (6in) long pancreas. This produces a fluid called pancreatic juice that contains a range of enzymes – such as trypsin, which helps to digest proteins – and buffers, which help to neutralise stomach acid. Inside the pancreas, branches of the pancreatic duct collect the juice from hundreds of lobules – rather like a bunch of grapes – then join up into a single vessel that leads to the duodenum. In addition to its digestive functions, the pancreas manufactures hormones, such as insulin.

THE GALLBLADDER

Bile passes from the liver, via the cystic duct, to a small pear-shaped sac called the gallbladder. Up to 70ml (2½floz) of bile is stored here, and while it waits to be squirted into the duodenum via the bile duct, its composition changes. Water is absorbed by the walls of the gallbladder to concentrate the solution of salts – it can be up to 20 times stronger than the original bile manufactured by the liver. When a new load of chyme arrives in the duodenum, the gallbladder contracts and ejects its contents to help emulsify the fat globules.

You can lose up to 80 per cent of your liver and it will still function normally and regenerate the lost cells within about 10 days.

The liver *is the largest and heaviest organ in the body at 1.5kg (3⅓lb).*

The cystic duct *is the tube through which bile travels on its way to the bile duct and then the duodenum.*

The gallbladder *stores and concentrates bile.*

The pancreas would digest itself in a few hours if it weren't for a special substance called trypsin inhibitor, produced to inhibit its own enzymes.

The pancreatic duct *transports the pancreatic juices to the duodenum.*

The pancreas *comprises lobules made from units called acini. These manufacture and secrete highly digestive fluids – about 1.5 litres (2⅔ pints) (ten times its own weight) – into the pancreatic duct every day.*

The bile duct

The duodenum

The ampulla of Vater *is the 'meeting point' in the duodenum where the bile and pancreatic ducts empty their contents.*

The sphincter of Oddi *controls the release of the fluids in the now merged bile and pancreatic ducts.*

Up close in the pancreas
This scanning electron micrograph of a pancreatic acinar cell shows zymogen granules (yellow, brown and white circles), which are the inactive form of a digestive enzyme. The purple folds are membranes that synthesise enzyme proteins.

The biochemistry of digestion

Before your body can absorb the nutrients of your last meal, the bonds that hold their molecules together must be broken. Your body employs an army of special proteins called enzymes, which work at different stages of the digestive process.

What happens where?
Join us on a digestive journey to see how large molecules are gradually transformed into smaller ones, using the visual key below.

BIOCHEMISTRY BASICS

Food is made up of three basic nutrients – proteins, carbohydrates and fats. Each is a large molecular structure made from many repeating smaller units.

- **Proteins** Every protein molecule is made from amino acids. A molecule of two amino acids is called a dipeptide, while a long chain of amino acids is a polypeptide. A complex molecule containing many polypeptides is a protein.
- **Carbohydrates** The two basic groups – sugars (simple) and starch (complex carbohydrates) – are made from the same basic unit: a monosaccharide. Sugars contain one or only a few monosaccharides joined together; glucose, for example, is a monosaccharide and sucrose is a disaccharide. Starch molecules are complex as they comprise long chains of polysaccharides.
- **Fats** These are made up of two basic units – glycerol and fatty acids.

Enzymatic digestion

In order to break the long chains of nutrient molecules into units small enough for your intestines to absorb, you need some means of 'snipping' the bonds holding the units together. This is where your digestive enzymes come in. These complex proteins latch onto a target substance, break it into smaller bits and then move on to the next target. Each enzyme works on one substance only; for example, the enzyme dipeptidase chops up dipeptides into amino acids. Furthermore, different enzymes work at different locations: amylase works on starch in the mouth, pepsin on proteins in the stomach and pancreatic lipase breaks up fats in the small intestine.

Sugar crystals
Probably the most familiar form of sugar in everyday life, sucrose (shown here in crystal form, magnified 60 times) is a disaccharide, that is two monosaccharide molecules joined together.

Monosaccharide

Starch

Amino acid

Protein

Fatty acids and glycerol

Fat droplet

Amylase

Stomach acid

Protein-attacking enzyme

Bile salt

Lipase

Water

Fibre

A bit of a mouthful
Enzymatic digestion begins in the mouth. Your saliva contains an enzyme called amylase, which starts the breakdown of starch.

A churning stomach *Hydrochloric acid, in conjunction with an enzyme called pepsin, starts to break up proteins into polypeptides; meanwhile the breakdown of starch continues. Fats are still largely unaffected at this point.*

Starting off in the small intestine
The main action is in the duodenum. Starch is broken into short chains and glucose units, and protein-attacking enzymes convert polypeptides into dipeptides and amino acids. Bile salts emulsify the fat into tiny droplets, small enough for the enzyme lipase to work on.

Finishing the job *The breakdown of starch into glucose and other monosaccharides is completed by the enzymes lactase, sucrase and maltase. Trypsin, chymotrypsin and dipeptidase, among others, turn poly-peptides into amino acids. Lipases have broken up fat droplets into units of fatty acid and glycerol, which are repackaged in water-soluble form. The basic units are now ready to be absorbed by the intestinal villi.*

The end of the tunnel
When the chyme is ready to pass into the large intestine, there is very little left except water, some vitamins and minerals and insoluble fibre.

The large intestine

Home to a thriving population of 'friendly' bacteria and the occasional bubble of pungent gas, your large intestine extracts the last drops of goodness from food and prepares whatever is left for departure.

GROSS ANATOMY

The final part of your digestive tract, the large intestine describes a 1.5m (5ft) circuit of your lower abdomen, framing the small intestine. Its main functions are the absorption of water, vitamins and minerals, and the compaction into faeces of what is left from the digestion process. It is divided into three main parts – the caecum, the colon and the rectum (see below).

Look who's coming to dinner

Thousands of millions of bacteria, collectively known as your gut flora, live in harmony in your large intestine. The bacteria feed off the material that passes through your gut, and in return they perform a number of important roles: they produce vitamins, including B_{12}, folic acid and thiamine, some of which your body cannot make for itself; they help to break down bile pigments, so that they can be reabsorbed and returned to the liver where they are reassembled and reused (leftover pigments give stool its colour); through competition for food with other bacteria, gut flora play a vital defensive role; and they feed off fibre that is too tough for digestive enzymes, producing fatty acids small enough for you to absorb – an important source of energy.

Wind power

Your digestive tract usually contains about 150ml (5floz) of gas; some of this is swallowed air and some results from the breakdown and fermentation of food. Most gas is absorbed through the intestinal walls into your bloodstream, but occasionally some builds up, causing discomfort and embarrassment. Gas in the lower intestine is mainly composed of hydrogen, carbon dioxide and methane, all of which are odourless. Unpleasant smells come from by-products of bacterial protein metabolism, such as hydrogen sulphide, indole or skatole.

Friend or foe?
Escherichia coli *bacteria are best known for causing outbreaks of food poisoning. But not all strains of* E. coli *are bad for your digestion; some strains, in fact, form a major component of a healthy gut flora.*

There are ten times more bacteria in your digestive tract than there are cells in the whole of the rest of your body.

A guide to the large intestine

a **The caecum** forms a pouch at the start of the large intestine. Here chyme is collected, fed in from the small intestine via the ileocaecal valve, and the process of compaction begins. Leading off the blind end of the caecum is the appendix, a slender 9cm (3½in) tube dotted with lymph nodules, where white blood cells congregate to fight germs.

b **The colon** is the main body of the large intestine. It is subdivided into four regions – (**1**) the ascending, (**2**) transverse, (**3**) descending and (**4**) sigmoid colon. Three ribbons of muscle that run along the colon – the taenia coli – pull the walls into a series of pouches called haustrae, allowing it to expand when a large load is passing through.

c **The rectum** is the last 15cm (6in) of the digestive tract; it is a muscular tube that stores faeces before they are excreted. The urge to defecate is triggered when material arrives from the sigmoid colon, but the exit from the rectum is controlled by two sphincters – the internal and external anal sphincters. The latter is under voluntary control.

A day in the life of the digestive system

Only the top and bottom of the digestive tract are under your conscious control. The rest depends on complex interactions between your unconscious brain and the different parts of the digestive system.

THE DAILY GRIND

The length of time it takes for a meal to work through your digestive system depends on a host of factors – the content and timing of the meal, the state of your digestive tract, how active you are, how much you've eaten recently. On average, though, food comes out of one end between 14 and 24 hours after it went in the other. For your digestive system to extract all the nutrients from a meal, its grinding, squeezing, mixing, secreting and compacting is carefully coordinated by a system of nervous and hormonal signals. Here, we follow the journey of your breakfast throughout the day.

07:30 Hungry? Feed me now

It's been 12 hours since you last ate, and receptors monitoring your blood sugar levels detect that you need rapid refuelling. Part of your brain called the hypothalamus gathers this information and sends signals to the conscious portions of your brain, producing the sensation of hunger. Your appetite drives you into the kitchen. The sight and smell of your partner's fresh toast activate some of the primitive parts of your brain, producing a barrage of nerve messages that literally make your mouth water and trigger the secretion of gastric juices in your stomach.

00:00 Chyme at midnight

Most of what is left of your breakfast has now reached your sigmoid colon. Arriving home late you treat yourself to a midnight feast. As food enters your stomach the gastrocolic reflex triggers a wave of peristalsis that pushes the remains of a ball of chyme – by now a stool – into your rectum. Stretch receptors in the rectal wall send messages to your brain, producing the urge to defecate. They also signal the internal anal sphincter to relax, allowing the stool to move into the anorectal canal. You visit the toilet to relax your external anal sphincter, and then toddle off to bed.

14:00 Move along now

The physical presence of chyme in the small intestine excites and irritates its walls. In response, the intestinal muscles twitch and contract, producing local movements that slowly mix and shift chyme along. By now the first masses of chyme from breakfast arrive at the caecum. Material moves very slowly from here on via powerful peristaltic waves, triggered by your body clock and the arrival of a new meal in your stomach.

11:00 What a gall!

As your pyloric sphincter squirts chyme into your duodenum, the acidic gastric juices stimulate hormonal signals that trigger the pancreas to produce its alkaline juices to counteract the stomach acid. When the fattier parts of your breakfast arrive, they trigger the production of a different hormone, which prompts the gallbladder to release bile.

07:45 A hearty breakfast

At last you sit down to breakfast: muesli with milk, croissant and milky coffee – a meal that provides carbohydrates in abundance, as well as some fat and protein. You tuck in, and receptors in your stomach wall detect the size and content of the meal. Signals to your brain produce an almost immediate loss of hunger (although not necessarily appetite), while your stomach itself responds by flexing its muscles to churn your meal into chyme and by secreting acid and enzymes.

2

Healthy digestion for life

LOOKING AFTER YOUR DIGESTIVE SYSTEM

In 400BC Hippocrates wrote that 'a bad digestion is the root of all evil'. For most of us, however, the digestive system is simply something that we take for granted – until it goes wrong. Over half of us will suffer from digestive problems at some stage in our lives, and yet many of these ailments could be avoided. By developing greater awareness of the health of your digestive system, what is good for it and what isn't, you can help to keep your digestive tract in trouble-free working order and minimise any problems that might occur.

 39 *Be aware of what is normal for you and your family, and be alert to any changes that may indicate a problem.*

 42 *Learn how to control your risk factors by eating well, not smoking and maintaining good food hygiene.*

 48 *Work with your GP to decide if you need to make serious lifestyle changes to prevent or treat digestive illness.*

Be aware of what is normal

Learning about your body's day-to-day workings is a great start to becoming more self-aware. By knowing what is normal for you, you can be alert to any unusual changes that might indicate a problem.

As with many aspects of looking after your health, when it comes to gut health awareness is the key: knowing what is normal and what is not. After getting food into your mouth, digestion is an unconscious process and so you are not really aware of it. The best bet, then, is to be on the lookout for unusual symptoms. An abdominal symptom could indicate something is wrong (for more information, see pages 50–53), but bowel habit is probably the most obvious indicator of how well the digestive system is working.

WHAT'S YOUR HABIT?
We're all unique when it comes to bowel habits. A UK survey of 1500 adults showed that all but 1 per cent had bowel movements ranging from three motions a week to three a day – a range that is entirely normal.

Look out for changes
Although variety is normal in the bowel habits of the population in general, when it comes to your own bowel motions a change may indicate a problem. Try to take note of the usual frequency and pattern of your own trips to the toilet, and be aware of the size, amount and consistency of the stools.

Some people are always 'regular', for instance they always pass a stool soon after getting up in the morning or after eating. But for others, bowel habits vary considerably. Diet has the most obvious effect – a particularly spicy meal, for example, produces a familiar change in bowel habit. In general, the more fibre you eat, the larger and more frequent the stools.

It's not just the food you eat that influences your bowel habit, the amount you drink – especially water, coffee and alcohol – also has an impact. So too do cigarette smoking and physical activity. Even your mood influences your trips to the bathroom: anxiety, for instance, tends to lead to 'the runs', while depression may cause constipation.

Women often find their bowel habits change when they are having a period, during pregnancy or at the menopause. This is due to changing levels of the sex hormones oestrogen and progesterone, both of which affect bowel function. Both prescribed and over-the-counter medicines can cause diarrhoea or constipation (see also page 50).

A CHANGE FROM THE NORM
How can you tell if you really are constipated or have diarrhoea? These terms often mean different things to different people. When doctors talk about constipation they mean infrequent motions – less than twice

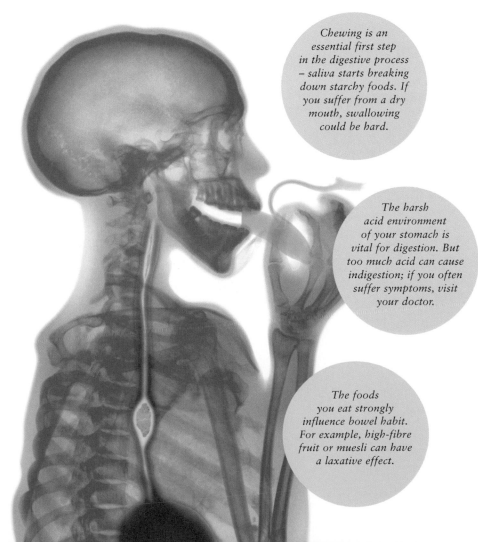

Chewing is an essential first step in the digestive process – saliva starts breaking down starchy foods. If you suffer from a dry mouth, swallowing could be hard.

The harsh acid environment of your stomach is vital for digestion. But too much acid can cause indigestion; if you often suffer symptoms, visit your doctor.

The foods you eat strongly influence bowel habit. For example, high-fibre fruit or muesli can have a laxative effect.

Digestion – an unconscious process
Once we have swallowed food and it enters the stomach, digestive enzymes and acid break it down into components that can be absorbed and used by the body.

Healthy teeth, healthy gut

Dental hygiene is important for your gut health – the whole process of digestion starts with chewing and the action of saliva on food. Look after your teeth and gums, and you probably won't need to worry. But if you think your dental hygiene routine is inadequate, ask your dentist or dental hygienist for advice on brushing technique and antibacterial products.

per week – or stools that are small, hard or difficult to pass. Diarrhoea means bowel motions that are very loose or frequent – in other words, more than three times per day. A change in bowel habit, especially if it lasts more than three weeks, is more worrying than the absolute frequency of bowel movements.

COMMON DIGESTIVE PROBLEMS

Among the most common conditions affecting the digestive system are constipation, gastroenteritis and irritable bowel syndrome.

Constipation

Women tend to be troubled by constipation more than men, and elderly people are particularly susceptible because of weakening muscles in the colon and pelvis as they age. Usually, the cause of constipation can be pinned down to a low-fibre diet, physical inactivity, long-term laxative use or a combination of the three. In people under 50, constipation is rarely a sign of anything serious. Above this age, however, the likelihood of a more serious cause, such as a blockage due to a tumour, is greater. If you are constipated a lot, it's worth seeing your doctor.

Constipation is a common cause of piles, also known as haemorrhoids. These usually improve if you increase your dietary fibre and fluid intake. But if you have persistent bleeding from the rectum, it's important to see your doctor so that a more serious condition, such as colon cancer, can be ruled out.

Acute gastroenteritis

This infectious condition causes abdominal pain, diarrhoea, nausea and vomiting. It usually starts suddenly, lasts for one to several days and then clears up of its own accord. The usual culprits behind a bout of gastroenteritis are bacteria (sometimes from food) and occasionally viruses (see page 43). Bloody diarrhoea and dehydration are worrying features and should prompt a doctor's visit.

Irritable bowel syndrome

Other than constipation, irritable bowel syndrome (IBS) is the commonest complaint affecting the intestines. About 7 per cent of men and 15 per cent of women have the condition at some time; symptoms include abdominal pain, bloating and altered bowel habit. The condition may be triggered by a gut infection or antibiotics, and it is often worse when under stress (see pages 52–53). IBS may last for years and can disrupt social life, travel and mood. Fortunately, though, IBS does not bring with it a higher risk of cancer.

UNDER-12s

A tummyache or something more serious?

Abdominal pain is very common in children – usually it is not a sign of anything serious, but there could be a number of different causes.

If your child has tummyache, it might help to ask yourself the following questions.

- Has the pain come on before or after a stressful situation, connected with school, friends or parents?
- Is the pain similar to any previous episodes of tummyache?

In these cases it's unlikely there's a serious underlying cause.

The presence of any of the following symptoms, or a new type of pain, however, should prompt you to call the doctor:

- high fever and/or a racing pulse;
- being much quieter than usual or suddenly listless;
- a tender-to-the-touch abdomen;
- other associated symptoms, such as pain going to the toilet, vomiting, diarrhoea, constipation or abdominal swelling.

Is chewing gum good for your teeth?

Chewing gum boosts the amount of saliva produced after eating – a good thing for two reasons: saliva contains bicarbonate to neutralise the acid produced by dental plaque and it is antibacterial. So it's worth chewing (sugar-free) gum after a meal for the health of your teeth. Chew on both sides of the mouth to release saliva on both sides. The downside to gum is that it encourages your stomach to make acid – you fool it into expecting food – and you may feel bloated. If you have stomach ulcers, it's best avoided.

ASK THE EXPERT

Diverticular disease

This disorder, in which small pockets protruding from the lining of the large intestine become inflamed and infected, can cause abdominal pain, diarrhoea or even passage of blood. About one in every three people above the age of 60 has diverticular disease. Unlike IBS, though, it's more common in middle age and beyond. Diverticular disease mainly affects people living in developed countries, and experts believe it results from relatively low fibre diets, combined with the lowered muscle strength that accompanies ageing.

Kiddie tummy trouble

About 10 per cent of children have recurrent tummy pain – and in most cases no physical cause is found. The commonest causes are stress or constipation. But there may be a more serious cause, such as gastro-enteritis (with diarrhoea and/or vomiting), urinary tract infection, IBS and appendicitis.

HAPPY TOILET TRAINING

Two tight bands of muscle around the anus, called anal sphincters, are responsible for preventing faecal incontinence. The internal sphincter relaxes of its own accord when the rectum fills up with faeces. The external sphincter is under your control and it is this that you keep squeezed tight until you find a toilet. Babies and young children have no control and respond to the sensation of a full rectum by immediately soiling their nappies. It's not until the second year of life that infants gradually learn to exercise control over their external sphincter, usually before they control the bladder. The next stage is potty training where the child must develop the social skill of using a toilet. Don't be tempted to start potty training before your child is ready, and be prepared for accidents; try to maintain an attitude of relaxed encouragement. A delay in gaining control of the bowels is common and there should be little concern until about four years of age. If your child still has no bowel control after this age, it's worth seeing a doctor.

On the potty
Potty training can start as soon as a child has developed conscious control of his or her bowels. This normally happens some time during the second year of life – before this time attempts at potty training are futile.

TRIPS TO THE TOILET

The cardinal rule regarding toilet habits is to follow the dictates of your body, not dictate to it. The intestines are a sophisticated and complex but finely tuned system that works like clockwork. It will tell you when it needs emptying. Don't feel that you must take a trip at a certain time each day. On the other hand, the urge to pass a bowel motion should be obeyed within a short time wherever practicable – constantly delaying such signals can result in constipation. It is important to avoid straining to excess. If you do, you'll be increasing the pressure in the rectum and you're more likely to develop haemorrhoids.

FILL UP ON FRUIT AND VEG *Eating plenty of fresh produce can prevent and counteract all sorts of gut problems, from constipation to cancer.*

TACKLE STRESS AND LEARN TO RELAX *Some digestive problems are linked with stress. So try some yoga or massage to take the pressure off.*

EXERCISE REGULARLY *A sedentary life is bad news for your digestive health. Build activity into your everyday life and you'll soon reap the digestive benefits.*

Control your risk factors

What steps can you take to safeguard the health of your digestive system? The first thing you can do is to look at whether you need to make lifestyle changes. Then it's just a matter of taking sensible precautions when dealing with food.

Certain factors make digestive disorders more likely. Knowing what these factors are and what you can do about them can help you to avoid some common gut problems and spot the dangers of food and drink-related hazards.

UNMODIFIABLE RISK FACTORS

As with heart disease, some digestive disorders tend to run in families. These include colon cancer, inflammatory bowel disease and coeliac disease. About 20 to 25 per cent of colon cancer cases are caused by inherited abnormalities in genes. Having a parent with one of these conditions does not mean you'll definitely develop it as well, but you are more likely to.

Although you obviously have no control over your genetic background, you can still take effective action to reduce your risk of digestive disorders: you can avoid lifestyle behaviour of the type known to contribute to triggering a disease; you can adopt a preventative approach through diet; and your doctor can enrol you on a regular screening programme to detect any disease at an early and much more treatable stage. For example, if you are at risk of colon cancer because of a strong family history of the disease, you can have regular screening by a procedure called colonoscopy (see pages 48–49 for more details on screening). Age is a contributory factor in some diseases: colon cancer and diverticular disease, for example, both become more common after the age of 50.

MODIFIABLE RISK FACTORS

Although you can't control your age and inheritance, there are other factors that you can influence, which can make a real difference to your future digestive health.

- **Stop smoking** Smoking increases the risk of a range of digestive complaints – heartburn, oesophageal and mouth cancer, peptic ulcers, chronic diarrhoea and Crohn's disease. Every year smoking causes more than 13,000 deaths from cancer of the oesophagus, stomach, throat and pancreas. If you smoke cigars, you still run the risk of developing cancers, particularly mouth, throat and oesophageal cancers.
- **Limit alcohol consumption** People who regularly drink more than the recommended limit (2–3 units a day for women; 3–4 units for men) are at risk of developing gastritis – inflammation of the stomach lining – peptic ulcers and cirrhosis of the liver. Heavy drinkers are also more likely to develop cancer of the digestive tract.
- **Cut fat intake** Researchers estimate that more than a third of cancers may be related to eating habits. Diets high in fat have been linked to increased risk of various cancers, including colon cancer.

The main culprits – food-poisoning micro-organisms

Many different micro-organisms cause food poisoning. Some organisms are ubiquitous, others tend to be found in particular types of food. The timing between eating a contaminated food and the onset and duration of symptoms varies widely depending on the particular organism responsible. Check out the chart below for the most common culprits.

Bacterium	Symptoms	Common foods	Time from eating	Duration of symptoms
SALMONELLA	Diarrhoea, vomiting, fever, headache, abdominal cramps	Raw meat, poultry eggs and egg products	12–24 hours	1–7 days
STAPHYLOCOCCUS AUREUS	Diarrhoea, vomiting, nausea, abdominal cramps	Cold meat, poultry, custard, trifle and cream	2–6 hours	6–24 hours
CLOSTRIDIUM PERFRINGENS	Diarrhoea, abdominal cramps	Cooked meat, poultry, fish, stews, pies and gravy	8–22 hours	24–48 hours
BACILLUS CEREUS	Vomiting, diarrhoea, abdominal cramps	Boiled or fried rice that has been kept warm or inadequately reheated	1–16 hours	12–24 hours
ESCHERICHIA COLI (E. COLI)	Diarrhoea, vomiting, mild fever, abdominal cramps.	Many raw foods	12–72 hours	1–7 days
CAMPYLOBACTER JEJUNI	Diarrhoea, abdominal cramps, fever, sometimes bloody stools	Milk and raw poultry	3–5 days	Days to weeks
VIBRIO PARAHAEMOLYTICUS	Mild abdominal cramps, diarrhoea	Seafood and fish	12–18 hours	2–5 days
LISTERIA	Mild fever. In pregnancy, can result in miscarriage or stillbirth	Unpasteurised milk and dairy products, cold meats	2–49 days	Days to weeks

Current guidelines recommend a total fat intake of no more than 30 per cent of daily calories, which converts to about 95g fat for a man and 75g for a woman.

• **Eat plenty of fresh fruit and vegetables** A diet rich in fruit and vegetables seems to protect against cancer of the oesophagus, stomach and colon. Eating a high-fibre diet also reduces the risk of diverticular disease – a sometimes painful condition that affects the large intestine. Some fruit and veg may be better than others: research suggests that oranges, spinach, corn, strawberries, bananas and apples are especially good as they are rich in antioxidants, chemicals that neutralise cancer-causing free radicals. But don't worry about matching your fruits to a specific disease, just focus on eating five or more servings a day from a variety of fresh produce – leafy greens, carrots, broccoli, tomatoes, garlic, onions and fruit of all kinds. Other risk factors for gut health are stress (see pages 52–53), caffeine (see page 60) and a lack of exercise (see page 84–89).

A GUT HEALTH RISK?

Food is a common source of gastrointestinal illness. Bacterial contamination of food is usually to

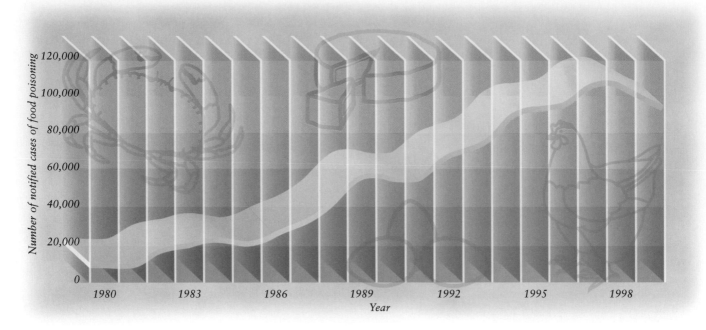

120,000
100,000
80,000
60,000
40,000
20,000
0

1980   1983   1986   1989   1992   1995   1998

Year

The rise of food poisoning

The incidence of food poisoning has increased sharply. In 1980 10,432 cases were reported in the UK. By 1999 the figure had risen almost tenfold to roughly 97,000.

blame for acute gastroenteritis (see chart, page 43), but viruses can also be the cause. It can take a few hours or several days before symptoms of food poisoning develop so it can be hard to pin down the offending food.

The time between eating infected food and getting ill varies according to a number of factors: the organism responsible, the number ingested and the presence of toxins – poisonous substances produced by certain bacteria. A person's age and general health also come into the equation. If vomiting starts within an hour of eating a food, the cause is usually a bacterial toxin or, rarely, chemical poisoning from metals from tins.

A matter of numbers

Food poisoning has escalated in recent years. There are an estimated 2 million cases of diarrhoea and/or vomiting in the UK each year due to food poisoning, although only a fraction of these are reported to doctors. The micro-organisms most commonly found in food-poisoning outbreaks are *Clostridium* (from cooked meat and meat products, poultry and fish) and *Salmonella* (from raw meat, poultry and eggs and egg products). The finger of blame has been pointed squarely at modern intensive farming methods, which allow the spread of bacteria between animals and encourage drug-resistant strains through the routine use of antibiotics. Battery-reared poultry are also under prolonged stress, which is believed to lower their immunity to infection.

The multiplication factor

Bacteria multiply at an astounding rate: each bacterium may replicate every 10–30 minutes, so a single organism may become many millions within just a few hours. Bacteria need a food supply (almost any will do but meat, milk, eggs, poultry, fish and seafood and their products are favourites), warmth (a temperature between 20°C and 37°C), moisture, air and sufficient time.

You never know if bacteria have grown on food, as there may be no mould, no smell or change in taste. So don't be tempted to use something that is way past its use-by date because it still looks and smells okay. You could be putting your digestive

Could 'clean' intestines cause inflammatory bowel disease?

TALKING POINT

More people than ever have inflammatory bowel diseases such as Crohn's disease. These diseases are thought to result from the immune system attacking proteins in cells of the large intestine. One theory holds that immune system development is linked with our early exposure to micro-organisms. With improved sanitation we now meet fewer micro-organisms in childhood and the immune system overreacts to harmless organisms.

SIMPLE STEPS TO SAFE EATING

Some aspects of food hygiene are common sense but others may be new to you. Cast your eye over the simple measures to limit bacterial spread in your kitchen that can make the difference between an upset-free digestive system or one in persistent trouble.

PERSONAL HYGIENE

- *Wash your hands before touching food. If you handle raw meat, fish or poultry, wash you hands again before touching any other food. Always wash hands after handling waste food and after visits to the toilet.*
- *Dry hands thoroughly, because dry hands have fewer bacteria.*
- *Any cut, burn or skin break on the hands – no matter how small – may contain additional bacteria and should be covered with a dressing.*

PREPARING AND STORING FOOD

- *Kitchen surfaces and utensils should be cleaned thoroughly and frequently with hot water and detergent.*
- *Use separate chopping boards for raw and cooked meat and vegetables.*
- *Salad, vegetables and fruits should be well washed or peeled.*
- *Wash all surfaces and utensils with detergent after contact with raw food, especially meat, and before using them for anything else.*

- *Ideally, meat and fish should be cooked or frozen on the day of purchase.*
- *Frozen food should be thawed properly in the refrigerator (not left out on the worktop) before cooking. Once thawed, the food should be cooked and eaten within a short time.*
- *Be particularly vigilant when dealing with high-risk foods, such as meat, eggs, poultry and dairy products, as they all require extra care.*

SAFE COOKING

- *The safest methods of cooking are pressure-cooking, grilling, roasting or frying because of the high temperatures that are reached.*
- *To destroy potentially hazardous bacteria, cooking must be thorough; if you are roasting a large joint of meat, use a meat thermometer to check that it has reached the right temperature.*
- *Avoid 'part-cooking' in advance. This can create the ideal conditions for bacterial growth. It is safer to keep raw meat*

in the refrigerator overnight and then cook it the next day.
- *If you can't eat food when planned, cook it while the food is fresh then freeze it, rather than freezing the raw foodstuffs and cooking at a later date.*
- *Once cooked, either eat food straight away or cool it rapidly and refrigerate within 1½ hours to avoid the multiplication of any surviving bacteria or heat-resistant spores.*

system at risk. Traditionally, people pickled foods or stored them in salty water to preserve them and discourage bacterial growth. These extreme conditions – acidic vinegar or high salt concentrations – prevent bacteria from multiplying. Other sterilisation techniques involve extremes of temperature. High temperatures (above 63°C for at least 30 minutes, as in the pasteurisation of milk) or low (refrigeration at 1–5°C, which slows bacterial growth, or freezing, which halts bacterial growth but doesn't kill bacteria) also prevent any possible bacterial colonies from growing.

Eating out? Spot the danger signs

Eating at home is under your control, but what about eating out? Look for obvious signs of poor hygiene in restaurants, such as unclean surfaces and poorly washed crockery and cutlery. Beware of food served less than piping hot. If you are at all concerned about hygiene in a restaurant, either leave immediately or avoid dishes that contain poultry, meat, fish or seafood.

TRAVEL HEALTH

Today, more people than ever before travel for work or pleasure to worldwide destinations. With travel comes the need for awareness on diseases you might contract abroad and advice on how you can avoid developing them.

TUMMY TROUBLE-FREE HOLIDAYS
DAN AND EMILY ARE HOLIDAYING ON THE EASTERN INDIAN COAST. THEIR DOCTOR CHECKED THEIR JABS WERE UP TO DATE AND GAVE THEM PRACTICAL ADVICE ON HOW TO LOOK AFTER THEIR DIGESTIVES SYSTEMS ABROAD.

8.00 EMILY BRUSHES HER TEETH AND RINSES WITH BOTTLED WATER. DAN CHECKED THE SEAL WAS IN PLACE WHEN HE BOUGHT IT. THEY NOW HAVE A SUPPLY TO KEEP THEM GOING FOR A FEW DAYS.

8.30 THEY TUCK INTO A FRUIT SALAD THEY MADE THEMSELVES FOR BREAKFAST. DAN PEELED THE FRUIT FIRST. THEY DRINK BLACK TEA AS THEY HAVE BEEN ADVISED TO AVOID MILK.

13.30 HAGGLING AT THE MARKET WORKS UP AN APPETITE AND THEY STOP AT A LOCAL STALL FOR LUNCH. THEY OPT FOR VEGETABLE CURRY AS THERE DIDN'T SEEM TO BE ANY KIND OF REFRIGERATION.

20.00 DAN TAKES EMILY BACK TO A RESTAURANT HE SPOTTED EARLIER AND IT'S BUSTLING AGAIN NOW. WHILE EMILY PONDERS OVER THE MENU, DAN POPS TO THE LOO AND CHECKS OUT THE KITCHEN ON THE WAY.

Travellers' diarrhoea

Every year more than a million people have diarrhoea while on holiday. Usually it lasts no more than four days and is caused by bacteria in the locale that are new to your stomach, although harmless to the locals. Often, travellers' diarrhoea is due simply to a change in diet, which disturbs your gut flora, or from eating too much fruit or drinking too much alcohol. But some cases are due to intestinal infections. The most common culprit is a toxin released from the bacteria *E. coli*. This toxin causes stomach cramps, vomiting and watery diarrhoea. Dysentery, a particularly severe form of diarrhoea, comes from ingesting food or water contaminated with *Salmonella*, *Campylobacter* or *Shigella* bacteria. Other causes are rotavirus, *Giardia lamblia* and *Entamoeba histolytica*, but one-quarter of cases have no identifiable cause.

So what should you do if you develop diarrhoea? Your main concern should be to avoid becoming dehydrated, so drink plenty of fluids. Oral rehydration salts are best – you could take some with you, just in case – but add them to bottled or boiled water. By combining salt and sugar in a specific ratio, these rehydration salts maximise the water absorbed in your large intestine to restore your hydration status (see page 120 for a simple recipe).

While recovering, stick to a bland diet – plain rice, bread and soup are good. If you don't have time to wait for the rehydration salts to take effect, you might consider using antidiarrhoeal drugs to control the symptoms. They are useful if you have to travel but may prolong the diarrhoea by retaining organisms in the gut. They can also cause constipation. Consult a doctor if your diarrhoea lasts for more than 12 hours, is blood-stained or if you have a high fever.

Avoiding tummy troubles

There are several positive steps you can take to avoid 'the runs' on holiday.
- When eating out, choose places used by travellers as well as locals, and stick to those that are busy.

12.00 DAN IS TEMPTED BY AN ICE-CREAM, BUT EMILY REMINDS HIM THE TRAVEL GUIDE WARNED AGAINST DAIRY FOODS. INSTEAD HE OPTS FOR A BOTTLE OF COLA, WHICH HE ENJOYS SIPPED THROUGH A DRINKING STRAW TO AVOID CONTACT WITH THE RIM.

23.30 BACK IN THEIR ROOM, THEIR EMERGENCY MEDICAL SUPPLIES BOX STILL HAS ITS FULL QUOTA OF ORAL REHYDRATION SACHETS, WATER PURIFICATION TABLETS AND (THE LAST RESORT) ANTIDIARRHOEAL DRUGS.

Can you take drugs to prevent diarrhoea on holiday?

Most people taking a two-week holiday in the Mediterranean will find antidiarrhoeal drugs completely unnecessary. But if you're travelling to a remote region where it's unlikely you'll find medical help, you may want to consider talking to your doctor about taking a course of antibiotics, such as ciprofloxacin, to prevent diarrhoea. This can be taken beforehand or as soon as symptoms occur.

ASK THE EXPERT

- Fast-food stands are a matter of judgment – check that a stand seems hygienic and that meat is kept cool and cooked thoroughly.
- Ice-cream and dairy products such as curd and yoghurt are best avoided in developing countries.
- Travel guides usually say whether tap water is safe to drink, but water that is safe for locals may contain bacteria that upsets your gut simply because it is unfamiliar. If in doubt, buy bottled water (with the seal intact), boil water or use purification tablets.
- If you are not drinking the local water, try to avoid ice cubes in drinks as these are often tap water. Avoid salads, which will probably have been washed in tap water, and fruit, unless it can be peeled.
- Don't assume that it is safe to eat and drink everything in your hotel because it has 4 or 5 stars. Stick to the advice given above to be sure.

Be involved in your healthcare

Your health is your most vital asset, and by working in partnership with your GP you can help to maintain your digestive health. Your doctor can give you advice on how to prevent and pick up on any problems early.

CHECK OUT ANY SYMPTOMS

All of us from time to time suffer a bout of constipation, diarrhoea or excessive bloating. Normally, if we think about it, we can put it down to a few days of an unusually low-fibre or high-fibre diet. Short-lived symptoms are usually nothing to be concerned about. But there are symptoms that you should take seriously and consult your doctor.

- **Abdominal pain** This can be associated with a multitude of conditions. The severity of the pain doesn't always reflect the severity of the condition. Severe abdominal

Salad days
Living a gut-friendly lifestyle is not just about keeping to a healthy diet – it also includes learning when to visit your doctor and when to deal with things yourself.

pain can be due to something as innocuous as wind or the cramping of viral gastroenteritis, while relatively mild pain may be a symptom of early appendicitis. Pain that is persistent should alert you to consult your doctor.

- **Indigestion** While common and usually harmless, indigestion that continues for more than one to

two weeks, especially in over-50-year-olds, may be a sign of a more serious condition such as oesophageal or stomach cancer.
- **Difficulty or pain swallowing** Although this might be due to simple inflammation of the oesophagus, this is an important and serious symptom. Always consult your doctor if it persists for more than a few days.
- **Change in bowel habit** If you have diarrhoea or constipation that continues for more than five days, see your doctor because you may have an obstruction or other significant problem.

Use the 'Help your doctor to help you' box opposite to think about questions your doctor may ask you.

SCREENING FOR ALL?

Your general practitioner can advise you on any tests that might be useful, especially as you get older. Many doctors run regular clinics, such as well-woman and well-man clinics, at which you can have a general medical check-up – the aim being to pick up problems before they become serious or difficult to treat successfully. The frequency of screening tests depends on your previous health, your family history of digestive problems and your present state of health.

The 50-year milestone

From the age of 50 the risk of digestive problems, such as colon cancer, increase and you might want to talk to your doctor about a check-up or screening test.

Your doctor can get a lot of information from doing a general examination of the digestive system, and if you have any digestive problems this will be the first step in finding out what's wrong. This examination usually includes looking at your physical appearance: the hands, eyes, face and abdomen. Your doctor may also carry out a physical examination of your rectum, which involves placing a gloved finger inside to feel for any abnormalities.

blood in the stools – the faecal occult blood (FOB) test. A positive result will lead to more precise, but invasive, investigations such as a colonoscopy, in which a doctor looks inside the colon with a special instrument (see page 115), flexible sigmoidoscopy (see page 114) and barium enema (see page 108).

> *In the UK, 30,000 people are diagnosed with colorectal cancer annually; nine out of ten people treated at an early stage survive for at least five years.*

Your doctor may also arrange blood tests to look for anaemia and to check liver function, especially if you drink alcohol to excess.

Screening for colon cancer
The emerging consensus is that everyone should be screened for colon cancer from the age of 50, although this is not done routinely in the UK. General screening uses a simple test to detect tiny traces of

One problem with the FOB test is that it produces a lot of 'false positive' results – it may detect blood in people who are actually healthy. However, treatment for colon cancer has a much higher success rate if it is detected and treated early, so screening tests are still used.

Family fortunes
Some people are at higher risk of colon cancer than others. If there's someone in your family with colon cancer you may need to be tested at regular intervals before you reach 50 (see page 97). If a parent or sibling has had colon cancer (especially at a fairly young age), doctors often advise people to have a colon-oscopy once every five years, starting ten years before the age the relative was diagnosed. People who have conditions that affect the large intestine, such as ulcerative colitis or

Is it serious?

Any of the symptoms below warrant a prompt visit to the doctor. Before the appointment, it may help to write down details of when symptoms started, their severity or frequency.

- *Prolonged diarrhoea. When did it start? Do you have any other symptoms?*

- *Bleeding from the rectum, bloody stools or vomiting blood. When did it start?*

- *Persistent abdominal pain. Is it sharp, crampy or dull?*

- *Unexplained loss of appetite and weight loss.*

- *Change in bowel habits, such as persistent or alternating diarrhoea or constipation, especially if you are over 50.*

- *Yellow discoloration of your skin or whites of the eye.*

A question of taste
Papillae (red) surround a central taste pore (blue), which leads to a barrel-shaped taste bud underneath. Taste bud numbers go into decline as we get older.

Crohn's disease, may also need to be screened more often than the general population because they are at higher risk of developing colon cancer. Doctors recommend that people with extensive ulcerative colitis have a colonoscopic investigation every two to three years, starting about ten years after their initial symptoms.

THE AGEING GUT
As we get older, subtle changes take place in the gut. We may feel inclined to add extra salt or spices to food, for example, to compensate for a

Absorbing medicines

Medicines are usually swallowed and absorbed in the gut. Some drugs are absorbed straight from the stomach, but most are absorbed in the small intestine. The rate of absorption depends on whether or not there is food in the stomach and what formulation of drug is taken. Prescribed medicines usually come with an instruction to take them before, with or after food. Some medicines don't damage the stomach mucus lining and are best taken before a meal. Others can irritate the stomach, making you feel nauseous; they must be taken with or after food, which reduces their irritant effects. Soluble drugs whiz through the intestinal lining and are absorbed rapidly. Next in terms of speed are suspensions, followed by tablets, which have to be broken down before the drug can be used.

natural decline in numbers of taste buds. The tongue can also help us to spot dietary problems: vitamin B_{12} deficiency may cause it to go pale, while a shiny tongue may reflect a lack of iron, B vitamins or folic acid.

A dry mouth

A common complaint among older people is dryness of the mouth, sometimes associated with painful small ulcers. If you have this problem check with your doctor, because medication could be to blame. Other causes include diabetes, infections or skin diseases. Chewing gum can stimulate saliva production.

Slowing down

The production of stomach acid and digestive enzymes often declines with age, leading to poor absorption of nutrients from food into the body. There is a gradual sluggishness of the bowels, and specific bowel disorders such as diverticular disease are more common in older people.

MEDICINES AND YOUR GUT

Some medicines, especially when taken everyday, can have damaging effects on your digestive tract. If you take medicines regularly and often suffer from digestive complaints, alert your doctor so that you can discuss available alternatives.

Aspirin and related drugs

Non-steroidal anti-inflammatory drugs (NSAIDs), which include aspirin and ibuprofen, are prescribed for arthritis and other inflammatory conditions, but can also be bought over the counter as painkillers. When taken regularly, these drugs may cause stomach ulcers. They have a direct irritant effect on the stomach

lining and also inhibit formation of chemicals known as prostaglandins, which in the stomach are responsible for maintaining the protective mucus lining. When these are inhibited by prolonged NSAID treatment, normal stomach acid may dissolve the weakened mucus and cause ulcers.

The problem is a worrying one because millions of prescriptions for NSAIDs are written in the UK alone every year. Over 2000 people die each year from bleeding related to this type of ulcer.

Try to take NSAIDs with food to minimise the irritant effect on the stomach. Also, ask your doctor for the 'gut friendlier' formulations.

Other drugs

According to one study, 30 per cent of over-60-year-olds take laxatives, probably in the mistaken belief that

Astonishingly, 15 per cent of Britain's population take a laxative at least once a week.

a daily bowel motion is necessary for health. Long-term use of laxatives, particularly those derived from senna pods, may cause degeneration of the nerves supplying the colon, making the constipation worse.

Antacids are taken to ease indigestion and heartburn. Long-term use can cause diarrhoea or constipation, but occasional use should not cause problems.

Antibiotics may adversely affect the natural population of bacteria in the large intestine – the gut flora – and diarrhoea is a common side effect of antibiotic treatment.

HEALTHY LIVING FOR YOUR DIGESTIVE SYSTEM

The simple fact that digestive illness varies so dramatically around the world suggests that lifestyle is a key element in maintaining digestive health. Factors that have the potential to wreak havoc with your finely tuned digestive system are explored over the following pages, together with the positive ways you can take your digestive health into your own hands and give yourself a real appetite for life.

52 *Psychological factors such as stress can have an extensive effect on your gut. Learning how to handle and reduce this stress is vital.*

54 *Even a couple of drinks can upset your delicately balanced digestive system. Discover what you can do to soften these effects.*

58 *Tobacco and nicotine provoke diverse actions on your gut in both the short and the long term, but very few of them are positive.*

60 *Consumed in moderation, the effects of caffeine are mild – in fact drinks such as tea can even be good for your gut health.*

Combating stress

Long-term stress can be particularly harmful to your digestive system, contributing to stomachaches, diarrhoea and irritable bowel syndrome. For some of these problems, the remedy lies in learning to relax and keep the pressure at bay.

A GUT REACTION

Stress affects us all to a greater or lesser extent, be it through work, a busy lifestyle or even from being bored. Physical and emotional stress switch the body to a heightened state of alertness to get ready to fight or else make a run for it – but at the expense of digestion.

At times of stress, blood supply to the gut is virtually shut down and digestion is sacrificed in favour of faster heart rate and breathing. So the gut is deprived of essential blood and nutrients, and digestion is temporarily brought to a halt. Saliva production falls – resulting in a characteristic dry mouth.

Curbing hunger

Diversion of blood from the gut can also affect appetite. Reduced blood flow is thought to slow or even stop the stomach from emptying completely. This may make us feel either not hungry or nauseous. At the same time, the body starts to mobilise reserves of fuel (in the form of the carbohydrate glycogen) that have been stored in the liver, converting it to glucose and then transporting it to where it's needed most. This glucose may also directly suppress the brain's appetite centre. Once the stress is gone, hunger and digestion restart and continue.

The rewards of relaxation
The abdominal breathing used in many Eastern techniques helps to exercise the diaphragm and relax both body and mind.

The litmus test

Exposure to stressful stimuli may alter the secretion of gastric acid and pepsinogen, an enzyme that stimulates acid production. As a result, the pH of the stomach falls – becoming more acidic – and secretion of the protective mucus layer of the stomach itself is reduced. At the same time, reduced blood supply to the gut and excessive production of the chemical prostaglandin can cause erosions in the stomach wall, and small areas may be worn away. This reaction can occur following extreme stress, such as after road accidents, and may aggravate peptic ulcer disease.

In the long term

Though these changes are beneficial for coping with serious immediate 'threats', repeated or prolonged stress may be harmful in many ways.

Long-term psychological stress has been linked with deleterious effects on the immune system, for example, which increases the risk of acute illnesses such as viral infections. At the lower end of the digestive system, the stress response can make the large intestines sluggish. If the stress is prolonged, this reaction can be a be a major cause of constipation.

Mint – a natural remedy
With its natural antispasmodic properties, mint is a great remedy for digestive complaints. Infused in boiling water to make tea, it can be helpful for people with IBS.

IRRITABLE BOWELS

Stress is one of the many factors that have been linked with irritable bowel syndrome (IBS). IBS is very common and affects more women than men. It causes a number of symptoms, such as lower abdominal pain, bloating and episodes of constipation or diarrhoea. So how can stress have such a dramatic effect?

Some studies have shown that individuals with IBS have overly sensitive muscles in the wall of the large intestine. These muscles react excessively to nerve impulses from the brain when under stress. These nerves control the intestinal muscles that squeeze and relax, which propels food along its journey.

This hypersensitivity to the stress response may account for some of the feelings of bloating, pain or altered bowel habit in people with IBS. What's more, a vicious circle can develop: while the gut muscles are overstimulated, pain messages are relayed from sensory nerve endings in the digestive tract to the brain, and the brain responds with the classic stress response, stimulating the hyperactive gut even further.

CALM DOWN YOUR GUT

Techniques to relieve stress can help to alleviate some of the symptoms of IBS in some people. So if you suffer from IBS, try this simple relaxation technique. Find somewhere to sit or lie down quietly for 20 minutes. Begin by concentrating on your breathing: breathe deeply, filling and emptying your lungs as completely as possible. Now concentrate on tensing and relaxing each part of your body one at a time. Start at the toes and work your way up to your eyebrows. Try doing this exercise every day.

De-stressing therapies

Some people benefit from more specific therapies, especially if they are also anxious or depressed. Some people benefit from psychotherapy or cognitive behavioural therapy, which attempts to modify behaviour and your response to certain situations. Others find hypnosis helpful or biofeedback, where you learn to control bodily functions through direct feedback about them.

Massage can sometimes help to relieve cramping abdominal pains, especially in children. Slow, rhythmic and firm massage strokes are applied in a clockwise circling motion around the perimeter of the tummy – following the outline of the large intestine. A hot-water bottle may provide some welcome pain relief.

Calming medicines

Antispasmodic medicines act on the wall of the gut, reducing the transmission of nerve signals to the wall of the large intestines and thus helping to stop gut spasms.

Mint is a natural antispasmodic. Peppermint tea has long been used as an aid to digestion, and for those that can't stomach the tea, peppermint oil capsules deliver directly to the lower part of the large intestine for pain relief. See pages 76–77 for more remedies for digestive problems. If you have persistent pain or symptoms such as a change in normal bowel habit, weight loss or vomiting, it is important to seek medical advice.

IT'S NOT TRUE!

'Stress is the main cause of ulcers'

It's a widely held belief that stress causes peptic ulcers, but research has shown that there are other more important factors at work. Infection with *Helicobacter pylori* bacteria, smoking and taking aspirin or other nonsteroidal anti-inflammatory drugs for a prolonged time all increase the risk of peptic ulcers. While day-to-day stress may result in a small increase in gut acidity – and consequent feelings of discomfort or indigestion – it doesn't cause actual ulceration.

Alcohol: ally or culprit?

Is alcohol a friend to your digestive system? After all, a moderate alcohol intake has been shown to be good for your heart. Or is every alcoholic drink simply a bad influence on your digestive health?

Much folklore surrounds the drinking of alcohol and its impact on digestion. All sorts of alcoholic drink have been claimed to aid digestion, but there is little evidence of this.

AN ALCOHOLIC HISTORY

The idea of the apéritif, the before-dinner drink, came from Sweden, when in the 18th century a pre-dinner snack, called a smörgasbord, consisting of herring, cheese, bread and aquavit (an alcoholic spirit made from potatoes) was served. The idea spread to France and strong spirits were served before dinner to stimulate the appetite.

Spirits were believed to have medicinal properties long before they were drunk for pleasure. As far back as biblical times, people valued wine as a medicine, believing it kept the digestion working well and protected the body from bad 'humours' and cleared 'maggots from the brain'. Bénédictine liqueur, for example, was originally produced as a way of preserving herbs (growing around the Benedictine Abbey in Normandy) for an elixir to combat local diseases.

AN ABSORBING TALE

Once you've swallowed a mouthful of an alcoholic drink, it flows down the oesophagus through a sphincter (an opening controlled by a band of muscle) and into the stomach. This is where absorption into the bloodstream begins. Up to 10 per cent of the alcohol you've drunk will be absorbed through the mucus-lined stomach wall. The rest passes into the small intestine – the main site of alcohol absorption.

Lining the stomach

The contents of your stomach influence what happens next in alcohol's journey. If you've recently eaten, the pyloric sphincter between the stomach and the small intestine will be closed. This shut sphincter keeps food in the stomach long enough to be broken down by acids released through the stomach wall. It also keeps alcohol from passing straight through to the small intestine and so it doesn't get absorbed so quickly.

The rule is, then, that if you line your stomach before drinking you are less likely to end up under the table after a few drinks. Instead, your blood alcohol level will reach a slower, lower peak. If you drink on an empty stomach, your blood

Wine-loving nations
UK wine consumption has increased from 13 to 17 bottles per person per year over the last decade – still well below the French average of 78 bottles per person.

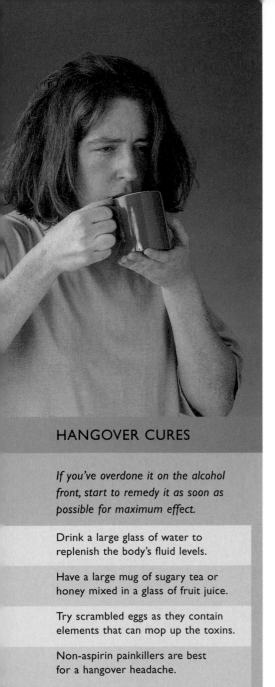

HANGOVER CURES

If you've overdone it on the alcohol front, start to remedy it as soon as possible for maximum effect.

Drink a large glass of water to replenish the body's fluid levels.

Have a large mug of sugary tea or honey mixed in a glass of fruit juice.

Try scrambled eggs as they contain elements that can mop up the toxins.

Non-aspirin painkillers are best for a hangover headache.

alcohol level will reach a peak level after only one hour. But if you've recently eaten, especially a fatty meal, the absorption of alcohol into the bloodstream is much slower – peak alcohol levels aren't reached for three to six hours, and the levels may be reduced by 25 per cent.

On an empty stomach, alcohol passes straight through the stomach into the small intestine where it is absorbed quickly through the millions of tiny finger-like projections called villi. Alcohol is then transported in the bloodstream, directly to the liver and from there to the rest of the body.

Breaking down the poison

The body sees alcohol as a poison so it does its best to get rid of it as quickly as possible. The first step in the detoxifying process is under the control of an enzyme called alcohol dehydrogenase, which is present in the stomach wall and in the liver. Another liver enzyme, aldehyde dehydrogenase, completes the conversion of alcohol into harmless constituents. The liver contains 17 varieties of aldehyde dehydrogenase, and within an hour it can handle 15ml (½floz) of pure alcohol.

We don't all have the same levels of these enzymes, however. In fact, some races have very little aldehyde dehydrogenase and are particularly vulnerable to the effects of alcohol. Half the population of Japan, for instance, don't have enough effective aldehyde dehydrogenase enzyme – just one or two drinks leads to the nausea and headaches normally associated with a bad hangover.

Regular drinkers also seem to metabolise alcohol faster. This is the result of another set of detoxifying enzymes being activated in regular drinkers – as a result, a lower peak alcohol level is achieved than in an average drinker. This is termed tolerance and accounts for the fact that regular drinkers can drink more before becoming drunk.

Why do people have an apéritif before eating?

It's a commonly held view that a small drink before a meal – a glass of dry white wine or small sherry – may stimulate the appetite. Most traditional apéritifs are slightly bitter and contain a relatively low percentage of alcohol. Apéritifs supposedly 'open' the digestive system and stimulate the appetite before a meal. The small amount of alcohol gets acid production started so that the stomach is ready to digest food straight away. However, there's no real evidence that one particular type of alcoholic drink is any better than another as an appetite stimulant.

ASK THE EXPERT

WHAT'S YOUR POISON?

Another factor in the absorption equation is alcohol concentration. Drinks with a low alcohol concentration, such as beer, are absorbed more slowly than the high percentage spirits. This is all to do with the concentration gradient between one side of the small intestine and the other. If the alcohol concentration in the lumen of the small intestine is 10 per cent, the alcohol passes through the walls at a slower rate than if the alcohol concentration were 40 per cent. In

The strongest known alcoholic drink was an Estonian spirit, distilled from potatoes, which measured a staggering 98 per cent on the alcohol content scale.

Whisky *has a similar alcohol content to brandy and cointreau* **40%ABV**

Vodka *has a similar alcohol content to gin* **37.5%ABV**

Red wine *is usually 11–14% ABV, whereas white wine is usually 8–12%ABV*

Champagne *measures* **12%ABV**

Mild/light beer *has a low alcohol content* **3.1%ABV;** *a strong lager may measure* **5.5%ABV**

How strong is your poison?
Drinks with a high alcohol content (ABV – alcohol by volume) are more rapidly absorbed through the small intestine than low-alcohol drinks. You can use this list to see the alcoholic content of your favourite tipple.

addition, the greater volume of liquid present when drinking beer slows the emptying of the stomach. High alcohol concentration drinks also irritate the stomach lining, causing secretion of mucus and a slowed emptying of the stomach. Whereas carbonated drinks, like champagne, speed up the emptying of the stomach into the small intestine, where alcohol is quickly absorbed.

WOMEN VERSUS MEN
Women are more susceptible to the effects of alcohol than men for a number of reasons. One difference is they have a lower level of alcohol dehydrogenase, which breaks down alcohol, so more is absorbed into the bloodstream. But there are other differences too. Women have a lower percentage of their body weight as water compared with men of the same weight. So, if a man and a woman both drink three glasses of wine, women will have a higher percentage of alcohol in their bodies.

FAT OR THIN?
Broadly speaking, the heavier you are, the greater is the volume of water in your body. More water means that any alcohol consumed is more diluted in the blood and body tissues. This would seem to give the overweight person an advantage when it comes to dealing with alcohol, but this is lost if the excess weight is fat rather than muscle. Fat

PERIODIC DRINKING

Alcohol absorption is affected by the menstrual cycle. Many women find they succumb to the effects of alcohol faster in the couple of days around ovulation and in the time leading up to menstruation. This coincides with low levels of progestogen, which tends to speed the emptying of the stomach. When progestogen dominates (after ovulation) the stomach empties more slowly and so there is more time for alcohol to be broken down.

cells contain less water than muscle cells, so the body's water volume is correspondingly less in a person with more fat and less muscle.

THE WEIGHT CONNECTION
All but 5 per cent of the alcohol you consume at one go is broken down in the liver. The rest is eliminated in the breath, sweat, saliva and urine. A side product of alcohol breakdown in the liver is heat – in other words calories – for the body to use as energy. Alcohol has a calorific value of 7kcal per gram. These calories are often referred to as 'empty calories' – because they contain no nutrients. Someone drinking large amounts of alcohol as well as a full diet puts on weight due to the high sugar content of most alcoholic beverages.

People who regularly misuse alcohol are three and a half times more likely to die in a given time than the general population.

THE LONG-TERM VIEW

In past centuries, fermented alcoholic drinks were about the safest form of liquid intake – the fermentation process got rid of otherwise harmful bacteria in contaminated water. Now, other health reasons are used as an excuse to drink: namely that it may be good for the heart. But when it comes to the digestive system alcohol does nothing but harm.

Gut-damaging effects

Research has shown alcohol to be one of the worst stomach irritants we can ingest. It increases the production of stomach acid, upsetting the balance of acid to mucin – the protective substance lining your stomach walls.

The effects of this imbalance vary from mild heartburn or nausea, to a condition called gastritis where the stomach actually begins to digest its own lining. Any alcohol over 40 per cent ABV directly erodes the stomach mucosa, but all forms of alcohol can inflict similar wear and tear on the body if you drink enough.

As well as damage to the stomach, alcohol also causes inflammation and ulcers in the intestines – especially the first part, the duodenum.

Wreaking havoc with the liver

In the UK, liver disease is commonly caused by alcohol misuse. The first sign of liver damage is the deposition of fat in the liver, which can occur within days of heavy drinking. Abstinence from alcohol reverses this stage. If a person carries on drinking, fibrous scarring ensues, followed by irreversible damage. Cirrhosis may develop over a short period of time or, despite drinking sizeable amounts over a lifetime, may never develop.

The cancer risk

Experts believe there is a link between alcohol consumption and cancers of the digestive system, breast, throat and liver. This link particularly holds true for high-alcohol drinks such as spirits, as opposed to beer or wine. Researchers believe this to be due to the higher content of nitrogenous chemicals in spirits, and therefore drinking them with mixers will not reduce the risk.

Drugs and digestion

Most drugs, whether prescribed, bought over the counter or taken recreationally, have some effect on the gastrointestinal tract. The commonest side effects are nausea or diarrhoea. Some recreational drugs have more specific effects.

Cannabis

This is probably the most commonly used recreational drug in the UK. It creates a mood of relaxation, increased sociability and awareness of colours and sounds. It can cause hallucinations, nausea and vomiting. It also tends to cause a dry mouth and an increased appetite – known as the cannabis 'munchies'. While cannabis is currently illegal in Britain it was a prescribable drug until 1928.

Amphetamines (speed)

These drugs were developed during the 1920s as a stimulant for soldiers to prolong their periods of wakefulness and activity. Subsequently they were used in the 1950s and 1960s both for their antidepressant properties and for their ability to suppress appetite and cause weight loss. The appetite-suppressant effect is short-lived and once the effects of the drug have worn off the person is likely to feel extremely hungry.

Ecstasy (3,4 methylene-dioxymethamphetamine)

The amphetamine derivative Ecstasy is popularly believed to be a safe recreational drug. After an initial feeling of stomach butterflies a state of calm euphoria develops for about six hours. During this time the appetite is suppressed and there is usually a sensation of a dry mouth. Once the effect has worn off there is usually a state of increased hunger and tiredness as the body 'catches up'. There have been several deaths related to Ecstasy usage, usually from dehydration and overheating.

Tobacco and tummy trouble

Most people know about the big health risks from smoking – heart disease and lung cancer. But do you know how tobacco affects your digestive system? The nicotine that gets you hooked also has some diverse actions on your gut.

Since tobacco was first brought back from America over 500 years ago, billions of people around the world have spent a life hooked to one of nature's most addictive drugs. Within a week of smoking an individual can become both tolerant (needing more each time for the same 'hit') and dependent on tobacco. If the effect is so immediate, then it's no wonder that smokers find it so tough to quit.

Tobacco smoking is responsible for about 3 million deaths worldwide each year, yet people continue to smoke. The health-damaging effects of tobacco are well known and stem not just from nicotine but also from the hundreds of other chemicals that are inhaled when you smoke.

By the time the humble tobacco plant has been processed into cigarette tobacco, it contains over 400 different chemicals, some of which are poisons.

NICOTINE AND THE GUT

With each puff on a cigarette, 90 per cent of the nicotine (plus other chemicals) remain within the lungs while the remaining 10 per cent whisks its way into the bloodstream and then around the body.

Nicotine itself has a number of actions on the gut. Many smokers have distant memories of the first time they tried smoking: physical sensations of nausea and dizziness are a common theme; some people are even physically sick. Although such noticeable effects of this gastric stimulation fade, inside the body of a smoker the nicotine is wreaking havoc with the digestive system. The long-term picture is worse: higher risks of digestive disorders such as ulcers and cancer of the mouth, oesophagus, stomach and, possibly, the pancreas.

The ulcer problem

Many smokers particularly enjoy a cigarette after meals, claiming that it helps their digestion. But, once nicotine is in your system, your stomach suffers the consequences.

Does smoking a cigar really aid digestion?

Traditionally, cigars are smoked after dinner, but they do not contain any particular digestive agents. The real reason for the tradition has more to do with the time large cigars take to smoke – up to two hours – so that a person has longer to relax, which in turn may help digestion.

ASK THE EXPERT

Nicotine reduces blood flow in the stomach and slows down the speed at which the stomach empties into the small intestine. Nicotine also lowers the production of protective chemicals called prostaglandins so that the lining is more vulnerable to attack by gastric acid – leading to heartburn and indigestion. In the long term, smoking makes you more likely to develop peptic ulcers – and less likely for ulcers you already have to heal. Twice as many smokers as non-smokers have peptic ulcers.

Speedy gut syndrome

Nicotine's powerful chemical actions also target the nerves supplying the muscles of your digestive tract. This boosts the peristaltic transport of food, which may sound like a good thing, but speeding up the transit time can lead to diarrhoea.

The nicotine conundrum

Long-term smoking also has repercussions on inflammatory bowel diseases such as Crohn's disease and ulcerative colitis. While some research shows that nicotine (in patch form not tobacco) relieves ulcerative colitis; other studies have yet to confirm this. Smoking does, however, exacerbate Crohn's disease.

SMOKING AND SNACKING

Many people rely on the often used reason that when they stop smoking their appetite will run out of control, leading to an inevitable weight gain. Nicotine is an appetite suppressant and it probably works by prolonging the sensation of having eaten (satiety), which means that smokers are less inclined to snack or pick at food between meals. Once smokers quit, though, their appetite returns and some may start to snack more. Some individuals complain of constipation when they quit, which is probably related to the downturn in the stimulation of the intestinal muscle.

THE CIGAR CASE

Cigar smoking is often believed to be less dangerous than cigarette smoking because cigar smoke is not usually inhaled. However, there is a similar incidence of cancer of the mouth, throat, oesophagus and lungs among cigar smokers – partly due to the fact that many cigar users are ex-cigarette-smokers and still inhale.

EFFECTIVE STEPS TO QUIT

On average, people who have just stopped smoking eat 300–400 kcal more a day. But don't let this put you off – the benefits of quitting greatly outweigh the health problems from any small weight rise. Try these tips so that your no-smoking plan is also a no-weight-gain programme.

- **Pick out the benefits** Make a list of all the health benefits of giving up and keeping it in a prominent position; plan a date when you're going to stop and stick to it.
- **Enlist support** Encouragement from friends and family can make all the difference to whether you succeed or fail.
- **Snack healthily** Keep a stash of low-calorie snacks (carrots or celery are ideal) to nibble on when you feel the urge to snack.
- **Top up on OJ** Try drinking plenty of orange juice. Oranges contain citric acid, which makes your urine acidic too and helps to speed nicotine removal from your body. The tangy taste should also make you less likely to crave for a cigarette.
- **Drink lots of water** This can have a dual effect: flushing nicotine out of your body and preventing the constipation that is common in the few days after giving up.
- **Cut down on caffeine** Reduce the amount of coffee and tea you drink. There's some evidence that caffeine can make the nicotine craving worse.
- **Avoid contact with alcohol** For many people, alcohol and smoking go together. So it helps to stay away from bars for a while (it's also another way to reduce your calorie intake).

Work it out of your system
Increase the amount of exercise you do. Not only will this make you feel great, it will also boost your metabolism so your body burns off more of the calories you consume. You'll also start to notice how much easier exercise becomes once you've stopped smoking.

Caffeine, the double-edged sword

The caffeine in your tea or coffee may give your brain a lift, but does it do the same for your digestive system? In moderation, it seems its gut effects are mild and pose little cause for concern – but there are limits.

As well as stimulating your brain and boosting alertness, caffeine has irritant properties when it comes to your digestive system. Caffeine's diuretic action (it makes you produce more urine) can leave you feeling dehydrated, which in turn may lead to a lack of water within the intestines and so to constipation.

STIMULATING THE GUT

Caffeine boosts your metabolism slightly through stimulation of the autonomic nervous system, with a corresponding rise in heart rate and blood pressure. This metabolic increase means that food you eat is burnt more quickly. Caffeine may also have a slight influence on suppressing the appetite.

Gut commotion

As well as making you produce more urine, caffeine also promotes more visits to the bathroom by stimulating the bowels. Even relatively moderate amounts of caffeine have a mild laxative effect – which can be a godsend if you're suffering from a bout of constipation.

Caffeine blocks receptors for adenosine – a signalling chemical that controls the balance between

Refreshing herbal tea
Instead of your usual cup of caffeine-loaded coffee or tea, try drinking a herbal tea such as camomile tea instead. Fruit teas are also caffeine-free and can be drunk hot or chilled.

muscle contraction and relaxation. Adenosine promotes the relaxation of the intestinal muscles. When caffeine occupies adenosine's spot by blocking receptors, the smooth muscles of the intestinal wall contract more easily and fall into a characteristic peristaltic rhythm. This contraction and relaxation speeds the transit of intestinal contents along

the gut. Although this effect is well documented, no-one has ever reported any harmful results due to this mild laxative effect.

Paradoxically, if you're not a regular coffee drinker, caffeine could actually cause diarrhoea.

Interfering with minerals

Caffeine can influence how certain substances are absorbed within the intestine. In particular, caffeine interferes with the absorption of iron. If you are taking iron supplements for any reason, don't slosh them down with a cuppa because you won't benefit at all. Caffeine can also reduce the absorption of other minerals too, including calcium – important for bone formation – and zinc.

SENSIBLE CAFFEINE LIMITS

The average person in Britain today drinks about three or four cups of tea or coffee per day– that's about 400mg caffeine. The major sources of caffeine are coffee (containing anything between 40 and 180mg per cup), tea (about 50mg per cup) and cola drinks (12–40mg). The level of caffeine in diet drinks is the same as in standard cola drinks; so unless the label states that it's caffeine-free assume it isn't.

How much caffeine do you think you drink on an average day? If the answer is over five cups of coffee, then maybe it's time to consider cutting down.

Rather than suddenly stopping drinking caffeine altogether, try to reduce your caffeine intake by about half a cup of tea or coffee per day, substituting with another caffeine-free hot drink such as herbal tea.

Babies lack the liver enzymes necessary to deal with caffeine, so breastfeeding mums should limit their caffeine intake.

EATING FOR HEALTHY DIGESTION

We hear and read so many conflicting stories through the media telling us what we should or shouldn't eat, it can be difficult to know who or what to believe. Food is not the enemy of your gut, however, and the overall message is really a simple one. A well-balanced diet that contains sufficient fibre can represent a potential fountain of good health, without compromising the great pleasure that food gives us. Where problems do occur, adjustments to the diet or increased intake of certain 'superfoods' can often provide the answer.

Foods for your digestive system

The health of your digestive system depends on the inclusion of a number of basic food groups in your diet. Simple nutrients obtained from food can have profound effects on the functioning and efficiency of your gut.

Your diet is composed of three primary food groups: proteins, fats and carbohydrates. The first two of these groups are indirectly essential for the healthy functioning of your gut – proteins supply the building blocks for the cells, enzymes and hormones of your digestive system, while fats (eaten in moderation) are a vital energy source. They also supply important components for hormones, cell walls and other parts of your body. The third group of foods, carbohydrates, are used by your digestive system mainly to power the energy-intensive processes of digestion. In addition, one subgroup of carbohydrate – fibre – is particularly significant for your digestive tract, directly affecting its health and function.

Fresh fruit vs fruit juice
Fruit juice is a nutritious drink but it doesn't provide much fibre, most of which resides in the skin of the fruit. An apple provides about 1.6g of fibre whereas a 100ml glass of apple juice scores a big zero on the fibre scale.

THE FIBRE FACTOR

Doctors first began to find evidence that a high-fibre diet could protect against constipation, haemorrhoids and colon cancer more than 30 years ago. Dr Denis Burkitt and Dr Hugh Trowell looked at the diets of people living in rural African villages, who rarely suffered from these problems. The typical diet in these villages was based on unprocessed foods and contained around four times as much fibre as the typical Western diet. The research led doctors to propose that a high-fibre diet (which allows food to pass through the gut much faster and produces larger, softer faeces that are easier to pass) promotes healthy gut function and was responsible for the lower incidence of digestive disease.

What is fibre?

Dietary fibre used to be called roughage. Recently, it's had yet another name change – the correct scientific term now is non-starch polysaccharide (NSP). Most people, however, continue to use the name fibre. The term describes a number of substances, including cellulose, hemicellulose, pectin and gum (all of which are found in plant cell walls) plus algal substances (found in seaweeds and algae) and mucilages (from cell secretions). Another plant component, lignin from the woody part of plants, is a fibre provider.

There are two groups of dietary fibre: insoluble and soluble fibre. Many foods contain both types.

The origins of fibre
Plant cell walls, shown as solid ribs between the polygon cells, are the source of the fibre we get from eating fruit and vegetables. Cell walls contain cellulose, hemicellulose, pectin and gum, all of which are types of fibre.

Studies carried out at Bristol University have discovered that butyrate – a fatty acid formed when fibre is fermented by bacteria in the gut – can trigger the self-destruction of malignant tumours.

Insoluble fibre

Found mainly in cereals (especially bran and wholegrain wheat) fruit, vegetables and pulses, insoluble fibre absorbs water and holds it in the large intestine. This accounts for the health-giving properties that Burkitt and Trowell noticed – the resulting stools have a higher water content, making them larger and softer. Insoluble fibre also speeds up the rate at which waste material passes through the digestive system. Faster passage is believed to play an important role in preventing colon cancer by reducing the length of time that cancer-causing toxins are in the digestive system.

Soluble fibre

Great sources of soluble fibre include oats, oat bran, beans and pulses. This type of fibre can help to lower high blood cholesterol levels by binding to it in the gut and preventing its absorption. The bacteria that live in your large intestine can use soluble fibre as a substrate for fermentation (their way of making energy); the byproducts are volatile fatty acids, which may be protective against colon cancer, and gas. Soluble fibre also seems to help to regulate the absorption of sugar into the bloodstream.

How much fibre do we need?

About 80 per cent of the adult population in the UK do not eat enough fibre. While nutritionists recommend an average intake of 18g fibre a day, most people manage only 12g. For those adults who are prone to chronic constipation the recommended intake is much greater at 32g a day. But reaching the recommended target of 18g is easier than you think. The following sample menu for one days provides more than 23g of fibre.

- Breakfast of a glass of orange juice (0g), muesli with semi-skimmed milk (3.8g) and one slice of wholemeal toast (2.1g) adds up to 5.9g – a great start to the day.
- A quick and tasty lunch of baked beans (5.1g) on wholemeal toast (2.1g) clocks up another 7.2g.
- An evening meal of chicken casserole, accompanied by a jacket potato with skin (4.9g) and steamed broccoli (1.7g), followed by fresh fruit salad (1.0g) adds another 7.6g.
- Four dried, ready-to-eat apricots makes a tasty snack whatever the time of day and adds another 2.5g.

The fibre 'shopping list' on the right rates different fibre providers so you can choose those that are higher in fibre. If you're eating a high-fibre diet, it's best to make sure you're getting your fibre from a wide variety of foods.

Too much of a good thing?

While fibre is important for most people, there are some groups in whom too much fibre can cause problems. People with poor appetites may find it difficult to eat enough because high-fibre foods are very bulky. Some people with irritable bowel syndrome may find a high-fibre diet aggravates this condition.

Young children don't need a high-fibre diet – it will make them feel full without providing enough nutritional value and energy. Too much fibre will cause stomachaches and wind. Children under two need very little fibre; after this age, encourage them to eat fruit and vegetables, which supply fibre in manageable amounts.

FIBRE PROVIDERS	
PRODUCT	GRAMS OF FIBRE PER SERVING
FRUIT	
8 prunes	5.2g
8 dried apricots	4.9g
1 medium orange	2.0g
1 medium apple	1.8g
1 medium banana	1.1g
1 tbsp raisins	0.6g
VEGETABLES	
1 medium jacket potato (with skin)	4.9g
1 portion peas	3.6g
1 portion carrots	1.4g
2 tbsp sweetcorn	1.2g
BEANS AND PULSES	
3 tbsp red kidney beans	6.0g
1 small can baked beans	5.1g
3 tbsp chickpeas	3.9g
BREAKFAST CEREALS	
1 bowl (30g) branflakes	4.5g
2 Shredded Wheat	4.3g
2 Weetabix rusks	3.9g
1 bowl (50g) muesli	3.8g
BREAD	
1 slice wholemeal bread	2.1g
1 slice of granary bread	1.5g
1 slice white bread	0.6g
PASTA AND RICE	
Average serving wholemeal pasta	8.1g
Average serving pasta	2.8g
Average serving brown rice	1.4g
Average serving cooked white rice	0.2g

EASY WAYS TO BOOST YOUR FIBRE INTAKE

BREAKFAST Eat wholegrain cereal such as porridge, muesli or branflakes. Choose one that provides 3g of fibre or more per serving. Adding fresh or dried fruit provides even more fibre.

SNACKS Fruit, preferably with its skin, is a great way of increasing your fibre intake, and an easy snack. Try to eat a minimum of five servings of fruit and vegetables a day.

LUNCH Wholemeal or granary bread with a bowl of vegetable soup is a good high-fibre choice. When buying bread, look on the label for the words wholegrain, wholewheat or wholemeal. Try to use wholemeal flour for baking wherever possible.

SNACKS Ready-to-eat dried fruits such as apricots or raisins are good snack foods. They are also high in fibre.

DINNER Eat more beans and pulses – try adding them to soups and casseroles. Use brown rice instead of white rice and choose wholemeal pasta.

Bran on everything?

Bran is well known as a rich source of fibre but sprinkling it over everything you eat to increase your fibre intake is not a good idea. Bran contains high levels of phytate, a substance that binds with minerals such as iron, zinc, copper and calcium, blocking their absorption. Just two tablespoons of bran a day can be enough to cause a deficiency of these minerals in some people, although this is more likely to be a problem in the elderly and people with poor appetites.

Rather than boosting your fibre intake with bran, it is much better to eat a variety of foods that are naturally rich sources, such as wholegrains, fruit, vegetables, beans and pulses. This way you'll also be raising your intake of other health-promoting substances – vitamins, minerals and phytochemicals – at the same time. As another added bonus, people who switch to a high-fibre, low-fat diet often find they lose weight without restricting their food intake. High-fibre foods are bulky and slow down the rate at which the stomach empties, helping you to feel full for longer.

Too much too soon

If you're not used to eating a high-fibre diet, suddenly increasing the amount you eat can cause bloating and wind. Your digestive system needs time to adjust, so increase your fibre intake gradually and give your body time to adapt. If you do this, painful wind and bloating won't be a problem. If your current diet is not high in fibre, it can take a few weeks for the enzymes needed to digest fibrous foods to develop; if undigested foods pass into the large intestine they are fermented by the gut bacteria, producing gas. Wind-generating food culprits include beans and pulses, cabbage, brussels sprouts, grapes, raisins and apples.

FIBRE AND WATER – A HEALTHY PARTNERSHIP

To do its job properly fibre has to have fluid. Insoluble fibre passes through the digestive system pretty much unchanged. Once it arrives in the large intestine, however, it acts like a sponge absorbing large quantities of water – up to 15 times its own weight. This process helps to prevent constipation and problems such as diverticular disease by creating bulky, soft stools that are then easy to pass.

Food combining – diet fact or fiction?

TALKING POINT

Food combining – or the Hay diet as it is sometimes known, after its inventor Dr Howard Hay – is based on the idea that proteins and carbohydrates should not be eaten together at the same meal. The theory is that these food groups require different conditions for digestion, so if you eat them at the same meal inefficient digestion results, leading to a build-up of toxins in the body. Many people claim that abiding by the Hay diet gives them increased energy and a sense of well-being, although there is no scientific evidence to support this.

The maximum capacity of the colon is approximately 5–6 litres (8¾–10½ pints) of water; on an average day the colon absorbs between 1 and 2 litres (1¾–3½ pints).

Your large intestine absorbs water from drinks and food. In a low-fibre diet, more water can be absorbed from food as it moves slowly through the gut. Upping your fibre intake (especially insoluble fibre) means that the fibre 'competes' with the large intestine for available water and so less is absorbed. Aim for a fluid intake of at least 1.75–2 litres (3–3½ pints) every day to satisfy your body's need for extra water when on a high-fibre diet.

CARBOHYDRATES FOR ENERGY

Carbohydrate is a term used to describe a type of food composed of sugar molecules. Carbohydrates include simple sugars, such as glucose and sucrose, and complex substances such as starch (known as complex carbohydrates). Foods rich in carbohydrates also supply fibre, protein, vitamins and minerals, but their main job is to provide energy.

For a healthy diet, experts recommend that at least half of your daily energy requirements should come from high-starch carbohydrate foods such as bread, rice, breakfast cereals, pasta and potatoes. For most people in the UK this means doubling their current intake. Choose fibre-rich varieties such as wholemeal bread and wholegrain cereals whenever possible – these help to keep the digestive tract working efficiently and provide a slow-release form of energy that helps to keep blood sugar levels stable.

Starchy foods are not fattening

Some people mistakenly believe that starchy foods are fattening. In fact, they are low in fat and are also good sources of fibre. It is only when eaten in conjunction with fat – pasta in a rich creamy sauce, potatoes fried in oil – that these foods become high in calories. A 125g (4oz) serving of boiled potatoes contains only 80kcal, but the same weight of chipped potatoes contains 250kcal!

ARE VEGETARIAN DIETS HEALTHIER?

Vegetarianism is becoming increasingly popular – in fact, numbers have trebled over the past 15 years in the UK. Studies have shown vegetarians are less likely to suffer from several diseases including diverticular disease, irritable bowel syndrome, haemorrhoids and colorectal cancer. Like any diet, there are healthy and balanced, and unhealthy vegetarian diets. But on the whole, vegetarians tend to have diets that are higher in complex carbohydrates and fibre than meat eaters, which probably explains why they are less likely to suffer from intestinal problems.

BALANCING FOODS IS KEY

Remember that while fibre and carbohydrate are crucial for a healthy digestive system, eating a balanced diet containing protein, vitamins and some fat is vital for your body to function properly. Don't go to extremes and fill up completely on fibre-rich food.

A healthy gut for life

Maintaining a healthy gut doesn't simply depend on what you eat, but also on how you eat. Good eating habits benefit the long-term well-being of your digestive system, and the sooner you start the better off you'll be.

The process of eating is something that most of us take for granted, so it may come as a surprise to learn that the way you eat – from the timing of your meals to your activities while you are eating them – can affect your digestion and, in turn, your general health. Developing good eating habits is a major step towards a healthy lifestyle, benefiting your digestive system both directly and indirectly. Habits learned during childhood will last a lifetime.

Babies have more taste buds than adults, not just on the tongue but everywhere in the mouth. They also prefer bland foods, while adults will tend to enjoy many flavours as they 'acquire' tastes.

THE FIRST FOOD

It's great to know that the first food we have is perfectly formulated for an immature digestive system. Breast milk and formula milk both contain all the essential nutrients and are easily digested to release what a tiny body needs. Health visitors and doctors always encourage mothers to breastfeed at least for a few weeks since it helps to boost the newborn's immune system and stimulates bonding. But even if breastfeeding is not a success, a baby will thrive on formula milk.

STARTING ON SOLIDS

Weaning, sometimes called 'mixed feeding' or 'starting on solids', is the gradual process that begins when parents start to introduce solid foods into their baby's diet. Throughout weaning, milk should continue to be an important food, but as a baby's digestive system gears up it is vital to start to increase gradually the amount, texture and variety of foods in your baby's diet.

The process of weaning takes place over many months. At first (from the age of four to six months), foods are introduced one at a time to avoid upsetting the immature digestive system. After about six months you should be able to combine foods for your baby – although it's still best to introduce any new food one at a time before mixing them.

By about 9–12 months, as the digestive system matures and becomes more able to cope, a wider variety of foods of different types and texture can be added. Around the time of a baby's first birthday, the digestive system should have developed enough to be able to handle much the same sort of food as the rest of the family. Remember, however, not to include any salt in your baby's food.

Why do babies need weaning?

As babies get older milk alone cannot satisfy all their nutritional needs. Their stores of certain nutrients – such as iron, which is built up from the mother's supplies

A LIFETIME OF EATING

The food we eat changes through life, from our first milk feeds through to the adventures of weaning and discovery of enticing new foods, which can continue well into adulthood and later life.

It's not just what we eat that changes, but also how we eat and how often. In part, this is dictated by the way our digestive systems handle food. For example, the large meals that we may easily have coped with in our young adult life can become a cause of indigestion; so older people often opt for smaller more regular meals. Social and cultural influences also play a huge part in what and how we eat – as we enjoy making mealtimes a special occasion with our friends and families.

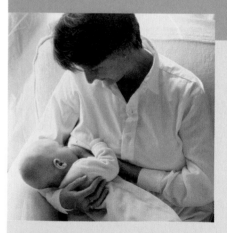

Milk – the first food of life
Our first eating habits are very much a one-to-one experience with our parents, most usually our mothers, at either the breast or the bottle.

Finger foods

Once toddlers have teeth, chewing foods is no longer a problem. Finger foods allow toddlers to enjoy feeding themselves, and older children can enjoy these as snacks – preferable to biscuits and salty snacks.

Developing exotic tastes

Teenagers may start to become more adventurous in their eating habits. A child who may have shunned any type of spicy food may become a teenager who tops everything with hot chili peppers.

Anyone for cake?

As we grow older, we tend to eat little and often, rather than in three big meals throughout the day. Some people also develop a definite 'sweet tooth' as their taste buds become less sensitive.

of iron before birth – start to run out and need to be supplemented by a more varied diet. Energy needs also increase. In addition, moving on to more solid foods also helps to develop the muscles necessary for chewing and for speech.

The process of weaning usually begins some time between the ages of four and six months, but the exact age depends entirely on the individual baby. Every baby is different and what suits one baby isn't necessarily right for another.

TODDLER TAMING

As children get older it's not unusual for them to become faddy about what they eat. They soon learn that refusing to eat is a powerful weapon and a good way of gaining attention. Usually, food fads are only a passing phase, but most parents are understandably concerned about the immediate effects of food refusal on their child's general health. This period is also significant in the longer term, as it can be a time when deep-seated attitudes to food and eating are laid down, such as associations between food refusal and control, or between eating and attention seeking.

Be food wise

Don't allow mealtimes to turn into a battle of wills. Never bribe, force or coerce a child to eat – this can make the problem worse. If your child refuses a certain food or meal, simply clear it away without any comment. Be aware that children often pick up bad eating habits from other members of their family. Discourage older siblings from being fussy and make sure that your own eating habits set a good example.

HAM AND PEA TORTILLA
Make a tortilla using eggs, ham and peas; complement the tortilla with a nutritious and fibre-rich carrot salad with dressing. Add some fruit juice for a complete and healthy meal.

PEANUT BUTTER AND APPLE SANDWICHES
Made with granary bread, peanut butter and sliced apple sandwiches are great for kids and adults alike. A cereal bar and fruit juice provide added nutrients for a perfectly balanced packed lunch.

PITTA BREAD LUNCH
Pack a wholemeal pitta bread with hummus and coleslaw and add a packet of low-fat crisps, a small box of raisins, a kiwi fruit, juice or sugar-free drink – perfect for kids.

PASTA, FETA AND CHERRY TOMATO SALAD
Mix cold pasta shapes with roughly chopped black olives, crumbled feta cheese, cherry tomatoes and diced cucumber for a balanced lunch. Include a drink of fruit juice or water too.

Snacks aren't all bad – young children may need 'top-ups' between meals in order to obtain sufficient energy. But offer sandwiches, fruit, scones or a fruit yoghurt rather than biscuits or salty snacks.

HEALTHY EATING FOR OLDER KIDS

Older children and teenagers often eat a lot of unhealthy snacks and processed foods. You can help to improve their diets by providing them with nutritious packed lunches, but preparing healthy food that children and teenagers will enjoy can be a challenge.

The main rule is to make food quick and easy to eat. Don't fall into the routine of providing the same packed lunch day after day – try to make the meals fun and imaginative. With children, it's important that food looks attractive – raw vegetables washed and cut into strips are colourful, easy to prepare and eat, and they provide all-important vitamins and minerals.

Sandwiches are the mainstay of most packed lunches. It's best to use wholemeal or granary bread, but if your child doesn't like them use high-fibre white, or compromise and use one slice of white and one slice of wholemeal. Introduce variety by using a selection of bread and bread rolls. Lightly toasted pitta bread splits easily to provide a natural pocket to take generous portions of salad and a range of different fillings.

Most children want something sweet in their lunch box. Home-made cakes and biscuits made using wholemeal flour are a healthier option than shop-bought varieties. Dried fruits such as raisins and apricots are also good options.

Avoiding indigestion and heartburn
Try some of these tips to reduce the chance of having indigestion and heartburn. As well as thinking about what you eat, also consider how and when you eat – eating too quickly or late at night are common causes.

DEVELOP HEALTHY ATTITUDES TO EATING

Eating habits developed in childhood lay the foundation for your attitude to food as an adult. But it is never too late to change your eating habits.

As well as paying attention to the kinds of food you eat, there are a number of tips you can follow to improve the way in which you eat. These simple measures can help to control your appetite and calorie intake; they can also help to make your diet more balanced and give your digestive system a helping hand.

Focus on your food

If you are distracted when you eat – by watching television, for example – you are are more likely to miss your body's 'fullness' signals. It takes about 15 minutes for messages from your stomach to turn off your brain's eating drive. If you eat too quickly, your stomach fills up before your brain knows that you are full and you will overeat, ending up feeling uncomfortable.

Try to make the time to sit down and eat your meals at a table – even

FOR THE OVER-80s

How to counteract poor appetite

Many older people find they don't feel like eating as much as when they were younger. Poor appetite can be a problem if it leads to inadequate nutrition.

- **Take a tipple** A small glass of sherry or your favourite alcoholic drink half an hour before you eat might help to get your appetite going. If you are taking any medicines, check first with your doctor or pharmacist.

- **Exercise** A short walk before your meals will help to stimulate the appetite.

- **Eat smaller meals** Three small meals a day will provide good nutrition in more manageable amounts than one or two larger meals.

- **Pop a vitamin pill** At this age, it's probably a good idea to take a multivitamin and mineral supplement. Ask your doctor or pharmacist for a recommendation.

- **Use 'build-up' drinks** As well as being nutritious snacks, the unflavoured varieties can be added to soups to enrich them.

CHANGES IN APPETITE AND DIETARY NEEDS

As we grow older physiological and psychological changes occur that have a direct effect on our nutritional needs. The body becomes less efficient at absorbing and using many vitamins and minerals. In addition, the long-term use of some prescription drugs can reduce the ability of your body to absorb certain nutrients. At the same time, many people find that as they get older their appetite decreases. Yet the need for vitamins and minerals stays the same with age, or in some cases increases. So it becomes even more important for you to make sure that the food you do eat is healthy and that it supplies all the important nutrients your body needs.

Spice up your life

As you get older your sense of smell and taste becomes less acute and this can have a negative effect on both your appetite and your enjoyment of

if you are on your own – rather than grabbing food while you are busy doing something else. If you eat on the move, you are more likely to get indigestion and heartburn because blood that is needed for digestion is diverted away from the digestive system towards the muscles.

Chew properly

Chewing food thoroughly gets the whole digestive process off to a good start. It breaks food down into smaller, more manageable pieces, and mixes food with saliva, beginning the breakdown of carbohydrates into simple sugars. Chew each mouthful carefully before you begin the next. If you eat too quickly you swallow air, and this can lead to painful wind.

Less tea with meals, vicar

Caffeine and tannin – a substance found in abundance in tea – interfere with the absorption of iron from food as it passes through the gut.

Iron deficiency can result in tiredness, lack of energy and increased susceptibility to infection.

Cutting out tea, coffee and cola drinks with meals could help to boost your iron reserves. Vitamin C increases the absorption of iron from foods, so eating fruit and vegetables or drinking fruit juice at the same time as iron-rich foods (such as lean red meat or spinach) is a good idea.

Delay brushing

Don't brush your teeth immediately after eating or drinking acidic foods. The acid from fruit juice and foods like pickles can weaken the enamel of your teeth. Brushing your teeth straight after consuming such foods or drinks can make things worse. Instead, rinse your mouth with a little water and wait at least 45 minutes before brushing.

Good guys
The Lactobacillus acidophilus *bacterium is one of the 'good' bacteria that thrive in the healthy gut. They help to keep harmful bacteria in check and contribute to efficient digestion.*

food. Try compensating for these effects by pepping up the flavour of your meals with herbs and spices (don't overdo the spices), garlic, lemon juice, mustard or vinegar.

Enjoying your food

Eating should be a pleasure, so it's worth making an effort each day to plan your meals and enjoy them. Choosing a healthy diet doesn't have to be expensive or involve elaborate cooking. A well-planned snack can be just as nutritious as a cooked meal, while frozen vegetables and canned beans are as nutritious as fresh ones. Different foods provide different nutrients, so eating a varied diet is the best way to ensure that you get a good mix of all the necessary nutrients.

Bad guys
Although prolific in your intestines, particular strains of the Escherichia coli *bacterium (the rod-shaped organisms) and streptococci (the spheres) can be potentially harmful and cause gastrointestinal infections.*

CULTIVATE HEALTHY GUT FLORA

At birth, a baby's sterile digestive tract picks up bacteria from the mother and within a few hours the newborn's intestine is home to millions of friendly bacteria collectively known as the gut flora. By the time you reach adulthood, your gut flora number in the trillions, with more than 200 species of bacteria competing for the resources that you provide by eating.

A balanced gut flora

Your gut flora includes 'good' bacteria, the most prolific of which is a harmless strain of *Escherichia coli,* that help in the digestion process and produce important nutrients, and 'bad' bacteria that can cause illness. These good and bad bacteria coexist in a fine balance, which is extremely vulnerable to disruption. Stress, poor diet or taking antibiotics can all upset the bacterial balance allowing the 'bad guys' to gain the upper hand. Problems such as candidiasis (see below) may result.

Bacterial imbalances

Candida albicans is a yeast-like organism that occurs naturally in the mouth, digestive tract, vagina and on the skin. Normally, it causes no problems because it is kept in check by 'friendly' bacteria. If the immune system is weakened, however, or if the protective bacteria in the gut are destroyed by stress, poor diet or antibiotics, *Candida albicans* can grow unchecked causing a condition known as thrush (usually in the mouth or vagina).

Alternative health practitioners relate an overgrowth of *Candida* to bloating, diarrhoea and constipation.

Probiotic foods

There are certain steps you can take to keep the balance in favour of the good bacteria and give your gut flora a helping hand. One such step is to eat what are known as probiotics – foods or supplements that contain 'friendly' bacteria. Eating probiotics regularly delivers a fresh supply of good bacteria, preventing the growth of the bad guys that can cause problems. Probiotic foods include live yoghurt, which supplies 'friendly' *bifidus* or *acidophilus* bacteria, and fermented foods such as sauerkraut, buttermilk and miso.

Prebiotics

Eating foods that promote good bacteria is another way of addressing the balance of bacteria in your gut flora: they stimulate the growth of good bacteria in the gut while inhibiting the growth of bad bacteria. Prebiotics include the dietary fibre oligosaccharide, found naturally in Jerusalem artichokes, onions and chicory. Food manufacturers are looking into the possibility of adding these ingredients to a range of foods.

Some also believe that, in the digestive tract, *Candida albicans* can cause damage to the mucus that lines the gut, allowing waste products to leak into the blood, a condition that has been called gut dysbiosis.

Complementary practitioners believe that candidiasis and dysbiosis are extremely common and cause a range of problems such as chronic fatigue, headaches, skin problems and depression. However, this is not based on any scientific evidence or properly controlled trials.

Banish harmful micro-organisms

Candida albicans feeds on sugars and refined carbohydrates in the digestive tract. For this reason, one way of treating candidiasis is to follow a strict sugar-free diet. At the same time eating prebiotic foods and probiotic supplements can encourage

The food of cravings
Chocolate is the focus of many food cravings and is believed to stimulate the release from the brain of 'feel-good' hormones.

the gut to become recolonised with friendly bacteria. Other helpful foods to combat candidiasis include garlic and dark green leafy vegetables – these all have natural antifungal properties. Olive oil, which is rich in oleic acid, is also thought to be helpful because it inhibits the growth of *Candida albicans*.

FOOD CRAVINGS

Many women find that their monthly menstrual cycles are linked to food cravings. One in four women notice an increase in appetite just before their period is due – this is often accompanied by a craving for carbohydrates, in the form of sweets and, in particular, chocolate.

Chocoholics

Some scientists suggest that a craving for chocolate is caused by desire for a compound called phenylethyl-amine, a substance that stimulates the release of the 'feel-good' hormone dopamine. There is some evidence that the minerals chromium and magnesium can help to ease this sort of craving. Try adding foods to your diet that are naturally rich in these minerals. Foods to include are wholegrain cereals, brewer's yeast, meat, kidneys, cheese, nuts, pulses, bananas and green leafy vegetables.

Cravings during pregnancy

Women often experience weird and wonderful food cravings during pregnancy, probably an effect of changing hormone levels. Most of these food cravings are nothing to worry about. Be aware of your general diet, however, and make sure you eat all the nutrients you need.

Craving for non-food substances is known as pica and can be a sign of iron deficiency. You should mention it to your doctor or midwife. Make sure your diet includes enough iron-rich foods and vitamin C, which aids iron absorption.

Theories on cravings

Some people believe that cravings or aversions are signs of food sensitivity (see pages 78–82). For example, a person who hates milk may be lactose intolerant; others find they crave the substance that causes the sensitivity. Another theory is that your body craves foods that contain nutrients in which it is lacking, but no study has proved this to be true.

Should you eat the foods you crave?

Some people believe that cravings are the body's way of making sure that you eat foods providing specific nutrients that are lacking in the diet. There is, however, very little scientific evidence to support this view. Whether or not you should succumb to cravings depends to some extent on how often they occur. Provided your diet is generally healthy and balanced, go with the flow. If your cravings become bizarre or you're lusting after certain foods all the time, discuss this with your doctor.

ASK THE EXPERT

A healthy attitude to weight

Maintaining a consistent, healthy weight benefits your general well-being and the health of your digestive system. Diet fads aren't the answer to weight problems; the key is to develop a sensible attitude to weight and eating.

Weight is a modern obsession. In theory, this obsession could encourage people to maintain a healthy weight. But, in practice, the incidence of obesity has grown to epidemic proportions and more and more people have health-damaging attitudes to food and eating.

The issue of weight is of particular importance for your digestive system, because its workings and body weight are intimately related. Being overweight can seriously affect your gut health, while looking after your digestive system is one of the best ways to control your body weight.

WHAT IS A HEALTHY WEIGHT?

Our views on what constitutes an ideal weight and shape have changed dramatically over recent decades. In the 1950s Marilyn Monroe was considered to be the perfect female form. But today's waif-like catwalk models are a far cry from her more generous size 14 figure.

Magazines and fashion designers may promote thin models, but the true ideal weight is that at which people remain healthiest and live longest. Check out whether you are a healthy weight using the chart below.

Weight expectations

While no-one can deny that being overweight and obesity are growing problems in many Western countries, many women – and a growing number of men – have unrealistic ideas about what constitutes an ideal weight. Obsession with weight can itself cause serious health problems. One UK survey found that for every six women who regarded themselves as overweight only two were correct about their assessment.

How you feel about your weight can have a fundamental effect on your self-esteem and happiness and can have an important, long-lasting impact on your health. Eating disorders such as anorexia nervosa and bulimia can result in severe nutritional deficiencies and long-term problems like osteoporosis.

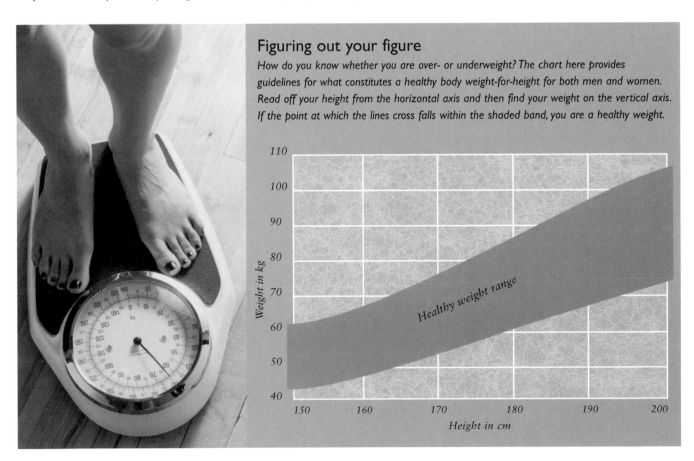

Figuring out your figure

How do you know whether you are over- or underweight? The chart here provides guidelines for what constitutes a healthy body weight-for-height for both men and women. Read off your height from the horizontal axis and then find your weight on the vertical axis. If the point at which the lines cross falls within the shaded band, you are a healthy weight.

Weight in kg: 40, 50, 60, 70, 80, 90, 100, 110

Healthy weight range

Height in cm: 150, 160, 170, 180, 190, 200

Reduce the amount of high-fat foods you eat. Try to combine any high-fat foods with high-fibre foods – fibre helps to reduce the absorption of fat by your gut. For example, eat full-fat cheese with wholemeal bread or full-fat yoghurt with slices of banana.

MAKE SMALL CHANGES FOR A MAXIMUM EFFECT ON YOUR WEIGHT

Making small changes to the way you eat and the type of food you choose can have a significant impact on your weight. The good news is that this doesn't have to mean missing out on your favourite foods. In fact, it is important to include foods that you enjoy eating. A diet that leaves you feeling deprived, unhappy or dissatisfied is a diet that's very quickly going to be abandoned.

Build some exercise into your daily routine. For example, walk up the stairs rather than taking the escalator or lift. If you travel by bus, hop off one stop earlier than usual and walk the rest of the way home.

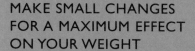

Never skip meals and don't allow yourself to get too hungry. If you do you'll be more tempted to snack and you are more likely to overeat at your next meal. Aim to eat three small to medium-sized meals. Using smaller plates can help you stick to smaller portions!

Try to reduce the amount of meat you eat and choose lean meat over fatty types. Trim away any visible fat from meat before cooking. When preparing or eating poultry, remove the skin first – this is where most of the fat lies.

Choose low-fat cooking techniques as much as possible – poach, braise, steam, dry-roast, grill or stir-fry.

Be prepared for snacking urges – make sure your cupboard is full of healthy foods and have plenty of low-calorie snacks available, such as fruit.

Write a list of food you want to buy, and try to stick to it when you go out shopping. Don't be tempted to buy crisps and biscuits if you know you won't be able to resist them the minute you get back home.

Freeze or throw away leftovers as soon as you've finished eating. That way, you won't be tempted to come back for more.

Can detox diets help in losing weight?

People use detox programmes for a number of reasons, which may include weight loss. These types of diet are said to rid the body of toxins and poisons and allow the digestive system a rest. Most doctors, however, claim that detox diets are unnecessary and potentially dangerous. Any weight loss that is achieved is likely to be temporary (it's just water) unless you adopt a new set of healthy eating habits for life.

ASK THE EXPERT

Health risks of being under or overweight

There's no doubt that being overweight increases the risk of several serious health problems. Heart disease, diabetes, high blood pressure, stroke, reproductive disorders, gallstones, osteoarthritis and certain types of cancer are all more common in people who are overweight. People who are underweight also have increased health risks, such as a greater risk of infection and poor general health.

In particular, being overweight can affect your digestive system. Hiatus hernia, heartburn and indigestion are all more common in people who are carrying too much weight. Several simple measures can help you to avoid heartburn and indigestion (see page 69). But, for many people, the most effective solutions to these common digestive problems is to lose the excess weight.

SLOW BUT SURE

The best and safest way to lose weight is slowly and steadily – between 0.5 and 1kg (1–2lb) a week is the ideal rate. If you lose too much weight too quickly, there's a danger that you may lose lean muscle tissue as well as fat. Your metabolic rate is related to the amount of lean muscle tissue you have, which means that losing muscle lowers the rate at which you burn calories, making it even harder to lose weight.

To achieve a steady, healthy weight loss you need to reduce your calorie intake to around 600 calories less than the average recommended daily intake. Between 1200 and 1500 calories a day should be sufficient for most women; 1750–1950 calories a day for men. It's important that you spread your calorie allowance throughout the day – eating little and often helps to maintain blood sugar levels and makes it easier to resist the urge to snack or binge.

Long-term change equals long-term success

Losing weight is relatively easy – keeping that weight off is the real challenge. Most diets provide a short-term fix to what is a long-term problem, with the result that many people who lose weight quickly regain it once they stop dieting.

If you really want to lose weight, you need to change your eating habits on a long-term basis – crash diets don't teach you how to change these. So forget about dieting – instead, think about a whole new way of eating. Successful dieters are those people who learn how to change both their eating habits and their attitude towards food on a permanent basis.

TRYING TO GAIN WEIGHT

Gaining weight can be as difficult as losing it. The healthiest route to weight gain involves a combination of muscle-building exercise and a balanced diet. Choose high-protein foods (such as lean meat, fish and dairy products), fibre-rich carbohydrate foods (such as bread, wholegrains and pasta) and foods rich in 'unsaturated' fats (such as oily fish, nuts and seeds).

Eating little and often will help to increase the total quantity of food you can manage. Try 'build-up' type drinks or smoothies between meals.

Blueberry and watermelon smoothie
Nutritious smoothies – fruit, milk and yoghurt or cream – can boost your calorie intake as 'mini meals' between meals; the bananas-and-cream varieties are especially calorific.

Eat to beat digestive problems

From the homely oat to the exotic fennel seed, nature has provided a medicinal treasure trove with the therapeutic power to help solve many digestive ailments and maintain the good health of your digestive system.

Around the late 5th century BC, Hippocrates, the father of Western medicine, advised his readers: 'Let food be your medicine, and medicine be your food'. The ancient Greek sage was building on a long tradition of using food as a potent therapeutic tool, and of using the digestive system as a vital delivery route for that therapy.

FOOD SOLUTIONS

Hippocrates was particularly keen on using food to treat digestive problems. He advocated wheat and barley bran to cure constipation, for instance, a strategy that still makes good sense today. Simply by eating and digesting food, you can deliver therapeutic foods directly to the site of trouble.

Nowadays a lot of food medicine is known to us as folk wisdom – you've probably had chicken soup fed to you to treat a cold, or heard of stewed prunes as a food that promotes regular bowel movement. But there are plenty of other foods that have health-giving properties that benefit your digestive system, of which you may not be aware.

Drink tea
In animal studies tea has been shown to help protect against certain types of cancer. Evidence that it has a similar effect in humans looks promising.

Foods for general digestive health

Probiotic and prebiotic foods, such as yoghurt, onions and Jerusalem artichokes, help to maintain healthy gut flora and fight problems like thrush and candidiasis (see page 71). There is even evidence that yoghurt can strengthen the immune system.

Studies that look at the incidence of colon cancer within different population groups suggest that people who eat more fruit and vegetables are less likely to get this type of cancer. Several studies show that a diet rich in fibre can help to prevent problems such as constipation, diverticular disease (a condition in which part of the lining of the colon forms small inflamed pouches) and haemorrhoids, as well as some types of cancer.

EATING TO BEAT CANCER

It has been estimated that up to one-third of all cancers in Western countries are associated with poor diet, and cancers of the digestive

DIGESTIVE *SUPERFOODS*

Certain foods are great for keeping your digestive system in good working order. By including some of these superfoods in your day-to-day diet, your gut will reap the benefits.

ASPARAGUS This vegetable is rich in fructoligosaccharides, which stimulate the growth of 'friendly' gut bacteria. In turn, these bacteria aid digestion.

PRUNES A substance called hydroxyphenylisatin, found in prunes, stimulates muscles in the bowel. This substance accounts for the mild laxative effect of this dried fruit.

SPINACH Several leafy green vegetables, including spinach, contain nitrates. These chemicals are converted within the body to a potent antibacterial chemical that helps to protect the digestive tract against infection.

TOMATOES These are another source of fructoligosaccharides and encourage the growth of 'friendly' gut bacteria.

OATBRAN As well as being a good source of several important vitamins and minerals, oatbran contains fibre, which speeds the passage of waste products through the large intestine.

system are among the top killers. Experts suggest that dietary changes could prevent nine out of ten deaths from colon cancer, for instance. Fibre speeds the passage of food and may prevent potentially cancer-causing substances from remaining long enough to do harm.

Fruit and fibre

Fruit and vegetables are rich in antioxidants – substances that mop up harmful chemicals called free radicals and help your immune system to prevent and fight cancer. Fruit and vegetables are particularly effective at guarding against several digestive cancers, including stomach, large intestine and oesophagus.

Dietary fibre (see pages 62–65), from sources including fruit, is also important in the prevention of colon cancer. Official guidelines are that we should eat at least five servings of fruit and/or vegetables a day to maintain good digestive health.

A soya solution?

There is a growing amount of evidence to suggest that soya may play a major role in preventing certain types of cancers, including colon cancer. In countries where soya is an important source of protein in the diet, the population has a reduced incidence of colon cancer.

When you choose soya you may want to consider whether it has been genetically modified. Soya was one of the first crops to be genetically modified, but in the late 1990s claims were made that GM foods may be harmful to health. Until further research has cleared GM foods you may want to hunt out a supply of soya that has not been subject to modification.

Food remedies for digestive ailments

Peppermint and mint tea Infusing fresh mint or peppermint leaves in boiling water for a few minutes makes a refreshing drink that is said to improve digestion and relieve indigestion.

Fennel and fennel seeds Chewing or eating fennel or fennel seeds may relieve indigestion and stomach cramps. Fennel tea may relieve nausea, flatulence and bloating. Avoid these if you are pregnant since they may encourage menstruation.

Water This remains one of the best solutions for constipation or bad breath (which can be caused by constipation). You should aim to drink at least eight to ten glasses of water a day.

Live yoghurt Eating live yoghurt encourages 'friendly' bacteria to flourish in the gut and genital tract. It can help to control thrush, caused by an excess growth of the yeast *Candida albicans*.

Ginger Whether sucked as a piece of the crystallised form or drunk as ginger beer, ale or tea, ginger quells nausea. To make ginger tea, grate a 1cm (½in) piece of root ginger into a mug of boiling water and leave to stand for ten minutes.

Manuka honey Taken after meals and at bedtime, this honey – from the New Zealand tea tree – is said to help heal stomach ulcers and kill the *Helicobacter pylori* bacteria that cause them.

Cardamom This spice is said to be good for digestive problems such as stomach cramps, indigestion and flatulence. It helps prevent acid reflux and belching.

Food allergy and intolerance

In recent years there has been a growing awareness that eliminating certain foods from the diet may be the key to successful treatment of a range of health problems linked to food allergies and food intolerance.

Allergies are an increasingly common health issue in the developed world. Conditions such as hay fever and asthma are among some of the most common childhood ailments, and these are only the most well-known types of allergy. According to certain schools of thought, allergic, or allergic-type, reactions to foodstuffs, additives in foods and chemicals in the environment are the underlying cause of a number of chronic (meaning long-term or constantly recurring) conditions ranging from arthritis to depression.

A COMPLEX ISSUE

Unfortunately this area of medicine is highly contentious. Conventional medicine has a narrow definition of allergy, and only recognises a type of food reaction known as immediate food allergy, which has clear-cut symptoms and is comparatively rare. Alternative allergy practitioners believe that a closely related type of reaction, known as hidden food allergy, is responsible for a wide range of vague symptoms and is one of the most common causes of illness in the Western world.

To complicate the picture further, a type of food reaction called intolerance or sensitivity also exists. Such reactions have a different mechanism to allergies, but the terms are often used interchangeably.

ALLERGY OR INTOLERANCE?

Although food allergies and food intolerance can produce very similar symptoms, they occur as the result of different mechanisms.

The allergic mechanism

Both conventional and alternative allergy practitioners agree on the basic mechanism involved in

The rice alternative
If you are allergic to or are unable to tolerate gluten in wheat, try substituting rice-based products for wheat based – from boiled rice to cakes and breakfast cereals.

How to stop food allergy developing

Breastfeeding for at least four months, along with the gradual introduction of new foods, can help to reduce the risk of food allergies. For example, delay giving allergy-provoking foods such as wheat, citrus, dairy products, eggs, nuts, soya and fish until after six months. Introduce one new food at a time, so that you can see if a particular food causes a reaction.

If you think your baby is allergic to a food, the next step may be to try excluding it from his or her diet. Before you do this, however, seek professional advice from a paediatrician, health visitor or dietitian.

food allergy: a food allergy occurs when the immune system overreacts to a normally harmless food or ingredient. The body responds to the substance's presence by producing antibodies. These trigger the release of histamine and other chemicals into the bloodstream, resulting in an allergic reaction. But the two schools differ over the type of symptoms that such allergic reactions can cause.

Immediate food allergy

According to conventional medicine, food allergy reactions are responsible for only a narrow range of symptoms that come on very quickly after the trigger food is encountered. The typical signs are swelling of the lips, urticaria (nettle rash), vomiting and diarrhoea. In severe reactions, a condition called anaphylactic shock

Some foods contain such potent allergens that you don't have to eat them to get symptoms. Steam from cooking fish can trigger an asthma attack in susceptible people and even kissing someone who has eaten fish can cause problems.

can cause breathing difficulties, a sudden drop in blood pressure and, in some cases, death.

Hidden food allergy

Adherents to the hidden food allergy theory believe that food molecules are constantly leaking through our intestinal walls into the bloodstream, triggering low-intensity but pernicious immune reactions that result in chronic illnesses, typically including digestive problems such as diarrhoea, constipation, flatulence, irritable bowel syndrome and even diverticular disease. These reactions may not appear for hours or even days after the trigger food was eaten.

Intolerance and sensitivity

Food intolerance or sensitivity occurs when the body cannot digest a particular food. One classic example is lactose intolerance, where the sufferer does not produce the lactase enzyme needed to break down lactose, a major component of milk. Another common type of intolerance is coeliac disease. The intestines of people with this condition are such that they cannot deal with and absorb gluten, a protein found in wheat and some other grains.

Alternatively, sensitivity may be the direct result of the pharmacological effect of chemicals present in a food, such as caffeine in coffee or amines in cheese and chocolate. Food intolerance does not involve the release of antibodies, but can cause many symptoms that alternative allergists link to hidden food allergies, such as flatulence, headaches or fatigue.

BEATING FOOD REACTIONS

There are a number of steps that you can take to deal with the problems caused by food reactions, but the golden rule is 'avoidance'. The only sure way to avoid developing a reaction to a food or food ingredient is not to eat it. First, however, you need to identify what it is you're eating that is causing the problem.

Identifying food triggers

Immediate food allergy triggers are often easy to recognise, because they produce symptoms soon after being eaten. If you develop a rash, swelling, nausea, shortness of breath or itchiness of the lips, tongue and throat over a short period of time, you should suspect whatever you just ate. The most common food triggers for this type of reaction are peanuts, nuts, shellfish and eggs, although practically anything can cause a reaction in a susceptible individual.

Steering clear of a food that has triggered an immediate allergic reaction is essential, because subsequent reactions may be a great deal

Common allergy-provoking foods

Several foods and food groups are common triggers for food intolerance or allergy. Some foods are associated with mild reactions; others can cause life-threatening symptoms.

	Source	Reactions
	COW'S MILK	A common cause of allergic reactions in children causing vomiting, colic and diarrhoea. In 9 out of 10 cases, sensitivity disappears by the age of 3.
	HEN'S EGGS	Eggs are common allergy-provoking foods in children, causing rashes and stomach upsets, but sensitivity to them gradually disappears with age.
	FISH	Fish can produce severe allergic reactions within minutes of being eaten; they can cause rashes, asthma, vomiting, diarrhoea and anaphylaxis.
	WHEAT	Wheat, rye and barley usually cause gastrointestinal symptoms including diarrhoea. Wheat flour can provoke asthma.
	PEANUTS	One of the most potent allergens, even a trace amount of peanut can cause life-threatening anaphylaxis in susceptible individuals.
	SHELLFISH	Shrimps, lobsters, prawns, crabs and other shellfish can cause violent allergic reactions, such as urticaria (nettle rash) and swelling of the lips.

stronger. You could even be in danger of a life-threatening attack of anaphylaxis. People who know that they are at risk of extreme allergic reactions, whether to peanuts or bee stings, should always carry an adrenaline self-injection kit with them just in case they are exposed. You should check with your doctor if you are in any doubt.

The date, the time, the food...
Keeping a food diary can help you to identify possible food allergy triggers. Note down everything you eat for a week alongside any symptoms, such as headaches, rashes and stomach upsets.

Hidden food allergy triggers may be less dangerous, but are also much harder to identify. One of the reasons that conventional medicine is unwilling to accept that hidden food allergy is a genuine phenomenon is that it is so hard to pin down. Reactions may not occur until days after a food was eaten, involving apparently unrelated symptoms of varying severity that actually get

worse when the trigger is avoided, due to a kind of withdrawal reaction. Even more confusing, some reactions happen only when two or more foods are eaten in combination.

If you are experiencing a number of vague, chronic and apparently unrelated symptoms get them checked out by your doctor. If no conventional explanation can be found, you should consider the possibility that you might have a food allergy.

Keeping a food diary

A reliable aid towards identifying a hidden food trigger is to keep a food diary. Record the type and severity of your symptoms on a daily basis. At the same time, keep a record of everything that you eat or drink, including all the ingredients. It is important to be comprehensive, because even minute quantities of a trigger substance could be responsible for your symptoms.

You can use a food diary to identify suspect foods and then try to eliminate them from your diet. If a week's abstinence produces results, you could confirm your suspicions by eating a little of the suspect – if it is the trigger, symptoms should reappear, possibly quite strongly, within a couple of days. People with special dietary requirements, such as children, the elderly, pregnant women and vegetarians, should never restrict their diet without checking with a doctor first.

LACTOSE INTOLERANCE

Lactose intolerance is a condition in which the body fails to produce the enzyme lactase. Lactase is necessary for the digestion of lactose, a natural sugar present in milk. Without it,

lactose cannot be broken down and passes unchanged into the large intestine where it is fermented by intestinal bacteria causing bloating, abdominal pains and diarrhoea.

Most ethnic groups in the world are lactose intolerant; some would say this is the 'normal' adult state as we're not designed to drink milk after being weaned. In countries where dairy products are not regularly eaten, the body stops producing lactase at some point between infancy and adulthood. In the Western world, however, we include so many dairy products in our diet that we need to produce lactase to deal with the milk sugar.

positive health tips

Decoding ingredient labels

Many processed foods contain lactose, cow's milk protein, wheat or gluten. If you need to avoid any of these foods, check the list of ingredients on the label to see if they include any of the following.

- **Gluten-free diet** Watch out for barley, bran, cereal binder, cereal filler, starch, cereal protein, modified starch, edible starch, food starch, flour, rusk, rye, vegetable protein, wheat flour and wheat germ.

- **Dairy-free diet** Steer clear of milk protein, milk powder, animal fat, casein, caseinate, hydrolysed casein or whey, lactose, non-fat milk solids, lactalbumin, lactoglobulin, skimmed milk powder, whey and ghee.

Lactose-free eating

Foods to avoid	Substitutes
Cow's milk (including condensed milk, and evaporated milk), goat's milk, sheep's milk and buttermilk	Soya milk, rice milk, coconut milk, oat milk, almond milk, 95% lactose-free milk
Butter or margarine	Milk-free margarine – there are several brands to choose from, including some made from olive oil
Cheese (including cream cheese and cottage cheese)	Dairy-free cheeses, such as soya, are available in both soft and hard varieties
Yoghurt	Dairy-free yoghurts – there are lots to choose from
Ice-cream	Sorbet or soft non-dairy frozen dessert

Lactase deficiency can also occur as a rare inherited condition, which becomes apparent shortly after birth. Much more common is temporary lactose intolerance, which can occur after a stomach upset.

People with lactose intolerance should avoid milk, including sheep's and goat's milk, and dairy products such as cream, yoghurt, cheese and butter. Processed foods, monosodium glutamate, artificial sweeteners and medicines may also contain lactose.

Some people with lactose intolerance can handle small amounts of milk and dairy foods, such as milk in tea or coffee or the occasional cheese sandwich, without experiencing any ill effects.

For those people who cannot tolerate even small quantities of dairy produce, most health food shops and some supermarkets stock low-lactose and dairy-free

Lactose intolerance around the world
Many people from Asia and Africa cannot tolerate the quantities of milk consumed in Europe and North America because of a lack of the enzyme needed for its digestion.

■ *Regions of lactose intolerance*

alternatives, such as cream substitutes. If you have to limit your intake of milk and dairy products, you need to ensure you get enough dietary calcium from other sources.

GREAT GLUTEN-FREE MEALS

For most people wheat is an essential part of their diet, the basis of such staples as bread and pasta as an ingredient in countless other foods. But for people with coeliac disease, the gluten protein found in wheat, rye, oats and barley causes serious health problems. Even minute amounts of gluten can cause the intestinal tract to become inflamed and damaged – the result is abdominal pain and diarrhoea. What's more, important nutrients aren't properly absorbed.

A growing number of people claim that wheat allergy is a contributory factor in a health complaint, such as arthritis. Although there is little evidence that these people actually have true allergic reactions, eliminating wheat from the diet does sometimes seem to help.

A gluten-free/wheat-free diet means eliminating all wheat, barley, and rye and products made out of grain, such as pasta, bread, breakfast cereals and biscuits. But it's not always easy to identify products that contain gluten. Many manufactured foods contain flour as a thickening agent, so read the labels on products to double check.

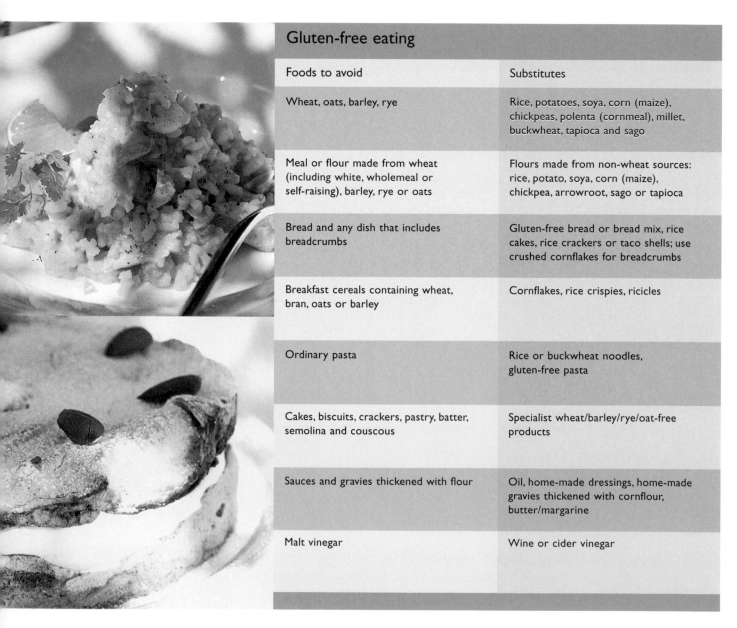

Gluten-free eating

Foods to avoid	Substitutes
Wheat, oats, barley, rye	Rice, potatoes, soya, corn (maize), chickpeas, polenta (cornmeal), millet, buckwheat, tapioca and sago
Meal or flour made from wheat (including white, wholemeal or self-raising), barley, rye or oats	Flours made from non-wheat sources: rice, potato, soya, corn (maize), chickpea, arrowroot, sago or tapioca
Bread and any dish that includes breadcrumbs	Gluten-free bread or bread mix, rice cakes, rice crackers or taco shells; use crushed cornflakes for breadcrumbs
Breakfast cereals containing wheat, bran, oats or barley	Cornflakes, rice crispies, ricicles
Ordinary pasta	Rice or buckwheat noodles, gluten-free pasta
Cakes, biscuits, crackers, pastry, batter, semolina and couscous	Specialist wheat/barley/rye/oat-free products
Sauces and gravies thickened with flour	Oil, home-made dressings, home-made gravies thickened with cornflour, butter/margarine
Malt vinegar	Wine or cider vinegar

EXERCISE AND DIGESTION

Your digestive system is surrounded and supported by a complex set of abdominal muscles, which play a vital part in the process of digestion. Just like all the other muscles in your body, these need looking after to ensure that they continue to function properly, so here we show you exercises that help to maintain abdominal muscles in good working order. What's best before a workout – a banana or an energy bar? Discover how best to fuel your body for exercise, as well as when and how to restore your energy afterwards.

We look at the internal and external ways of exercising your digestive system – and suggest ways to tailor them to your personal needs.

Make sure you are fully fuelled and hydrated when exercising, but do not let your fitness routine interfere with the process of digestion.

Exercise and your digestive health

You probably recognise the importance of regular physical activity for your heart and lungs, but did you know that the digestive system benefits from exercise? Regularly working out helps to keep your gut in good working order.

THE SUPPORT SYSTEM

Your abdominal muscles are part of the set of structures that keep your digestive organs in their proper place. The muscles form a complex web that extends from the diaphragm (which forms the roof of the abdominal cavity) to the muscles situated in the pelvis (which form its floor). Abdominal muscles also play a vital role in maintaining posture and producing twisting, turning and bending movements of the torso.

As well as helping to support your intestines, the muscles of the pelvic floor have a direct effect on your large intestine. As they contract and relax, they squeeze the colon (the main part of the large intestine), and help to move the contents along so that they can be eliminated.

Shaping up the gut
It's difficult to exercise the digestive system directly, but keeping your abdominal muscles in shape not only helps to keep you toned but also to keep the gut moving.

The walls of your intestines are partly composed of muscle fibres, allowing the intestines to contract and move food along by peristalsis. Intestinal muscle fibres are a special kind, known as involuntary – unlike those muscles in your arms or legs, they are not under conscious control.

WORKING OUT

By exercising or being moderately active for 30 minutes on most days of the week (brisk walking, for example), you can improve your gut motility – the amount and efficiency of peristalsis in your intestines. When you exercise regularly you indirectly affect the digestive smooth muscles as your abdominal muscles contract and relax. This affects gut motility, helping to ensure that food moves through your gut at the right speed. Lack of activity leaves your digestive system sluggish. The bad news for sedentary individuals is that they'll often suffer from constipation and increase their risk of developing diverticular disease.

Can massage improve gut function?

Massaging your abdominal muscles can increase the blood supply to your gut, aiding the movement of food along your digestive tract and is said to offer relief from indigestion and stomach tension. Massage in a clockwise direction to match the flow of the digestive tract. Use gentle strokes that work from the right to the left side of your body.

ASK THE EXPERT

TURNING UP THE THERMOSTAT

Your metabolism (the rate at which you burn up energy) is set by an internal thermostat. Being able to 'turn up' this thermostat would make you burn energy faster, using up carbohydrates and fats before they get laid down as fat and even consuming pre-existing fat deposits. One of the best ways to reset your metabolic thermostat is through moderate exercise.

Eating and exercising

Your body needs fuel to exercise, but eating too much before a session will cause a tug of war between your digestive system and your muscles. Time your eating to supply the energy your body needs without upsetting your digestion.

To exercise you need energy. This energy comes from the breakdown of simple carbohydrates, which the blood takes to the muscles ready to be used. Energy stores are also found, in limited quantities, in the muscles themselves (in the form of a substance called glycogen).

Carbohydrates come from the foods you eat, and one of the main jobs of your digestive system is to break down these foods so that they can be absorbed into the bloodstream. In order to exercise safely and effectively, you need to ensure that you maintain the level of carbohydrates available to your muscles, by supplying the right things to your digestive system.

FUELLING YOUR EXERCISE

UK guidelines for a normal balanced diet for general health recommend that we obtain 55–60 per cent of our calories from complex carbohydrates, such as bread, potatoes, pasta, pulses, fruit and vegetables; no more than 30 per cent of our calories from fats, avoiding saturated fats where possible and choosing low-fat milk cheeses and spreads; and only 10–15 per cent of calories from proteins in the form of lean meat, fish, eggs and pulses. In summary,

the greater proportion of your diet should contain fibre and complex carbohydrates, and only a small proportion should contain fats and simple carbohydrates (see pages 62–65 for more information).

FEEDING YOUR MUSCLES

These eating guidelines help to prepare you for exercise by improving your general health. If you are doing moderate exercise

every day, you may also need to boost your carbohydrate intake further in order to compensate for the increased amount of energy being used by the muscles.

In particular, your muscles quickly use up their stores of glycogen during exercise. These stores therefore need to be built up before, and replenished during and after exercise. Only about 600–800 kcal worth of glycogen is actually stored in the body at any particular time (mostly in the muscles but there is also some in the liver). If you allow your glycogen stores to become exhausted, your exercise performance will be impaired.

Eating after a workout
A light snack after taking exercise can replenish your muscles' depleted energy stores. A banana supplies about the right amount of carbohydrate.

HIGH GLYCAEMIC INDEX FOODS

These foods produce a rapid rise in blood glucose; they are useful after exercise to boost glycogen stores.

wholemeal bread

cantaloupe melon

diluted orange juice

carrot

processed breakfast cereals

raisins

LOW GLYCAEMIC INDEX FOODS

These are converted to sugar slowly so they are useful between workouts or a few hours before exercise.

cherries

skimmed milk

apples

dried apricots

wholewheat pasta

lentils

Meeting extra demands

In order to meet increased calorie demands, and build up and maintain stores of glycogen, you will need to increase your energy intake. The amount you need to eat depends on the intensity of your exercise programme. If you take regular exercise for general health maintenance, for example swimming or jogging for 30 minutes five days a week, you probably need to only slightly boost your food intake.

These increases should be met by eating more complex carbohydrates, which should account for a higher proportion of your diet – around 65 per cent – than in the normal scheme. You should avoid eating more fats or simple sugars than you already do, except possibly during or immediately after exercising when you need to replenish glycogen stores quickly. Active people also need more protein per kg of body weight than their couch potato cousins. Between 1.2 and 1.7g/kg body weight should be enough to promote healthy new muscle growth and for tissue repair.

The glycaemic index

How do you know whether a food is a good source of complex carbohydrates or is richer in simple carbohydrates? A good guide that also provides useful information for the diet-conscious exerciser is the glycaemic index (GI) of a food. The GI is a measure of the rate at which consumption of a food raises the level of blood glucose. In other words, it shows how quickly a food gets broken down by the digestive system, converted into glucose and absorbed by the blood. The fastest carbohydrate to be absorbed into the bloodstream is pure glucose and this is given a GI rating of 100.

Foods that have a low GI rating and are broken down slowly make you feel full for longer and keep blood sugar levels constant. This helps to prevent you craving more calories than you need and reduces the degree to which carbohydrates in your blood are converted into fat. Low GI foods include beans and pulses, apples, wholewheat cereals, dried apricots, pasta and oats. Foods with a high GI include bread, glucose energy drinks, sugar, honey, mashed potatoes and breakfast cereals.

But how does this help you plan a diet for exercise? The best way of ensuring a good level of carbo-hydrate intake in a healthy form is to eat foods that have a low GI – in other words, complex carbohydrates. This will ensure that your body is fuelled up and ready for exercise, with full stocks of glycogen. Immediately after a bout of exercise, when your muscle glycogen is depleted, you need to get your blood sugar levels up quickly. This is easily achieved by having high GI foods or drink, such as rice cakes and jam or a high-energy drink, in the two hours after exercise.

If glycogen is not replaced within two hours, it can take up to 48 hours for glycogen stores to refill. Glycogen is replaced quickest in the first 30 minutes after activity.

THE BATTLE FOR BLOOD – MUSCLES VERSUS DIGESTION

An important consideration in terms of meal timing and exercise is the issue of blood flow to the different areas of your body. You only have about 5 litres (8 pints) of blood to supply all of your body's needs.

During exercise your heart rate increases two or threefold, massively boosting the volume of blood pumped per minute (your muscles get up to 30 times more blood per minute than when you are at rest). Putting food into the digestive system before or during exercise can lead to conflicting demands, as your stomach and intestines compete with your muscles for limited resources.

Digestive needs

After a meal, your body begins the process of digestion and there is a greater need for blood in the gut so that nutrients can be absorbed and carried to the liver, and then on to the different parts of the body. The conversion and use of these nutrients becomes a priority to your body, and in order to transport them to your body tissues, the blood vessels in and around muscle tissues constrict while

Athletes in regular training need at least 5000kcal a day, compared with the average daily requirement of around 2000–2500kcal for most adults.

vessels supplying your digestive organs dilate. This directs blood away from muscles towards the digestive system, reducing the provision of oxygen and nutrients to the muscles. Assuming you are not too active after a meal, this is not a problem for your body.

Blood for working muscles

If you start exercising soon after eating a meal, your central nervous system attempts to redirect blood flow away from your digestive organs and towards the working muscles. This redirection of blood

flow slows the digestive processes and reduces gut motility. A sort of 'tug-of-war' between your muscles and digestion results, and both your digestive and your exercise performance are compromised. You may experience rapid breathing, abnormally high heart rate, nausea and dizziness during or after your workout. If these symptoms occur, you should slow down or stop your exercise session altogether.

For serious athletes, sports nutritionists recommend eating five or six smaller meals throughout the day, thereby ensuring that there is sufficient glycogen and blood-borne glucose in the system to supply the energy needed for an efficient workout, without straining the digestive organs.

MAINTAINING FLUID LEVELS

During exercise your muscles are burning fuel to produce energy at a tremendous rate. Unfortunately the system is not particularly efficient – only about 25 per cent of the energy stored in our food is converted to a

---

positive health tips

Remember the fluid factor

The simple steps given below outline how you can avoid dehydration.

- Ensure you are fully hydrated before beginning your exercise session. This does not mean downing a litre of water before you go on a run; although it's wise to have a glassful. Instead, ensure that you keep up your fluid consumption throughout the day and don't let yourself go thirsty.
- Start drinking early in your exercise programme – don't wait until you are thirsty. Take frequent small sips. A cyclist's water bottle is a good container.
- Put a teaspoon of sugar in your water bottle – a low-sugar concentration increases the rate at which fluid is absorbed by your digestive system and gets into your bloodstream.
- Take plenty of fluids on completion of your exercise programme. Ideally you should carry your own supply of fluid in your kit bag.
- Use isotonic/energy drinks with care. They can be useful for fluid replenishment and also provide additional carbohydrates. If used incorrectly, however, they may lead to nausea and stomach cramps and can actually inhibit fluid absorption.

EATING AND DRINKING PLAN FOR MODERATE EXERCISE

It's important to get the timing of food intake right when exercising. Drink plenty of fluids to prevent dehydration. Avoid exercising within two hours of eating a heavy meal.

Food and fluid before activity
One hour before exercise have a snack that is high in complex carbohydrates, such as a small sandwich or banana. Have a large glass of water or diluted fruit juice just before exercising.

Food and fluid during activity
There is no specific need to eat food if you are exercising for less than one hour; if you are exercising for longer than an hour, have small amounts of fruit or diluted fruit juice.

Food and fluid after activity
About 30–60 minutes following exercise eat some fruit, a small sandwich or a wholemeal scone. Drink a large glass of water or diluted fruit juice.

form that the muscles can use to contract and generate force. Most of the rest becomes heat, and your body needs to dissipate this excess heat. An effective way of doing this is through sweating.

As well as water lost through sweating, heat-laden moisture is also lost every time you breathe out. This means that over a prolonged exercise session you could very easily become dehydrated. This will impair your exercise performance more severely than a lack of glucose would. In other words, correct hydration (maintenance of fluid levels) is more important than nutrition.

The factors that influence your exact fluid requirements include the length of the exercise session, the intensity of the exercise and also the temperature in the environment (outside or inside). If you are just jogging for half an hour, there's no need to be concerned about dehydration. But it's good to get into the habit of having a large glass of water before any activity.

TIMING MEALS

The best time to eat and drink in relation to exercise depends on a range of factors – the GI of the foods you're eating (see page 86), fluid requirements and blood flow issues. In addition, each person is different in their eating habits and in their response to food, so it is important to listen to your body and develop a routine that works for you.

Putting all the advice together, however, we can derive some general guidelines to get the best out of any exercise regime (see above).

Exercising on an empty stomach

Choosing when to exercise is often a matter of individual preference, circumstances and opportunities. Some people like to snack an hour beforehand, while others find that they cannot tolerate anything in their stomach. Exercising on an empty stomach is quite safe. Fluid replacement is much more important than eating food during activity.

PREVENTING A HERNIA

If the muscles of your abdomen are weak, a sudden increase in pressure may cause a hernia – the protrusion of a loop of intestine through the abdominal wall. When working out with weights, do not try to lift too much or you could strain and give yourself a hernia. Sensible breathing and avoiding lifting more than you

EATING AND DRINKING PLAN FOR INTENSE EXERCISE

The correct timing of food intake is particularly important when you do strenuous or endurance exercise. Drinking plenty is important to prevent dehydration. Avoid exercising within two hours of eating a heavy meal.

Food and fluid before activity

About 15–30 minutes before exercise have a snack that supplies about 50g (2oz) carbohydrate – for example a handful of dried fruit, a 50g (2oz) bowl of cereal or else two to three bananas.

Food and fluid during activity

Consider having an isotonic drink to supply both fluid and glucose.

Food and fluid after activity

30 minutes after exercise eat some fruit, a banana sandwich or a baked potato with beans, and drink at least a pint of water. These are vital for replacing glycogen stores.

can realistically manage will keep your abdominal wall intact and prevent a hernia.

Abdominal breathing

The breathing pattern of the average sedentary person is one of small, shallow breaths, which use only the top portion of the lungs. As a result the lungs are never stretched to capacity – and the diaphragm is rarely exercised. Correct abdominal breathing allows you to fill your lungs from the bottom to the top. By breathing in this way, you extend and exercise the diaphragm, keeping it in good shape.

Exercising your diaphragm

Try this simple exercise to improve your abdominal breathing. Place one hand on your chest and one hand on your abdomen and take a deep breath. If you feel your chest rise first then you are filling only the top half of your lungs and are failing to exercise your diaphragm. Aim to get your abdomen rising before your chest rises. This not only benefits your diaphragm but also ensures you are using all your lung capacity. As you breath out concentrate on emptying the lungs and allowing your abdomen to push out. Abdominal breathing is a basic yoga technique: in addition to its beneficial effect on the diaphragm, yoga can also help to relieve stress.

EXERCISE FOR DIGESTIVE PROBLEMS

A number of gut-related disorders can make physical activity difficult, yet people with impaired physical health usually benefit the most from exercise. If you suffer from some form of digestive condition, staying active is one of the most important steps you can take to help your gut stay healthy and to prevent further problems. Whatever exercise you choose it is important that you enjoy it and that you feel comfortable taking part.

Stay fit without straining

If you have a hernia or a colostomy (a surgically created opening from the intestines to the abdomen), aim for 30 minutes of moderate activity on most days of the week. Walking is an excellent way to stay fit and healthy and is a good way for many people with digestive problems to remain fit without putting undue strain on the digestive system.

3

What happens
when things go wrong

Knowing what can go wrong

Digestive symptoms are extremely common and usually pretty harmless, but as we grow older the risk of developing a more serious digestive disorder increases, so greater vigilance is called for. Here we outline the main factors that cause or contribute to digestive complaints.

INFECTION

On a worldwide basis, infection is by far the most common cause of gastrointestinal and liver disease. Diarrhoeal diseases, for instance, are extremely common. In developed countries, diarrhoea is usually a short-lived problem, but in the developing world it kills about 3–4 million people each year, mostly pre-school children.

Helicobacter pylori infection is probably the commonest in the world. Many people live in harmony with this bacterial organism without it causing any disease; in some susceptible individuals, however, it causes peptic ulcers, while in others it can contribute to the development of stomach cancer over many years. Research efforts currently focus on understanding why some people with this infection suffer no ill effects, and indeed may be protected from other infections. As with many conditions, a person's genetic make-up may be the key.

Other causes of infection are parasites, such as liver flukes and tapeworms, which today occur mainly in developing countries where sanitation is poor.

Stomach ulcers are more likely to afflict people in blood group A, whereas duodenal ulcers mainly affect people in group O.

GENETICS AND HEREDITARY FACTORS

Inherited (genetic) factors play an important role in some common digestive disorders, although in most cases an inherited tendency is not the only factor required to develop the disease. The most common example is colon cancer, where genetic predisposition acts in a number of different ways (see page 97). For instance, in very rare cases members of a family carry an abnormal gene that predisposes them to develop colon cancer, conditions known as familial adenomatous polyposis or hereditary non-polyposis colon cancer. These types of cancers account for about 1 per cent of colon cancer cases. In such families, children of an affected person carry a 1 in 2 risk of inheriting the disorder. Screening programmes are now available so that people at risk in such families can be detected and preventative steps taken to stop any cancer developing.

Such straightforward genetic effects are rare, but even in the other 99 per cent of colon cancer patients, family history affects the risk status of an individual. Other digestive disorders that may run in families, include the inflammatory bowel diseases Crohn's disease and ulcerative colitis, and coeliac disease.

AGEING PROCESSES

In general terms, the digestive system can take a lot of punishment without significant loss of function, so that the effects of ageing do not usually result in serious damage. But there are more specific changes that may produce visible effects. For instance, advancing years result in metabolic changes, including decreased physical activity, increase in body fat and decrease in muscle bulk.

MORE COMMON

HAEMORRHOIDS PRESENT IN UP TO HALF THE POPULATION BY AGE 50	DUODENAL ULCER CHANCE OF DEVELOPING OVER LIFETIME BETWEEN 1 IN 10 AND 1 IN 7 Almost all (95 per cent) of duodenal ulcers are associated with Helicobacter pylori infection.	COELIAC DISEASE UK – 67 NEW CASES PER 100,000 (1 IN 1500) IRELAND – 333 PER 100,000 (1 IN 300)	COLORECTAL CANCER 50 PER 100,000 (1 IN 2000) The UK's second most common tumour.
IRRITABLE BOWEL SYNDROME 1 IN 3 PEOPLE SUFFER OCCASIONAL SYMPTOMS; 1 IN 10 SUFFER BAD SYMPTOMS			PANCREATITIS 15 PER 100,000 (1 IN 6666)

As people age, they produce less acid in their stomachs, probably due to long-standing infection by *Helicobacter pylori*. Reduced levels of stomach acid can interfere with the processes of digestion, which can make it more difficult to absorb certain vitamins and minerals, such as iron, folic acid, vitamin B_{12}, calcium and vitamin K. Some age-related digestive health issues are linked to the fact that older people typically eat a poorer diet. The reasons for this are complex, but may include poor general health and mobility, financial difficulties and state of mind as well as physiological changes, such as changing senses of smell and taste with age.

FUNCTIONAL DISTURBANCES

The brain and gut are intimately connected: we're all familiar with terms such as 'butterflies in the stomach' or 'gut feelings' that relate to our state of mind. The gut has its own branch of the peripheral nervous system – the enteric nervous system – which is extensive and regulates digestion. It is not surprising therefore, that the gut can reflect states of mind, such as emotional upsets or depression. When investigating and treating functional disturbances, doctors often work closely with psychologists to identify and address possible causes.

The enteric nervous system can play a more specific role in gut problems. Some doctors believe that events affecting the bowel, such as attacks of gastroenteritis, can sometimes cause the intestine to become more sensitive, resulting in abdominal symptoms. This disturbance of the bowel function is not strictly a disease, but it is a real physical phenomenon, which doctors sometimes refer to as a functional disturbance. The most commonly recognised form of functional disturbance is irritable bowel syndrome.

TUMOURS

Cancer of the digestive system is very rare in young people but becomes more common with age, most notably after 50. As elsewhere in the body, tumours may be benign or malignant. Stomach cancer is the second most common worldwide, after lung cancer. It has a particularly high rate of incidence in Japan, where it's thought to be linked with the high consumption of smoked, salty and pickled foods. Doctors now know a great deal about tumours affecting

parasites

genetics

drugs

'superhygiene'

infection

alcohol abuse

inactivity

Influences on digestive health
Throughout your lifetime, your digestive system has to cope with a variety of factors that can harm it. Some of the diseases that can result are shown below with their UK incidence rates (number of new cases per year).

LESS COMMON

ULCERATIVE COLITIS
9 PER 100,000 (1 IN 11,000)

CIRRHOSIS
7 PER 100,000 (1 IN 15,000)

CROHN'S DISEASE
5–8 PER 100,000
(1 IN 12,500–20,000)

ACHALASIA
1 PER 200,000

Aspirin – good for the heart, bad for the stomach
The group of drugs collectively known as non-steroidal anti-inflammatories (NSAIDs) can have a harmful effect on the stomach lining, in some cases causing ulcers when used for a long time.

the colon, in particular, and the molecular processes involved in the formation of benign growths (polyps) and cancer. What is less certain, is the role of external factors, such as diet, that may trigger the process.

LIFESTYLE – ALCOHOL, EXERCISE, DRUGS

Chronic heavy alcohol use can lead to many health problems. Liver damage is probably the best known, and typically follows one of three patterns: fatty liver, alcoholic hepatitis (inflammation of the liver cells) and cirrhosis of the liver. Alcohol can also cause a condition known as pancreatitis (inflammation of the pancreas).

Physical exercise keeps the bowels regular. In an increasingly sedentary Western lifestyle, more and more people suffer from constipation.

Prescription drugs often have an impact on the digestive tract. A common side effect of antibiotics, for example, is diarrhoea, while strong

Intestinal parasites
According to one theory, lack of intestinal parasites, due to improved hygiene, may be a factor in the rise of autoimmune diseases of the digestive system.

painkillers, such as codeine and morphine, can cause constipation. Aspirin and related drugs can cause stomach upsets, while long-term use can cause ulceration and worsen conditions such as existing peptic ulcers or inflammatory bowel disease.

INFLAMMATION

There are a number of conditions in which the body's immunological response is overstimulated, causing inflammation when there is no detectable infective agent, such as a bacterium, virus or parasite. Doctors believe that these auto-immune diseases may be triggered by childhood infections or imbalance in gut flora.

Inflammatory bowel disease is one such condition, manifesting in the form of ulcerative colitis (inflammation of the colon) or Crohn's disease (inflammation of any part of the gastrointestinal tract). Research shows that this class of diseases is increasingly common; some experts put this down to our 'superhygienic' lifestyle, which prevents any contact between children and 'bugs' – specifically certain types of bacteria, or intestinal parasites such as worms.

MOTILITY PROBLEMS

The digestive tract is supplied by a complex nervous system that coordinates the contraction of the gut muscles and therefore the movement of food through the digestive system. In a number of rare conditions these mechanisms do not work properly. In achalasia, for example, which has an incidence of just 1 per 200,000, the muscle at the lower end of the oesophagus does not relax normally in response to swallowing food, making it difficult to swallow.

CONGENITAL ABNORMALITIES

Occasionally, parts of the digestive system fail to develop properly in a fetus and the baby is born with a congenital defect. The most common congenital problems are cleft lips and palates. In the UK, about 1 in 1000 babies is born with a cleft lip and 1 in 2500 with a cleft palate. Today, these conditions can be successfully treated with plastic surgery while the baby is young (from 3 to 15 months).

Who's who – stomach and digestive system experts

Digestive disorders are extremely common, and unlike many diseases of the heart or brain, they can often be dealt with very effectively by your general practitioner without the need for a referral to hospital.

GENERAL PRACTITIONER

The general practitioner (GP) is in the best position to give a preliminary assessment of someone's symptoms and to judge according to national guidelines whether they are serious enough to refer the patient to hospital. After carrying out a physical examination, the GP can treat most disorders. Some GPs may also take a more active part in the gastroenterology team and some may even perform endoscopies themselves.

GASTROENTEROLOGICAL SURGEON

Working closely with the gastroenterologist, the surgeon has special expertise in digestive diseases that can be treated surgically. Increasingly, surgeons will specialise even further, often concentrating on a particular part of the digestive system such as the colon and rectum, or the liver and gallbladder. Common operations in this area are the removal of the gallbladder, hernia repair and appendectomy (removal of the appendix).

PATHOLOGIST

Not directly involved in dealing with patients, pathologists provide a support service to doctors and surgeons, assessing tissue specimens taken during surgery as well as biopsies from endoscopic procedures. The pathologist is often the person who makes the final, firm diagnosis and thus plays a vital role in the team.

NURSES

Many hospitals have nurses specialising in nutrition and gastroenterology who are experienced in treating patients with certain problems, such as those requiring artificial nutritional support, people with inflammatory bowel disease or those being treated for viral hepatitis. Nurses are also key to the running of an endoscopy unit. They admit the patient on arrival, assist with the endoscopy, look after equipment and care for the person undergoing the procedure. Some nurses undergo further training and perform some endoscopic examinations themselves.

GASTROENTEROLOGIST

The gastroenterologist is a hospital-based doctor who specialises in the diagnosis and treatment of diseases of the digestive system. The gastroenterologist will deal with most forms of gastrointestinal disease as well as diseases of the liver and pancreas. Most gastroenterologists perform endoscopies (looking inside the digestive tract) for further diagnosis and therapy.

DIETITIAN

Most gastroenterology teams will have a dietitian (nutritionist) who is trained to provide specialist advice on diet and nutrition. This may take the form of directly advising patients on dietary supplements and special requirements such as gluten-free diets for people with coeliac disease. They also work in close liaison with the medical team to provide nutritional support for poorly nourished patients, for patients requiring a liquid diet by tube into the stomach such as burn victims or other traumatic injuries, and for people who are unable to eat and therefore need feeding intravenously.

CLINICAL PSYCHOLOGIST

Digestive disorders may have a component that is related to stress and other emotional factors. In some units, therefore, a clinical psychologist may be employed as part of the team. A psychologist has training in theories of human behaviour and thought and possesses special counselling skills. These techniques can be a useful addition to the surgical, endoscopic, nutritional and drug treatments available from other members of the team.

FINDING OUT WHAT IS WRONG

The digestive system comprises approximately 8 metres (26 feet) of convoluted tubing – any part of which can potentially become damaged or diseased. Diagnosing the exact location and nature of a problem is therefore a daunting task, but one which has been made easier and more accurate in recent years with advances in X-ray techniques and endoscopic technology.

As well as these sophisticated investigations, procedures such as examining stool specimens and blood samples still provide doctors with vital diagnostic clues.

Medical history and examination

Initial diagnosis of digestive problems does not require sophisticated equipment or expensive tests. Skilful questioning and a thorough physical examination can provide the doctor with all the necessary information.

Symptoms in the digestive system are extremely common, often short-lived and are not usually due to serious disease. Despite this, they can be troublesome and uncomfortable and, if persistent, often lead to a visit to the GP; in some cases, the symptoms may be worrying enough to prompt a referral to a gastroenterologist – a hospital doctor who specialises in the digestive system.

The first priority of any doctor (whether a GP or a hospital specialist) is to take a medical history and perform a physical examination. Both of these basic procedures can provide a clear picture of the problem and give an indication of which diagnostic tests and investigations would be appropriate.

THE HISTORY

The medical history is the discussion between the patient and the doctor during which the patient 'tells their story'. Most diagnoses are made during this initial consultation – subsequent investigations and tests are mainly carried out to confirm the diagnosis.

The nature of the symptoms

Occasional episodes of the most common digestive symptoms – abdominal pain, diarrhoea, constipation, nausea and wind – are familiar to most of us and are either ignored or tolerated until they go away. Persistent or unusual symptoms that begin to affect everyday life, however, may indicate a more serious condition.

Describing the exact nature of a symptom, such as how and when it developed, can give doctors significant clues as to its cause. What brings symptoms on and what relieves them is particularly relevant. For example, pain in the stomach that starts before meals but is relieved by eating may be caused by a stomach ulcer. Unexplained weight loss should always be mentioned, especially if clothes are becoming noticeably looser – a good indication of significant weight loss.

Describing your bowel habits

One of the most important indicators of problems in the digestive tract is bowel habit. These symptoms can be rather embarrassing to discuss but it is vitally important to mention such details, even if they don't seem relevant. The doctor will probably want to know the answers to the following questions.

- *How often are your bowels opened? The 'normal' range is three times a day to three times a week.*

- *Is the motion loose and watery, hard and pellet-like, or pale and foul-smelling?*

- *Is there any blood or mucus in the stool? Is there any evidence of blood on the toilet paper after wiping?*

Colour, consistency and frequency

Be prepared for questions about the regularity, consistency and appearance of stools – the description provided may be helpful to the doctor. The trouble is that everyone is different and it is very difficult to define what is normal – the most important question is, therefore, whether the regularity, consistency and appearance of stools have changed. If bowel habit changes noticeably, keep a record of how often episodes of diarrhoea or constipation occur and, embarrassing as it may seem, always check the appearance of the stools.

Bleeding from the rectum is particularly important, as it could be a sign of cancer. Far more commonly, however, rectal bleeding is due to haemorrhoids, which although uncomfortable are not serious.

Constipation is not usually a symptom of serious disease but it is important to mention if it is difficult to pass a motion, whether or not laxatives help and, if so, how often they are used.

Health history

In order to get a complete health picture, the doctor will want to know about any other existing illnesses, such as diabetes, high blood pressure or heart disease. He or she may also ask about any previous surgery or blood transfusions, which may be of relevance. Some symptoms, such as diarrhoea or nausea, could be side effects from drugs, both over-the-counter or prescription ones, so it is helpful to give a list of these to the doctor.

Knowledge of a family history of illness is of particular relevance as a number of digestive disorders, for example inflammatory bowel disease and cancer of the colon, can affect more than one member of the same family.

Psychosocial history

The behaviour of the digestive system can reflect a person's state of mind. Stress and anxiety, for example, can lead to symptoms such as pain and diarrhoea. Stress is also known to contribute to the development of certain conditions, such as irritable bowel syndrome. Symptoms in the digestive tract are also a feature of certain

Family history and the risk of colon cancer

This chart shows your relative lifetime risk of colon cancer, in relation to the general population, if a member of your family has been affected.

RELATIVES AFFECTED	LIFETIME RISK OF COLON CANCER
General population (UK)	1 in 50
First-degree relative (parent and siblings) over 45	1 in 17
First and second-degree relative (grandparents, uncles and first cousins) over 45	1 in 12
First-degree relative under 45	1 in 10
Two first-degree relatives	1 in 6
Three first-degree relatives	1 in 2

Taking care of business
Learning to manage time and finances effectively can indirectly help your digestive health by relieving stress and anxiety.

psychological disorders. It is particularly important, therefore, that the doctor is aware of individual social circumstances. A high-stress job, financial struggles or an unhappy relationship could all give rise to symptoms, as could excessive alcohol consumption and recreational drug use.

THE PHYSICAL EXAMINATION

The most important part of the doctor's physical assessment is the abdominal examination, although the doctor will also routinely take a patient's pulse and measure his or her blood pressure.

Look, feel and listen

The doctor will ask the patient to undress down to underwear and will maintain privacy throughout the procedure by using a blanket. There are three parts to the examination: visually assessing the abdomen (inspection), feeling for abnormalities (palpation) and listening to the abdomen through the stethoscope (auscultation).

- **Inspection** Often, simply looking at the abdomen can provide a great deal of information. Some conditions, for example bowel obstruction, cause bloating or distension and if severe the abdomen will look swollen and tense. The doctor will also be on the lookout for any visible bruises, blemishes or operation scars.
- **Palpation** The doctor will gently feel the abdomen with the hands for tender areas, lumps or bumps or enlarged organs. The doctor may then percuss (tap with the fingers) over particular areas. Different sounds indicate hollow or solid tissue and it is possible to tell whether an organ, for example the liver, is enlarged.
- **Auscultation** Finally, the doctor will listen to the abdomen with a stethoscope to listen for 'bowel sounds' – the tinkling noises made by the normal working of the intestines – which may be unusually loud or quiet, or even absent, in certain conditions.

Examining the abdomen

a Tensing of the abdominal muscles in response to palpation is common in patients with pain or tenderness. It is known as guarding and is a symptom in itself.

b Bowel sounds should be present, but not too loud. A stethoscope can also be used to check the liver margins – scratching over the liver produces a soft sound.

Checking the rectum

If bowel symptoms suggest an abnormality in the rectum, and in particular if there is any sign of blood, a rectal examination may be necessary. The examination is quick and can be done in the doctor's office, with the patient lying on the left side with his or her knees drawn up. The doctor gently inserts a gloved and lubricated finger through the anus into the rectum to feel for any tender areas or lumps. Although the procedure may be uncomfortable it is not usually painful. Sometimes the doctor will perform a sigmoid-oscopy or proctoscopy, where a small, telescope-like device is inserted through the anus to allow the doctor to check the rectum visually.

Investigative tests

A doctor usually makes a tentative diagnosis after the initial examination. Further tests are then used to verify the theory and to help eliminate other possible causes of illness.

Digestive symptoms, although uncomfortable, do not necessarily require hospital admission. Many of these tests therefore, which are mostly straightforward and do not need complex equipment, can be carried out by a person's own general practitioner or in an outpatient clinic.

BLOOD TESTS

Blood analysis provides a wealth of valuable information and is simple and quick to perform. Using a needle and syringe, enough blood for several samples can be taken in one go from a vein in the arm and sent to the laboratory – each in a different coloured tube for ease of identification – to be tested.

When blood is spun at very high speed in a centrifuge, the blood cells separate from the plasma – the straw-coloured fluid in which they float. Some blood tests look only at the blood cells, while others measure substances that are dissolved in the plasma.

Counting cells

There are three types of blood cell, all of which carry out different functions: red cells, white cells and platelets. Red cells are responsible for carrying oxygen to the body's tissues. The white cells, of which there are several

Using a centrifuge
Different elements of blood have different weights. Spinning blood at high speeds in a centrifuge separates out the components so that they can be investigated independently.

different types, play an important role in defending the body from invaders such as infectious organisms. Platelets are a group of cells that help blood to clot if necessary. A severe reduction in the level of any of these blood cells could have serious consequences.

From only a small sample of blood, an automated machine can provide a count of each type of cell. This information can give doctors clues about a patient's condition. For example, a low red cell count indicates anaemia and may suggest that there is bleeding in the digestive tract. The white blood cell count may be raised in someone who has an infection or inflamed areas in the digestive tract. Platelets also increase in number if there is inflammation or bleeding in the bowel.

A test called the erythrocyte sedimentation rate (ESR) does not actually count the cells but measures how long it takes red blood cells (erythrocytes) to settle in a sample of blood. A raised rate of settling is a general indicator of inflammation or infection.

If I have a lot of blood taken for a test, will I feel ill and how does it get replaced?

You would need to have a great deal of blood taken before you felt unwell: blood donors lose slightly more than a pint each time – much more than in a blood test – with no adverse effects. In addition, your body won't really miss the blood. Blood cells are produced continuously in the bone marrow. If there is a significant drop in your blood volume, a feedback mechanism swings into action and the marrow speeds up production of blood cells.

ASK THE EXPERT

Milestones
IN MEDICINE

The first person to see bacteria under the microscope was a Dutch shopkeeper, Anton van Leeuwenhoek, who made lenses for a hobby and then examined very small things. On a normal working day in 1674, Anton took a scraping from between his teeth and observed it through one of his lenses: 'I then saw, with great wonder ... many very little animalcules, very prettily a-moving'. Presenting his findings to Britain's prestigious Royal Society, van Leeuwenhoek initially met with disbelief and hostility, but later became a member of the organisation. As his fame spread, the former shopkeeper, now a civil servant, received visits from the rich and famous, among them the Queen of England and the Russian Tsar.

Measuring substances in blood

As well as looking at blood cells, doctors may also need to measure various chemicals that are dissolved in the plasma. In a patient with suspected pancreatitis, for example, doctors may take a blood test to measure a substance called amylase, levels of which shoot up when the pancreas is inflamed. Often, a person with a digestive tract disorder is poorly nourished because of absorption problems or a loss of appetite. Measuring levels of proteins, such as albumin, in the plasma can confirm that a person is not absorbing nutrients because of gut disease or is not making sufficient proteins in the body.

In a condition called coeliac disease, the body produces antibodies as part of a sensitivity to gluten, a protein found in wheat, rye and barley. Using sophisticated equipment, experts can detect the presence of these abnormal antibodies in the

Coeliac disease
This intestinal wall is flat, pitted and without villi. Compare this with the healthy version on page 26.

blood. General practitioners sometimes use a blood test to detect antibodies against the bacterium *Helicobacter pylori*, which is known to contribute to the development of stomach ulcers. This confirms whether a person has been infected with the organism during their lifetime. It is not, however, useful in assessing the effectiveness of treatment, as even when the infection clears, the antibodies remain in the bloodstream.

Checking the liver

Some tests assess how well the liver is working and whether it is damaged by measuring substances that are either produced or broken down by the liver. Certain enzymes are excreted by damaged liver cells and these can also be measured. Testing the blood for levels of clotting factors can be an indicator of liver function. Many of the factors that produce normal blood clotting are made in the liver, and in some people with liver problems, levels of these may be abnormal.

Measuring minerals

Mineral salts are dissolved in the plasma and are necessary for the normal functioning of the body. Looking at the levels of some of these minerals in the blood, such as potassium, calcium and magnesium, can be very useful in the assessment of people with diseases of the digestive tract. Low levels of potassium are frequently found in people with long-term diarrhoea, while people with conditions such as Crohn's disease and coeliac disease, who are not absorbing food properly, tend to have low levels of calcium or magnesium.

STOOL TESTS

Apart from a simple visual inspection of the stool in the outpatient clinic or on the ward, which may reveal blood, mucus or an abnormal colour and consistency, specimens are sometimes sent for laboratory testing. A patient is given a clean container to take home or into the toilet, where a small amount can be collected in privacy. The sample is then sent to the laboratory for testing. There are three main signs that doctors will be curious about: how much

Bacterial test cultures

Bacteria from stool samples can be cultured, or grown, on a plate of nutrient-rich jelly known as agar. Each species forms a distinctively shaped colony on the plate. By placing paper discs soaked with different antibiotics on the plate and measuring the area cleared of bacteria, a laboratory technician can assess which treatment will be most effective for the patient.

stool is passed; whether there is blood in the stool, which could indicate a damaged gut; and whether there are any abnormal micro-organisms, such as viruses or parasites, that might be causing infection.

Looking for blood

Sometimes, the presence of blood is clearly visible to the naked eye. If the bleeding point is in the rectum, streaks of bright red blood will coat the stool. Blood from higher up in the system will cause the stools to look very dark and tarry, even black.

Sometimes, though, doctors may suspect that a digestive disorder is causing very slight bleeding that is not visible – this is technically known as occult ('hidden') bleeding. In these cases, faecal occult blood testing may be carried out. A tiny sample of faeces is placed on an absorbent card and a chemical added. The presence of even a microscopic amount of blood causes the card to change colour. The test is usually repeated three times over a few days because blood may not be present in every sample of faeces.

The major drawback of this test is that it frequently produces a positive result even when there is no bleeding from the gut. In fact, the test is so sensitive that even bleeding gums can produce a positive result.

Infectious organisms

There are some bacteria that are known to cause diarrhoeal illness if they are present in the gut. These bacteria include certain types of *Escherichia coli*, *Campylobacter*, *Salmonella* and *Shigella*. If the doctor suspects that a patient has been infected with one of these bacteria, a stool culture test may be arranged. For the test, the patient provides a small sample of stool, which is sent to the laboratory. It is then cultured on a Petri dish of agar jelly in warm conditions to encourage any bacteria to grow. After a period of time, the specimen is treated with staining agents and examined under the microscope – bacteria can be identified by their size and shape, and the way they react with the stains. If a pathogen is identified, it is possible to measure its sensitivity to a battery of antibiotics so that the appropriate drug can be prescribed.

BREATH TESTS

Currently, the only breath test routinely used in gastroenterology is the test for *Helicobacter pylori* bacteria, the organisms strongly associated with stomach ulcers. This is a simple test that can be done in a doctor's surgery or a hospital clinic.

Helicobacter pylori
This species of bacteria has characteristic flagellae – whip-like structures – at one end.

Saving your breath

To start with, the person swallows a small capsule containing a chemical called urea, which is labelled with a non-radioactive marker. A breath sample is taken to provide a control reading of carbon dioxide levels. After 45 minutes another sample of breath is collected and both breath specimens are analysed for the marker substance. If a person's stomach is infected with *Helicobacter pylori*, the organism metabolises the urea in the capsule. This process produces carbon dioxide, which is excreted in the breath and can be measured because of the marker. As well as detecting the presence of *Helicobacter pylori*, this test is ideal for assessing whether the bacteria have successfully been eradicated by a course of treatment.

About half the world's population is infected with Helicobacter pylori, but only a small proportion of people develop peptic ulcers.

pH MONITORING AND OESOPHAGEAL MANOMETRY

These specialised tests are used in people with severe heartburn who are not responding to normal treatment, or who are having difficulty swallowing that is not due to oesophageal narrowing. They are used to measure the pressure and the levels of acid in the oesophagus over a 24-hour period.

Acid test

In pH monitoring, a doctor or nurse passes a small pH-sensitive probe through the nose and down into the oesophagus where it is left in position. The person is then sent home, and over a 24-hour period the amount of acid reflux is recorded by a small device worn on the body. The person keeps a diary so that a correlation between heartburn and other reflux symptoms can be made.

Under pressure

Oesophageal manometry measures the pressure in the oesophagus during the process of swallowing and is useful in diagnosing conditions that affect motility, such as achalasia. During the normal swallowing process, a morsel of food is propelled down the oesophagus towards the stomach by muscular contractions called peristaltic waves. The muscle at the lower end of the oesophagus then relaxes to allow food to enter the stomach. If the muscles of the oesophagus are not contracting and relaxing properly, unusual changes in pressure result – oesophageal manometry seeks to measure these changes.

A doctor or nurse passes a small catheter through one nostril until it is positioned in the oesophagus, and the person is asked to swallow. Changes in pressure in the oesophagus are recorded by a gauge attached to the catheter. At the end of the procedure, the catheter is removed and the person sent home.

Scenting danger
Here a nurse assists a man as he breathes into a sample tube, in a test designed to detect the presence of Helicobacter pylori bacteria. Levels of carbon dioxide in the sample are measured.

Imaging the digestive system

Many of the soft tissue structures of the abdomen cannot be seen with traditional X-ray techniques. However, in the past two decades there have been exciting developments in imaging technology, and the field of digestive medicine has benefited particularly.

It is now possible to obtain detailed, real-time three-dimensional pictures of the organs of the digestive system. This makes diagnosis quicker, easier and more accurate, and helps to target and assess treatment options more effectively than ever before.

ULTRASOUND SCANNING

Ultrasound scanning is a simple and safe method of imaging abdominal organs without the use of radiation. Most people will be familiar with ultrasound as, because of its safety, it is routinely used to examine fetuses in pregnant women.

What is it used for?

Ultrasound scanning has limited ability to image hollow organs, such as the intestines, but it is usually the first choice of doctors for an initial look at the pancreas, liver, bile ducts and gallbladder. Abnormalities such as gallstones, tumours and abscesses are easily located, and doctors can measure the size of the organs.

If an abnormality is noted on an ultrasound scan, for example a possible tumour, doctors can use the technique to help guide a small needle to take a sample for further analysis. Ultrasound can also be used to guide the draining of abscesses or fluid from within the abdomen.

Echoes of stone
This coloured ultrasound scan shows a gallstone (see arrow), an accretion of fats and minerals, in a man's gallbladder. The stone could become stuck in the bile duct, causing excruciating pain.

How does it work?

Ultrasound works by firing rapid high-frequency sound waves – too high-pitched for the human ear to hear – at the body's tissues, measuring the echoes as they bounce back and converting them into visual images that are shown on a screen. Different types of body tissue reflect different echoes and, using modern equipment, a skilled operator can obtain extremely detailed images of the internal organs. Also, because images are produced in 'real time' – as they happen – movement can be detected.

An abdominal ultrasound is carried out with the patient lying almost flat on a bed, couch or trolley. The ultrasonographer or doctor covers the skin with conducting jelly and then moves a probe, known as a transducer, gently over the area being scanned observing the image on the screen and taking 'still' photographs when necessary. Usually, the patient can watch the screen during the scan. The procedure is painless and completely safe, and usually takes between 10 and 30 minutes.

AT THE LEADING EDGE

Endoscopic ultrasound

An ultrasound probe can be attached to an endoscope – a flexible viewing instrument – and passed into and down the digestive tract. This 'internal ultrasound' can be used to detect the presence of a tumour and measure the thickness of the oesophagus and stomach walls; it is one of the most accurate ways of diagnosing cancer of the pancreas. However, this technique is very difficult to master and not yet widely available.

COMPUTED TOMOGRAPHY (CT) SCANNING

CT scanning is a sophisticated X-ray technique that was introduced in the early 1970s – about 80 years after X-rays were first used to look inside the body. The technique is generally carried out only after an ultrasound scan or other investigation has raised the possibility that something may be amiss and warrants further inspection.

What is it used for?

CT scanning gives excellent images of the digestive tract and is particularly useful for the detection of structural abnormalities such as tumours and abscesses. Like ultrasound, CT scanning can be used as image guidance when an abnormal area is identified for the doctor to take biopsies using specialised needles.

How does it work?

The technique uses X-rays to produce a series of cross-sectional slices of the body using computerised reconstruction. A rotating X-ray source sends multiple narrow beams through the body. As they exit, they are detected and analysed by equipment that is sensitive to the variations in tissue density and reproduces these variations on the resulting image in different shades of grey. The many cross-sections are analysed by computer to form a 'map' of the body area.

Abdominal CT scans are often done to look at the organs of the digestive system. Because many of these are hollow, X-rays travel straight through them and the resulting images are unclear. To get over this difficulty, on arrival at the X-ray department, the patient is usually given a drink called gastrografin. This is a contrast medium that absorbs X-rays, outlining the stomach and small bowel so that they are easier to identify on the CT images. Sometimes, as well as drinking gastrografin, contrast is enhanced by injecting medium into the bloodstream during the procedure.

Are there any adverse effects?

The main concern about CT scanning is the exposure to X-rays. Because a series of images are required, it can add up to quite a high dose of radiation, even though the dose for an individual image is small. The risk, however, is minimal and exposure is carefully monitored (see box).

CT scanning: slices of life

a This scan shows a horizontal 'slice' through the torso of a pancreatitis sufferer. The spinal cord is visible at the top, with the kidneys on either side. The blue mass is an enlarged pancreas.

b This advanced 3-D CT image shows a healthy torso. The spine (beige), kidneys (blue–grey), gallbladder (green–grey) and a normal pancreas (yellow) are visible, ringed by the ribs.

Is radiation-based imaging safe?

Everyone is exposed to radiation in daily life, from cosmic rays from outer space to radioactive rocks in the earth. The important safety question about radiation exposure is therefore not 'whether' but 'how much'. The radiation exposure a patient receives from one session of CT scanning is not dangerous, especially as the radiation doses are kept as low as possible. However, special measures should be taken to protect reproductive organs, and pregnant women should avoid X-rays altogether as there is a very small risk that high doses of radiation may cause birth defects.

ASK THE EXPERT

MAGNETIC RESONANCE IMAGING

Magnetic resonance imaging (MRI) is a relatively new imaging technique that is rapidly becoming more widely used, where available, because of its ability to produce amazingly detailed pictures of the body's interior.

What is it used for?

In gastroenterology, doctors use MRI mainly to look at the bile duct, gallbladder and liver. Abnormalities such as gallstones, cysts, abscesses and tumours are very clearly defined on MRI. Because of the fine detail, the technique is also helpful in detecting abscesses around the anus.

How does it work?

MRI uses a powerful magnet and radio waves to create 3-D images on a computer screen. Human tissue is mainly composed of water, which contains hydrogen atoms. When a patient is exposed to a huge circular magnet, the pattern of the hydrogen atoms in the body is disrupted so that rather than existing randomly, they lie in rows pointing in the same direction.

The appropriate part of the body is then bombarded with radio pulses, which knock the atoms temporarily out of alignment. As they fall back into place, the nuclei in the atoms emit signals – the so-called 'resonance' – that

Sliced in half
This MRI shows a section through a torso, seen from the back. The spine runs down the centre, flanked by the lungs at the top, two lobes of the liver, two kidneys and a short length of intestine on the right.

MRI generates images on computer using a magnetic field that is between 10,000 and 30,000 times more powerful than the earth's magnetic field.

are picked up and analysed by a computer, according to their strength and source, to form clear images. Sometimes a contrast medium is used to enhance the definition of the pictures obtained.

What are the adverse effects?

Although the process of MRI sounds extraordinary, patients undergoing the procedure do not feel a thing. As far as the experts know, MRI is an extremely safe procedure, as no radiation is involved. However, the magnets can interfere with pacemakers, hearing implants and other artificial devices. The experience itself can be uncomfortable since the subject spends up to 30 minutes in a narrow tube while the image is obtained, and patients who suffer from claustrophobia may need a sedative beforehand to calm them.

Barium studies

For over a hundred years, barium studies have been the primary technique for imaging the gastrointestinal tract. They have the advantages of being cheap, quick and non-invasive. A century of development has led to better media, new methods and advanced X-ray equipment, which combine to provide extremely high-quality images.

BARIUM CONTRAST STUDIES

With the introduction of X-rays in 1895, doctors were finally able to look inside the human body without having to cut a patient open. However, the images obtained depended on the ability of the various body tissues to absorb X-rays. Those that absorb X-rays well, such as bone, are reproduced beautifully on the radiographs. But the amazing new technology appeared to have limited use in visualising organs such as the stomach and intestines, which did not show up at all well on the X-rays because they are hollow.

Within a year, however, the principle of a 'contrast medium' was developed. In 1896, it was discovered that when cavities are filled with barium, a substance that readily absorbs X-rays, a clear outline can be seen. To give an even clearer picture, air can be introduced into the cavity once the barium is in place, a technique known as a double-contrast X-ray.

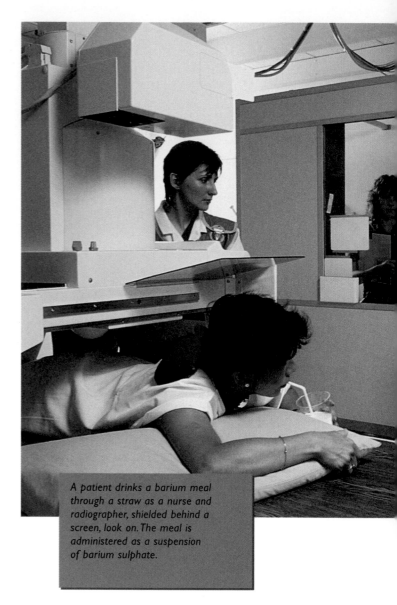

A patient drinks a barium meal through a straw as a nurse and radiographer, shielded behind a screen, look on. The meal is administered as a suspension of barium sulphate.

Walter Cannon was still a first-year medical student when, in 1896, he devised the use of barium as a contrast medium to outline the upper digestive tract.

What are they used for?

There are four main types of barium studies, each of which examines a different section of the digestive tract.

- Barium swallow This is mainly carried out to investigate patients who have difficulty swallowing. The test shows whether the process of swallowing is normal and indicates any abnormality of the oesophagus, such as a narrowing (known as a stricture). A barium swallow may also be used as a test for gastro-oesophageal reflux, a condition in which some of the contents of the stomach pass back up into the oesophagus.

- Barium meal This type of study has been shown to be effective in visualising abnormalities in the stomach and duodenum, for example a hiatus hernia or cancer.

- Barium follow-through The aim of this type of study is to follow the barium beyond the lower part of the stomach into the small intestine to look for inflammatory conditions such as Crohn's disease.

- Barium enema This procedure visualises the whole of the large bowel and is carried out if doctors suspect conditions such as ulcerative colitis or colon cancer. The technique does not always reliably image the rectum.

A monitor linked to the digital X-ray system allows both the patient and the radiographer to follow the progress of the contrast medium along the digestive tract, giving images first of the stomach and then the intestine.

Barium meal studies

a If doctors suspect a problem with the stomach or small intestine, such as an ulcer or some form of inflammatory condition, a barium meal can provide a good picture of the stomach and intestinal lining, highlighting damaged or deformed regions of the mucus membrane. Barium meals are usually followed by eating gas-producing effervescent granules, so that the digestive tract is filled with air while the barium forms a thin coating on the inside surfaces. This shows up features of the gut surface that could not otherwise be seen.

b This false-colour barium meal X-ray reveals an advanced cancer that has spread across almost the whole bottom half of the patient's stomach. The uniformly purple area at the top is the healthy part of the stomach, filled with barium. In stark contrast, the lower parts of the stomach appear strangulated and wasted where the cancer has taken over. At the left, the patient's spinal column is visible, leading down to the pelvic bones at the bottom of the picture.

c This false-colour double-contrast X-ray was taken after a carbonated barium meal was administered. The image shows the patient's duodenum, revealing the formation of a peptic ulcer, highlighted as a pink oval in the duodenal cap.

How do they work?

Barium sulphate is a chalk-like liquid that is either swallowed so that it coats the upper digestive tract or given as an enema into the large bowel. Once the barium is in the gut, X-rays are transmitted through the body onto a photographic plate. As the rays pass through, the contrast medium slows their progress and shows up as a white area on the film. At the same time, images are transmitted to a monitor for real-time viewing.

Barium swallow, meal and follow-through

For most barium studies, the patient is given a set of instructions on how to prepare for the test and where it will take place – which is usually in the X-ray department of a hospital. A period of fasting is always necessary for a few hours beforehand to ensure that the stomach or bowel are completely empty. Once they're underway, barium studies usually take less than an hour.

In a barium swallow procedure, the patient drinks some barium, initially while sitting up and then when lying down – changing position helps to move the barium through the gut. X-rays are taken as it passes down the oesophagus, and into the stomach. A barium meal is similar but only a small amount of barium is drunk, together with some effervescent granules or tablets, which produce gas to allow double-contrast X-rays to be taken.

For a barium follow-through a slightly different technique is used. The patient may be asked to lie in different positions on the X-ray table to help move the barium through the digestive tract. Some hospitals have specially designed tables that rotate and tip during the procedure, which is important for immobilised patients.

HELP YOUR DOCTOR TO HELP YOU

Preparing for a barium enema

In order to get a good outline on the X-rays taken during a barium enema, the large intestine should be completely clear. The procedure used to achieve this can be unpleasant in that it produces frequent watery stools, but it is vital that you stick to the preparation schedule so the investigation goes smoothly. Different hospitals vary slightly in their procedures.

- *On the day the barium enema takes place you should not eat any solid food – just drink plenty of clear fluids.*

- *Drink the oral laxative supplied to you. This is usually in the form of salts, which are dissolved in a great deal of water.*

- *Stay close to a toilet as the laxatives will cause frequent episodes of watery diarrhoea.*

Barium enema

Looking at the large intestine is a more complicated procedure than the other studies – it is a long and convoluted organ, which has to be empty in order to get a good view. Consequently, a bowel preparation procedure is necessary (see left).

The investigation involves placing a small tube into the rectum through the anus and injecting barium liquid and air to outline the entire colon so that X-rays can be taken.

Are there any adverse effects?

The main side effect of barium investigations is a feeling of bloating and flatulence. In addition, because of the chalky nature of the barium, some people suffer constipation for a day or two after the test.

As X-rays are a form of radiation, there is a certain amount of exposure. However, this dose is not high enough to cause damage, and exposure is closely monitored by radiologists and radiographers.

HAVING A BARIUM ENEMA

Three days before the procedure the doctor gave me a leaflet about following a low-fibre diet. She also gave me some strong laxatives to empty my bowel the night before the test.

On the morning of the test I had to skip breakfast – having food in my gut might ruin the picture – but I did have a large glass of fruit juice, which kept me going. At the hospital I changed into a gown (completely open at the back, of course).

The doctor asked me to lie on a special table and warned me that the next part of the procedure would feel

a bit uncomfortable. First, I had an injection to relax the muscle of the bowel wall, then a special tube was inserted into my back passage. This was used to run a special dye that shows up on X-rays into my intestines, which were also pumped up with air. Again, this was uncomfortable, as it caused some sharp, colicky pain in my abdomen.

Once the air and dye mixture was right the staff retreated behind a screen and took lots of X-rays, moving the table (and me) into a different position for each one. It only took about ten minutes.

After the X-rays were finished, I was taken into a side room with a toilet to recover. I passed a lot of dye and air into the toilet straight away, but as the muscle relaxant wore off I got a bit of discomfort – along with embarrassing noises – from being bloated with gas.

Looking inside the digestive tract

The development of endoscopy over the past 30 years has revolutionised the medical specialty of gastroenterology. Video-endoscopes can now produce high-quality images and allow direct imaging of both the upper and the lower digestive tract.

Endoscopy literally means 'looking inside' and endoscopic procedures of the digestive tract do just that. For nearly 40 years, these techniques have been used mainly for diagnosis – to check for abnormalities and to take samples for further examination – but they are now increasingly used to carry out treatments. Although, in some procedures, light sedation may be necessary, there is no need for surgery, a general anaesthetic or surgical incisions. Because of this, endoscopic procedures can often be carried out on an outpatient basis.

Flexible endoscopes

These are narrow, bendy tubes that can be manipulated round tricky corners. They consist of bundles of optical fibres, made from either glass or plastic, that transmit light signals using reflection. Some of the fibres carry light to the gut to illuminate it and others transmit the image back. The doctor then views the images through an eyepiece or on a monitor. Over the last few years, a new type of endoscope – the video-endoscope – has effectively supplanted the older model. This endoscope has a miniature camera at its tip, which relays high-quality video images to a monitor screen.

Both types of endoscope usually have several channels – one for viewing, one for lights, and one for sucking out fluids and blowing air. This channel can also carry instruments, such as biopsy forceps.

Inside an endoscope

Shown here are the different parts of an endoscope.

a The endoscope being connected to the light and power source. Steering controls on the hand unit allow the operator to move the tip of the endoscope left and right and up and down.

b Fibreoptics channel light through the flexible tubing to illuminate internal spaces and structures.

c The tip of the endoscope, as the air channel is tested by blowing bubbles in saline – the same channel can suck fluids and carry surgical instruments.

Channel for water, air and instruments

Viewing lens

Fibreoptic lights

— Endoscope

Looking at the upper digestive tract

The easiest way to reach the small intestine using an endoscope is by passing it down the oesophagus and into the stomach, and then negotiating the sharp bend at the pylorus to pass into the duodenum.

— Oesophagus

a

Stomach ———

Pylorus ———

Duodenum ———

b

c

Endoscopic views

Shown here are three views obtained with an endoscope: **a** *the entrance to the stomach, viewed from the oesophagus;* **b** *the folded lining of the stomach;* **c** *the pylorus – the exit from the stomach to the duodenum.*

LOOKING AT THE UPPER DIGESTIVE TRACT

There are three parts to the upper digestive tract, each of which can be examined individually using an endoscope: the oesophagus, the stomach and the duodenum (the first section of the small intestine). The endoscopy procedure for looking at the upper digestive tract is called an oesophagogastroduodenoscopy – a term that doctors usually shorten, understandably, to gastroscopy.

The first attempts at endoscopy began in the early 1900s, with a rigid instrument similar to a telescope. Flexible gastroscopes were invented in the 1930s.

What is it used for?

The need for endoscopy usually arises when a patient has symptoms such as upper abdominal pain or persistent nausea and vomiting, especially vomiting up blood – a condition known as haematemesis. The technique may also be used when barium studies (see page 106) have confirmed an abnormality that needs closer inspection. Without looking inside the stomach, it is very difficult to diagnose the nature of a problem, and using an endoscope gives doctors the opportunity to inspect the stomach directly and take tissue samples if necessary. There are some conditions that can be both diagnosed and treated during an endoscopy session, for example narrowing in the oesophagus, bleeding ulcers, or tumours (see page 124).

How does it work?

Endoscopy is usually carried out in a specially designed 'endoscopy unit'. The doctor will ask that the patient does not eat or drink for at least four hours beforehand so that the gut is as empty as possible. Once in the endoscopy unit, local anaesthetic spray is squirted onto the back of the throat to help prevent discomfort as the endoscope is passed down. The patient can choose to be lightly sedated; although this does not induce sleep, it means that most patients retain no memory of the procedure. After the endoscopy, it is advisable not to eat or drink for an hour as the local anaesthetic can affect the ability to swallow properly and food may go down the wrong passage.

ENDOSCOPIC RETROGRADE CHOLANGIO-PANCREATOGRAPHY (ERCP)

Sometimes, doctors take upper digestive tract endoscopy a step further so that they can examine the ducts draining the gallbladder and pancreas. This technique is also extremely useful in the treatment of patients with gallstones and bile duct strictures who would otherwise need to undergo major surgery.

How does it work?

ERCP combines endoscopic and radiological techniques to provide clear images of biliary and pancreatic ducts and is generally carried out in the X-ray department of a hospital. For this procedure, the patient is given sedation, which induces a light sleep. It is unusual for the patient to remember the procedure afterwards.

Before the ERCP takes place, the patient fasts for about four hours to make sure that the stomach and duodenum are completely empty. The anatomy of the bile ducts can make the procedure technically difficult – to make it easier the patient lies stomach down on the table, with shoulders turned to one side. Throughout the procedure oxygen is given, and pulse and blood oxygen levels are monitored using a pulse oximeter, attached to the finger. The doctor passes an endoscope through the mouth and oesophagus into the stomach and duodenum. A long, thin catheter is then threaded down one of the channels in the endoscope and positioned at the point at which the ducts enter the duodenum (see page 28).

Once the catheter is in position, a radio-opaque iodine dye that absorbs X-rays is injected back into the ducts – hence the procedure is termed 'retrograde' – and a series of X-ray images is taken. Two different types of dye are used: a low contrast one for the bile duct, so that the dye does not obscure gallstones that may be present, and a

Imaging the parts that other scopes cannot reach
Running diagonally across this contrast X-ray is an endoscope. Visible behind it is the bile duct, filled with radio-opaque dye. Running down the right of the picture is the spine.

AT THE LEADING EDGE

Ingestible camera capsules

It may soon be routine for doctors to examine the insides of the digestive system with a wireless endoscopic camera capsule the size of a vitamin pill. The disposable capsule consists of a battery, a camera on a chip, a light source and a transmitter. A patient will simply swallow one and continue with normal activities. The camera is 'live' for five to six hours and relays information to a video-recording device worn around the waist. Peristaltic movements propel it through the digestive tract and it leaves the system after 10 to 48 hours.

higher contrast dye for the pancreatic duct. If the doctor finds gallstones or a narrowing in any one of the ducts, it is possible to use the endoscope to carry out treatment there and then (see page 124).

After an ERCP investigation the patient is often able to go home the same day. If treatment has been carried out, however, an overnight stay in hospital may be necessary.

Gastroscopy – looking inside the stomach

In the late 1960s the introduction of techniques using flexible, manoeuvrable endoscopes revolutionised the diagnosis of gastrointestinal disorders. Gastroscopy is one such technique, providing a quick and easy way of investigating problems with the stomach.

Before the invention of flexible endoscopes, only each 'end' of the digestive tract – the oesophagus and rectum – could be viewed through rigid tubes. Now, however, doctors can see almost the entire system.

The comfort and cooperation of patients is paramount, so after signing a consent form they are asked if they would prefer to be sedated during the investigation. If so, the doctor administers a sedative, which takes only a minute or so to kick in. The whole procedure is quick: a straightforward gastroscopy takes, on average, about five minutes from start to finish.

The endoscopy team

Two endoscopy staff nurses assist the endoscopist throughout: one talks the patient through the procedure and monitors the pulse rate and blood oxygen levels. The other nurse helps with procedures such as taking biopsies, and cleans the scope once the procedure is finished. The unit is equipped with two or three scopes to allow time between patients for disinfection.

Home within 30 minutes

Most endoscopic procedures are carried out on an outpatient basis. Patients who choose to have the procedure without a sedative can go home within 20 or 30 minutes after having something to drink, like a cup of tea. Those who opt for a sedative have to wait for 45–60 minutes before being taken home by someone, such as a friend or family member.

Taking a biopsy

If a growth or other abnormality is found during an examination, the doctor can insert biopsy forceps into a special instrument channel and take a small sample of tissue or cells. The biopsy is brought out through the same channel, and the sample is sent to the pathology laboratory, where technicians can examine it to determine whether the growth is malignant.

The gastroscopy procedure, step by step

1 The endoscopist sprays some local anaesthetic on the back of the patient's throat to numb the area and make the passage of the endoscope easier and less uncomfortable. The patient is then positioned on his left side.

2 The doctor will, if requested, administer a small dose of sedative through a vein in the back of the hand. The nurse attaches a pulse oximeter, which looks like a high-tech 'peg', to the patient's forefinger; this device measures how much oxygen is in the blood and takes the pulse throughout the procedure.

3 A mouth guard is put in to prevent biting of the endoscope. To make it easy to breathe while the endoscope is in the mouth, a tube supplying oxygen may be gently inserted into one nostril.

4 The endoscopist first lubricates the endoscope with KY jelly and then gently guides it into the mouth, down the oesophagus and into the stomach, at the same time observing the monitor. Wheels on the handset allow the doctor to move the endoscope around to examine the internal surfaces; it can even bend right back on itself to view the top of the stomach.

5 Pictures picked up by the lens in the tip of the gastroscope are relayed back to the TV monitor, which displays and records them, together with the date, time and patient's details. The video can be replayed to review significant findings.

6 Sometimes endoscopic biopsy forceps are used to obtain tissue samples, which are carefully labelled and sent to the laboratory for testing by a pathologist.

EXAMINING THE LOWER DIGESTIVE TRACT

Just like the upper digestive system, the lower gut can be examined in sections, depending on the symptoms.

- Proctoscopy provides information about the rectum only. It is often carried out if the patient has noticed bright red blood in the stools, which can be an indication of a problem, such as haemorrhoids, in the very last part of the gut.
- Sigmoidoscopy is used to look at the left side of the colon only and is usually done to investigate persistent diarrhoea or someone who has noticed blood in the stools.
- Colonoscopy enables doctors to carry out an examination of the colon from the rectum to the small bowel and is a very effective tool for diagnosing all kinds of digestive system disorders.

For most types of lower digestive tract endoscopy, the doctor carrying out the procedure will ask the patient to lie on his or her left side. This is because the bowel curves to the left, so it is easier and more comfortable to insert the endoscope in this position.

How do they work?

Both rigid and flexible endoscopes are used to look at the lower gut. The proctoscope is a short, rigid tube about 15cm (6in) long. A rigid sigmoidoscope is a plastic tube with a light source and a magnifying glass at one end and is used to examine the lower 25cm (10in) of the gut only. The flexible sigmoidoscope is able to turn corners and can therefore extend to about 70cm (28in). Colonoscopes are similar to flexible sigmoidoscopes but longer.

Colonoscopes can be up to a metre and half (5 feet) in length.

Proctoscopy

This 'on the spot' examination can be done with no preparation at all, either in an outpatient clinic or in the doctor's surgery. A proctoscope with an obdurator – a central piece that makes insertion more comfortable – is lubricated and inserted through the anus. The obdurator is removed and air is pumped in to inflate the passage for a better view. The doctor then shines a light down the tube to examine the rectum. This investigation takes only a few minutes and is not painful unless there are tender or inflamed areas in the rectum.

Sigmoidoscopy

This technique can be rigid or flexible, depending on the type of endoscope used. Either procedure is slightly more complex than proctoscopy and is usually performed on a hospital ward or in the outpatient clinic. They require little preparation but sometimes an enema is given to clear the lower end of the gut. Sigmoidoscopy takes slightly longer than proctoscopy as it views a larger part of the gut. The endoscope is gently inserted into the

HAVING A SIGMOIDOSCOPY

The first step in the procedure was an enema, following which the doctor examined my rectum with his finger.

I was a bit apprehensive about this but the doctor was very reassuring. He explained that he had to check that the passages were clear for the scope, and also that it would help to relax the sphincter. Once he'd given the all-clear, the nurse passed him the sigmoidoscope, already coated with KY jelly. I was a little uncomfortable when it was inserted, but the doctor did everything very gently as he guided the tip past the bends in my colon.

At the first bend there was a tiny stab of pain, but it quickly passed. The worst thing was a feeling that I needed to go to the toilet for almost the whole duration of the procedure. In just a few minutes the whole tube was in, and the doctor and I watched on the TV monitor as he slowly withdrew it. He assured me that everything looked normal and healthy.

Some blood appeared as the camera got near the rectum, which the doctor said was caused by an anal fissure. At the same time there was a raspberry sound, as some of the air that had been pumped in leaked out. Then the scope was out, less than ten minutes after we started.

Journey through the colon

a With the patient lying on one side, an endoscopist gently withdraws a colonoscope, watching the monitor as he does so to check for signs of disease. The image on the monitor shows the transverse colon.

b This X-ray shows the colonoscope in place, its curves following the course of the colon.

c An endoscopic view of a healthy transverse colon shows its typical triangular cross-section.

bowel and then gradually pulled back as the doctor looks through the magnifying glass. Side effects for the patient can include wind and tenesmus – a sensation of incomplete emptying of the bowels.

Colonoscopy

The most important part of a colonoscopy is the preparation to clear the gut, without which the test would be impossible to carry out. Different hospitals may vary, but patients are usually given the following guidelines.

• Follow a low-fibre diet for two days before the test.
• Take clear fluids only on the day before the test.
• The day before the colonoscopy, drink the sachets of laxative that have been provided with plenty of water.
• Stay close to a toilet after taking the laxatives as they cause frequent watery bowel movements.
• On the day of the test, don't eat or drink anything for a few hours before the test.

A colonoscopy is usually performed with light sedation, which causes drowsiness – most people are unable to remember anything about the examination afterwards. Oxygen is given throughout, and the pulse and oxygen concentration in the blood are measured continuously using a pulse oximeter.

As the doctor gently advances the endoscope along the intestine, images of the lining of the intestine are relayed to a nearby screen, and any abnormal areas that are spotted are investigated more closely. If the doctor finds something of concern, particularly a growth of some sort, a small sample of tissue – a biopsy – will be taken for laboratory examination. This is done by passing biopsy forceps down a special channel in the endoscope and snipping away a tiny piece of the lining (see page 112).

CURRENT TREATMENTS

Drugs have revolutionised the treatment of some digestive disorders. Peptic ulcers, for example, can now be cured by a simple triple-drug regimen of antibiotics and ulcer-healing drugs. Surgery has also advanced to the stage where a number of procedures can be carried out by keyhole techniques, in which only tiny incisions in the body are made. For some serious conditions, open surgery is still needed, but the risks that go with such operations have been minimised with advances in surgical practice.

Drugs for the digestive system

Drugs are now available to tackle most digestive disorders. Even where an outright cure is not possible, for example with inflammatory bowel disease, drugs can help to alleviate symptoms.

DRUGS FOR NAUSEA AND VOMITING

Vomiting is a reflex action for getting rid of harmful substances, but it may also be a symptom of disease. Nausea and vomiting can be caused by gut infection, travel sickness, pregnancy or vertigo, and can also be a side effect of some drugs, such as those used in cancer chemotherapy. Doctors try to diagnose the cause of sickness before prescribing drugs so that they can focus on treating the underlying cause. Although several drugs for nausea and vomiting – antiemetics – are available without prescription, they should not be taken for more than one to two days without consulting your doctor.

How do they work?

Antiemetics act directly or indirectly on the vomiting centre in the brain. The vomiting centre is activated by stimuli from several areas of the body, including the chemoreceptor trigger zone in the brain, which is sensitive to chemicals in the blood; the hearing and balance centre in the inner ear; and the gut. The vomiting centre and chemoreceptor trigger zone have receptors for several brain chemicals, which act as messengers to signal the sickness response. Antiemetic drugs act on receptors at one or more of these sites.

Mucus-producing cell

Mucus

Gastric gland

- **Antihistamines** These drugs, such as cyclizine, work at sites both in the inner ear and on the vomiting centre. They can be bought over the counter and are useful in preventing and treating motion sickness and dizziness.
- **Hyoscine hydrobromide** This is used to control motion sickness. It may be applied in the form of a tiny patch behind the ear to allow continuous release of the active ingredient.
- **Dopamine receptor antagonists** Domperidone and metoclopramide, two examples of this group, block receptors in the chemoreceptor trigger zone. They are often prescribed to prevent and treat chemotherapy-induced nausea and vomiting.
- **Phenothiazines** Drugs in this group include prochlorperazine, which blocks receptors in the chemoreceptor trigger zone. They are used to prevent and treat nausea and vomiting in people with cancer and in those taking drugs that cause nausea.
- **Serotonin receptor antagonists** These block receptors for the brain chemical serotonin and are effective against nausea and vomiting induced by anticancer drugs. An example is ondansetron.

Stomach acid is incredibly strong – if it came into direct contact with your skin, it would burn.

What are the adverse effects?

Some antiemetics, including prochlorperazine, cyclizine and hyoscine hydrobromide, may cause drowsiness and shouldn't be taken if driving or operating machinery. Some can also cause a dry mouth, blurred vision and/or difficulty in passing urine.

ANTACIDS

Antacids are one of the most widely used classes of drugs. People take antacids mainly to relieve indigestion or heartburn, known medically as dyspepsia. Often a change in diet or a glass of milk can prevent or relieve indigestion, but many people find antacids a huge help from time to time. Doctors often prescribe antacids for mild symptoms of dyspepsia in disorders such as inflammation or ulceration of the oesophagus, stomach and duodenum. They are usually taken when symptoms occur and relieve pain within a few minutes. The drugs may be prescribed by a doctor, but more often people buy them from a chemist or supermarket. Antacids are available as tablets (some of which are chewable) and suspensions.

How do they work?

The stomach lining is normally protected from the powerful stomach acid by a thin layer of mucus. There are several types of antacid – all are simple chemical compounds that are mildly alkaline and so help to neutralise stomach acid. Taking antacids on a regular basis reduces the acidity of the stomach, which is good for healing ulcers, but can be bad for digestion of food.

- **Aluminium and magnesium compounds** Both these groups of antacids have a prolonged action in neutralising stomach acid and are widely used for the treatment of indigestion.

Shield of mucus

The stomach produces two to three litres of highly acidic gastric juice per day. In order to prevent the stomach being eaten away by its own juices, cells at its surface produce a thick coating of mucus that forms a protective barrier.

a An electron micrograph of the stomach lining shows the entrances to gastric glands, which secrete hydrochloric acid. The actual surface of the lining is made of simple columnar cells, which produce mucus.

b A close-up shows the mucus-producing cells spiralling down into a gastric gland.

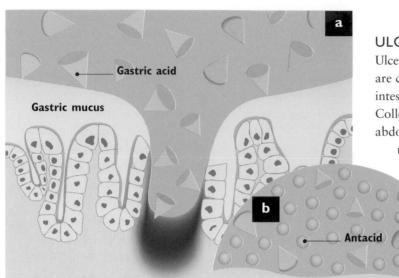

Gastric acid

Gastric mucus

a

b

Antacid

How antacids work

a *If there is too much acid, or insufficient protective mucus, the stomach lining may become irritated and inflamed, and eventually damaged.*

b *Antacids restore the pH balance of the stomach juices, neutralising excess acid. This reduces irritation of the stomach lining, giving it a chance to heal and allowing the mucus coating to re-form.*

- **Sodium bicarbonate** This antacid works rapidly to neutralise stomach acid but its action is short-lived.
- **Combined preparations** Some antacids are combined preparations: a neutralising compound, such as magnesium, along with other substances called alginates. Alginates float on the contents of the stomach and produce a neutralising layer that prevents acid from rising into the oesophagus and causing heartburn.

What are the adverse effects?

Aluminium compounds may cause constipation, while magnesium can cause diarrhoea; the two may be taken together to counteract their opposing effects. Aluminium compounds can also cause weakness and bone damage, and should not be taken at high doses for long periods.

Individuals with kidney problems should take extra care because levels of magnesium in the blood may become high, causing lethargy and drowsiness. Sodium bicarbonate produces gas and so may cause bloating and belching. People with heart or kidney diseases should not take sodium bicarbonate because it can lead to water accumulation and chemical imbalances of the blood.

ULCER-HEALING DRUGS

Ulcers most commonly form in the stomach, where they are called gastric ulcers, and duodenum (part of the small intestine), where they are called duodenal ulcers. Collectively known as peptic ulcers, they can cause abdominal pain, vomiting and changes in appetite. Left untreated, ulcers may erode blood vessel walls or perforate the stomach or duodenum with potentially fatal consequences. Although the symptoms of an ulcer may be relieved by antacids, ulcer healing is slow. Instead, the usual treatment is with a specific ulcer-healing drug. Some of these drugs are combined with antibiotics to treat *Helicobacter pylori* infection – now known to be the main cause of peptic ulcers (see page 122).

How do they work?

Most ulcer-healing drugs dramatically reduce acid secretion in the stomach. The result is that they both relieve symptoms and heal the ulcers. Some ulcer-healing drugs, such as cimetidine, can be bought over the counter. But since they may mask the symptoms of a more serious illness, such as stomach cancer, they should not be used for more than two weeks without consulting your doctor.

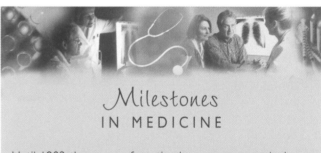

Milestones
IN MEDICINE

Until 1982 the cause of peptic ulcers was uncertain, but overproduction of acid was thought to be responsible. Then researchers discovered a bacterium – *Helicobacter pylori* – that could survive in acidic stomach conditions by burrowing into the mucus. There was still some doubt as to whether this bacterium caused ulcers, so to clarify the issue an Australian doctor, Barry Marshall, decided to infect himself with it. He developed gastritis, and a biopsy confirmed *Helicobacter pylori* as the culprit. This brave experiment led to antibiotic treatment for ulcers.

- **Histamine (H₂) receptor blockers** These drugs have structures that fit the histamine (H₂) receptors on the acid-secreting cells in the stomach. Histamine normally attaches to these receptors and stimulates acid secretion. It also mediates the action of other substances, such as gastrin and acetylcholine, which further increase acid production. H₂ receptor blockers prevent histamine from attaching to its receptor site and so reduce acid production, allowing the mucus lining to heal. Examples are cimetidine, ranitidine, famotidine and nizatidine. They are usually taken for four to six weeks.
- **Proton pump inhibitors** Acid secretion by cells in the stomach depends on the action of a group of enzymes that work together in a system known as a proton pump. Drugs that bind to the proton pump enzymes are known as proton pump inhibitors, and include omeprazole, lansoprazole and pantoprazole. They can reduce acid secretion by 90–100 per cent over 24 hours. Proton pump inhibitors are effective for oesophagitis (inflammation of the oesophagus) and oesophageal and peptic ulcers. They are particularly useful for ulcers that have failed to heal on other treatments. They begin to reduce pain in a few hours and usually allow the ulcer to heal within three to eight weeks.
- **Misoprostol** This drug is related to naturally occurring chemicals called prostaglandins. It reduces the amount of acid secreted in the stomach and promotes healing of peptic ulcers. Drugs such as NSAIDs have an antiprostaglandin action, which blocks certain prostaglandins and causes ulcers and bleeding in the digestive tract. Misoprostol can be used to prevent or cure such ulcers – treatment is usually effective within a few weeks.
- **Sucralfate and bismuth** Sucralfate forms a coating over the ulcer, protecting it from the action of the stomach acid and allowing it to heal. Bismuth may stimulate production of gut-protective prostaglandins or bicarbonate, which contribute towards the protective mucus layer of the stomach. It also kills *H. pylori* bacteria and is used in triple therapy with antibiotics.

A closer look at stomach ulcers

a This coloured electron micrograph of the surface of the stomach lining shows a smooth, round wound – an ulcer – in the otherwise pitted epithelial surface.

b This micrograph shows a section through a sample of tissue taken from a bleeding ulcer in the stomach. The mucus-secreting cells are stained green and seem fairly normal on the right, but towards the left-hand side of the image the cells are contorted with massive numbers of red blood cells.

What are the adverse effects?

H_2 receptor blockers can cause confusion in elderly people. On rare occasions, cimetidine can cause temporary breast enlargement and impotence in men. Proton pump inhibitors may cause headaches, diarrhoea and rashes and shouldn't be taken by anyone with liver problems, or by pregnant or breastfeeding women. Many people find they experience side effects (nausea, vomiting and a rash) with triple therapy using proton pump inhibitors and antibiotics, mainly related to the antibiotics. The most likely side effects from misoprostol are diarrhoea and indigestion. If they are severe, it may be necessary to stop treatment and find an alternative. Sucralfate can cause diarrhoea or constipation, as well as nausea and indigestion.

DRUGS FOR DIARRHOEA

An attack of diarrhoea usually resolves quickly without medical attention. The most important principle is to abstain from food and drink plenty of clear fluids.

Rehydration solutions (containing sugars as well as potassium and sodium salts) are available from chemists and can be used to combat dehydration and chemical imbalances due to lost body fluids. Alternatively, you can make your own (see below).

Diarrhoea bug
These Clostridium bacteria belong to one of the many species of micro-organism that can cause diarrhoea.

Several drugs are available to relieve non-specific diarrhoea when the diarrhoea is particularly severe and once it is certain that the diarrhoea is neither infectious nor toxic. These drugs include opioids and bulk-forming and adsorbent agents. Antispasmodic drugs may also be used to relieve cramping pain. If diarrhoea is found to be caused by an infectious agent, and the agent can be identified, a course of antibiotics may be prescribed (see page 122).

How do they work?

Antidiarrhoeal drugs act on the gut wall affecting the speed with which it moves contents along or boosting the large intestine's ability to absorb water, thereby making the stools less fluid.

- **Opioid drugs** The commonly used drugs are loperamide, codeine and co-phenotrope. These drugs act directly on the gut wall and slow down gut motility. Faeces then pass more slowly through the large intestine. They are very effective and are used when the diarrhoea is severe and debilitating. Some of these drugs – for example, Imodium (which contains loperamide) – can be bought over the counter.
- **Bulk-forming agents** These agents have a milder effect than opioid drugs and are usually used only when it is necessary to regulate bowel action over a prolonged period, especially in individuals who have had part of the intestines removed by ileostomy or colostomy (see pages 130–131). The agents contain particles that swell up as they absorb excess water, irritants and harmful chemicals from the intestines, making the faeces firmer and less fluid.
- **Antispasmodic drugs** These are anticholinergic drugs – drugs that act on the involuntary part of the nervous system – and include hyoscine. They are used mainly for the symptoms associated with irritable bowel syndrome. They reduce the transmission of nerve signals to the large intestine wall, thus preventing spasm.

Rehydration for diarrhoea
This easy-to-make recipe delivers optimum oral rehydration. In 1 litre (2 pints) of drinking or boiled water, add 2 table-spoons of sugar or honey, ¼ teaspoon of salt and ¼ teaspoon bicarbonate of soda. For a dose of potassium, add either some lo-salt (potassium chloride) or some mashed banana.

What are the adverse effects?

All antidiarrhoeal drugs should be taken with plenty of water and may cause constipation if used in excess. It is important not to take a bulk-forming agent together with an opioid or antispasmodic drug because a bulky mass could form and obstruct the large intestine.

LAXATIVES

The simplest remedy for constipation is to drink more fluid, eat a high-fibre diet and take more exercise. Sometimes, however, laxatives may be required. Laxatives are also used to prevent pain and straining in people suffering from hernias or haemorrhoids. Doctors may prescribe laxatives for the same reason after childbirth or abdominal surgery. Potent laxatives are used to clear the large intestine before investigative procedures such as a barium enema (see pages 106–108) or colonoscopy (see page 115). Although laxatives can be bought over the counter, anyone taking them regularly should consult a doctor, because they may have adverse effects if taken inappropriately.

Average daily stool weight in the West is 50–200g whereas in Africa it is about 500g.

How do they work?

Most laxative drugs work in one of three ways: they stimulate the gut wall to move the contents along faster, they help draw fluid into the faeces, or they bulk up the faeces to make stools easier to pass.

- **Bulk-forming agents** Ispaghula husk and methylcellulose take a while to work but are less likely than other laxatives to interfere with bowel action. These agents are usually taken after meals but are not absorbed as they pass through the gut. They contain particles that absorb many times their own volume of water to bulk-up the faeces and so encourage normal bowel action. They should be taken with plenty of fluids.
- **Stimulant (contact) laxatives** These substances, including senna and bisacodyl, act on the nerve endings in the intestinal wall that trigger muscle contraction. Faeces are moved through the large intestine faster so there is less time for water to be absorbed by the body. The faeces become more liquid and are passed more easily.
- **Osmotic laxatives** These laxatives act by increasing the amount of water in the large intestine. Faeces absorb the water with the result that stools become softer and more bulky. Osmotic laxatives are available as tablets

or as suppositories, which tend to act more quickly. This group includes Epsom salts (magnesium sulphate), given before surgery to clear the bowels.

What are the adverse effects?

In general, laxatives should be used only for short periods of time. Prolonged use may be harmful and may render an individual dependent on them for regular bowel motions. The colon can become 'lazy' and unable to contract normally. Long-term use of stimulant laxatives can cause abdominal cramps and diarrhoea, while osmotic laxatives used long term can cause chemical imbalances in the blood.

DRUGS FOR INFLAMMATORY BOWEL DISEASE

Inflammatory bowel disease is an abnormal immune reaction, and includes Crohn's disease and ulcerative colitis. Two main groups of drugs are used to treat these conditions.

How do they work?

Both drug groups come in tablet, enema and suppository forms, and they work by damping down the body's natural inflammatory response, although they do this in different ways.

Do-it-yourself prescribing

TALKING POINT

Mild bowel discomforts are so common as to be almost normal – the average adult suffers about one symptom a day. It is neither possible nor desirable to go to the doctor for every minor ache and pain, yet it is also entirely reasonable not to want to suffer unnecessarily. This means that self-care with home remedies and medicines that are available over the counter is an important part of healthcare. But can you overdo it? Almost certainly the answer is yes, and it's probably wise to talk over your symptoms with a friend or relative, before you take even as much as a simple antacid. If you find you need to self-medicate on a regular basis you should visit your doctor.

Inflammatory bowel disease
This false-coloured micrograph shows the colon of an ulcerative colitis sufferer, magnified 1100 times. The surface of the colon (pink) has been eroded, leaving the mucous glands (orange) abnormally raised.

- **Aminosalicylates** These drugs, which include sulpha-salazine and mesalazine, prevent chemicals called prostaglandins being released by the damaged lining of the intestine. Prostaglandins are part of the body's inflammatory response. Aminosalicylates are used for acute attacks of colitis (inflammation of the colon) but their main role is to prevent recurrent attacks.
- **Corticosteroids** These drugs act to prevent movement of white blood cells into the damaged area. In Crohn's disease or ulcerative colitis, corticosteroids (steroids for short) may be given as suppositories or foam enemas to

deliver the drug quickly to the site of action. Steroids can be used as a short high-dose course in severe attacks of inflammatory bowel disease.

What are the adverse effects?

Aminosalicylates can cause diarrhoea, nausea and headaches. There is also a small risk of blood disorders and people taking this drug are always told to report any unexplained bruising, bleeding or sore throats. Adverse effects of long-term use of corticosteroids include diabetes, osteoporosis (thinning of the bones) and indigestion. In children, corticosteroids can cause growth retardation. In adults, continuous high-dose usage may cause Cushing's syndrome – characterised by a moon face, acne, bruising, oedema (swelling) and fat deposition on the back. Anyone on long-term steroid therapy should carry a card giving details of the drug and dosage.

While a person is on long-term oral steroid therapy, the natural production of corticosteroids by the adrenal glands is suppressed. Withdrawal of steroid treatment should be gradual and in consultation with a doctor, to allow the glands to resume production of natural steroids.

ANTIBIOTICS

The use of antibiotics in gastrointestinal disease is confined to specific infections, and they are only given when the infective cause is known.

Infection with the bacterium *Helicobacter pylori* is present in nearly all patients with duodenal ulcers and in about 75 per cent of patients with gastric ulcers. For this reason, antibiotics are now used as part of the treatment for ulcers. Combining an ulcer-healing drug with two antibiotics has a major impact on preventing ulcers recurring – a significant problem when ulcer-healing drugs are used alone. This triple drug therapy is highly effective and needs to be taken for only one or two weeks.

About 50 per cent of British 50-year-olds are infected with Helicobacter pylori, significantly increasing their risk of developing ulcers.

How do they work?

Antibiotics act by interfering with metabolic pathways in the bacteria, especially the ones that bacteria use to make their cell walls, so that they disintegrate.

What are the adverse effects?

Antibiotics can cause diarrhoea, although it is not usually severe. They can also alter the balance of healthy gut flora and the yeast *Candida albicans*. Thrush, a vaginal infection caused by this yeast, is a fairly common side effect of antibiotic treatment in women.

DRUGS FOR ANAL AND RECTAL PROBLEMS

Several different types of drugs are used in the form of creams, suppositories or enemas to treat problems such as haemorrhoids (piles) and anal fissures.

How do they work?

Drugs for anal and rectal problems are a diverse group and mainly act as anti-inflammatories. These include anaesthetic creams and gels, and corticosteroid creams and suppositories.

- **Local anaesthetics** These act on nerves supplying the skin and prevent transmission of signals to the brain. Formulations are available as a spray, cream or gel.
- **Topical corticosteroids** These can be applied directly to the haemorrhoids using an applicator or in the form of a suppository and help to reduce inflammation. They can relieve itching and discomfort.

What are the adverse effects?

There are no major side effects associated with these agents, but they should not be used for more than a few days without consulting your doctor.

ANTIPARASITIC DRUGS

The human body provides a suitable environment for the growth of many types of parasite, including insects, worms and flukes. Some can be transmitted from person to person by direct contact, others are picked up through inhalation of infected air or consumption of contaminated food or water. Treatment with antiparasitic drugs is necessary in combination with hygienic measures to break

Terrifying tapeworms
Large suckers and a row of hooks are key features of how these tapeworms attach themselves to the intestine. Tapeworms affect some 4 million people worldwide.

the cycle of infection. Parasitic infections are most common in tropical countries and areas of poor sanitation. With the exception of threadworms, parasitic infections are rare in the UK.

How do they work?

Antiparasitic drugs work directly on the parasite by paralysing it or killing it outright, so that it passes out of the body. Others exert their effect on tissues bodywide.

- **Anthelmintics** Drugs such as mebendazole are used to treat roundworms, tapeworms and threadworms. They kill or paralyse the worm, which is then excreted.
- **Praziquantel** This drug is used for infection with flukes such as the liver fluke. These parasites live in the bile duct in the liver and can cause jaundice. Praziquantel is active against all species of liver flukes.

What are the adverse effects?

Taken as a single dose or short course, these drugs do not usually produce side effects. However, nausea, vomiting and abdominal pain can result.

Endoscopic treatments

As well as being used for investigations of the digestive tract, endoscopy can be used to treat particular conditions. Often the endoscopist will carry out any treatment that is needed as an extension of the investigative endoscopic procedure.

One of the most common investigative techniques used in gastroenterology today is endoscopy, using a telescopic device with a built-in camera to see inside the body. Thanks to the unique design of the endoscope, doctors can not only look at the structures of the stomach and small and large intestine, they can also treat many problems. As well as having their own lighting and video-recording systems, endoscopes contain channels down which instruments can be passed for an appropriate task: removing a polyp from the inside of the colon, for example, using polypectomy snares. A suction and water channel helps to clear debris and wash the lens.

PREPARING FOR THE PROCEDURE

At the endoscopy unit, a nurse asks a series of questions to check that the patient is generally healthy and ready for the procedure. To clear the gut of food, the patient usually has to fast for at least four hours beforehand and/or take laxatives to clear the bowels. A mild sedative may be administered to relieve anxiety.

Once in the endoscopy suite, the patient lies down on the bed and may be positioned in various poses – usually on the left side – by the nurses or doctors to assist the viewing process. A local anaesthetic is sprayed onto the back of the throat, for an upper GI endoscopy, to make the patient more comfortable as the endoscope is inserted into the mouth and down the throat.

The endoscope is fed slowly into the digestive tract so that the doctor can fully inspect the section of the gut in question using the endoscopic video camera. Once a full examination is completed, the doctor may want to sort out any potential or obvious problems visible during the endoscopy. Gastrointestinal conditions that are routinely treated in this way include:

• narrowing of the oesophagus;
• bleeding in the digestive tract and from ulcers;
• tumours or polyps.

Treating digestive system problems with an endoscope avoids open surgery and its associated risks. A general anaesthetic is not required, recovery is much quicker, patients experience much less pain and the chances of infection are generally lower. Endoscopic treatment also means that patients can be treated on an outpatient basis. The procedures are so quick – a gastroscopy, for example, can take as little as five minutes – a patient can often return home the same day. Endoscopy is easily repeatable, which is important for monitoring an ulcer, for instance.

CORRECTING A NARROWED OESOPHAGUS

Parts of the oesophagus can be constricted by conditions such as tumours. This can be corrected using balloons or stents (mesh tubes), passed down the oesophagus via the endoscope. A balloon is inflated once in place, widening the narrowed portion, or stricture. In some cases a stent may be inserted to keep the passage from closing again.

a   b

The right tool for the job
a The endoscopist can choose from a wide range of tools, which are fed down a special channel in the endoscope.
b Endoscopic microforceps, magnified 16 times, grasp a watch cog, demonstrating their precision of movement.
c A nurse assists an endoscopist during a gastroscopy procedure. They watch on a video monitor as he guides the instrument down the patient's throat and into the stomach.

STAUNCHING A BLEEDING ULCER

Endoscopy is routinely used to identify bleeding ulcers, but can also be used to treat them. Once the endoscopist has located an ulcer, the leaking blood vessels are either cauterised with a heating probe or injected with a diluted adrenaline solution. Adrenaline makes the blood vessels constrict and so slows and then stops the bleeding.

REMOVING A TUMOUR OR POLYP

Benign or malignant tumours can be cut out of the digestive tract during endoscopic procedures. Colon polyps, for instance, are generally excised during colonoscopy, either by burning or by cutting them out with a wire loop, known as a snare. It may take more than one procedure to do this if there are numerous polyps or if one polyp is particularly large.

If a condition warrants more extensive treatment, a surgeon may perform open surgery or, for selected problems, surgery using a type of endoscope known as a laparoscope (so-called keyhole surgery – see page 128).

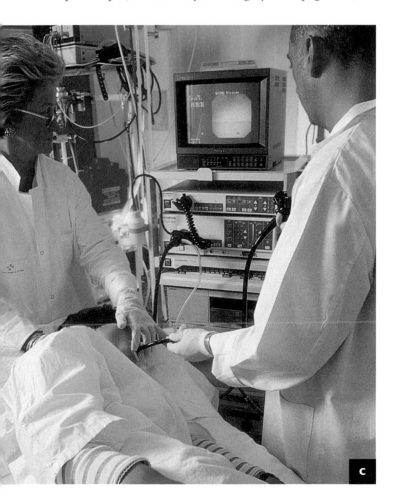

c

The inside track

Once the preserve of science-fiction movies, surgical procedures done from within the body are now routine in the treatment of many digestive tract disorders.

a

a A narrow tube leading away from the endoscopic camera carries air to a balloon lodged in a narrowed stretch, known as a stricture, further down the oesophagus. Inflating the balloon widens the stricture.

b

b An endoscopic view of an oesophageal stent holding open a stricture. Stents are tubes made out of wire mesh. They are inserted in collapsed form, and their mesh structure allows them to be expanded, like a concertina, once in place.

c

c Oesophageal varices are a serious complication of liver damage, in which high blood pressure causes weak blood vessels in the oesophagus to swell and protrude. They can be treated by banding, where rubber bands are placed around the base of the varix using endoscopic manipulation. This endoscopic view shows a large varix in the centre of the picture, with a blue band around a varix behind it. Banding cuts off the circulation to the protruding vessel, preventing it from bursting and haemorrhaging.

d

d Large polyps may be removed during colonoscopy. Here a polyp (right) in the sigmoid colon has been cut away from its base, leaving a small wound (left).

Surgical solutions

Surgery plays a major role in gastrointestinal treatment, either as the first-line treatment or after drug therapy has failed. Surgical advances allow some operations to be carried out as a day case. Newer 'keyhole' techniques mean fewer complications and faster recovery.

Abdominal surgery ranges from the simple – operations carried out on an outpatient basis – to major procedures in which large amounts of the digestive tract are removed because of disease. Most procedures are planned in advance (elective surgery), but sometimes emergency abdominal surgery is needed.

BEFORE AN OPERATION

For any operation the patient is examined before surgery and will meet the surgeon performing the procedure. This is the time when the patient can ask questions and give informed consent. For relatively minor operations such as hernia repair, the patient is usually admitted on the day of the procedure and can often go home that same day. If specific tests are needed – for example, full blood count, measurement of urea and electrolytes, chest X-ray and/or electrocardiogram (ECG), depending on the patient – patients may have to attend a pre-admission clinic a few days before the operation. If the operation requires general anaesthetic it may be necessary to go into hospital the day before the operation. For major abdominal

surgery, especially if this involves opening the intestines, doctors give an injection of antibiotics as part of the premedication an hour or two before the procedure. These antibiotics help to prevent possible infection from the intestine entering the abdominal cavity.

RECOVERING FROM ABDOMINAL SURGERY

After any major surgery, the patient wakes up in the recovery room, often with a number of tubes attached, which provide fluids and pain-relieving medicines. After major abdominal surgery, it can take more than two to three days for complete gastrointestinal function to return. During this time it is not possible to pass wind or stools. After the operation, doctors carry out a daily abdominal examination to check for tenderness and to make sure that the intestines have not become distended due to an obstruction resulting from the surgery. Any surgery on the oesophagus makes it impossible to eat for several days so the patient is fed through a nasogastric tube passed through the nose and into the stomach.

APPENDIX REMOVAL

Appendectomy – removal of the appendix – is the most common abdominal emergency procedure carried out between childhood and early adulthood. The appendix serves no known function in humans, but if this tiny finger-like organ becomes inflamed it can burst and cause life-threatening infection. The aim of appendectomy is to remove the inflamed appendix before it bursts.

The operation is carried out under general anaesthesia through a small incision (2.5–5cm/1–2in) in the lower right abdomen just above the groin. The appendix is tied at its base with thread then cut off. The whole procedure takes about 30–60 minutes, and the patient can go home after two or three days. Over the next couple of weeks, a patient can gradually resume normal activities.

Open abdominal surgery
Many surgical procedures on the digestive system involve opening up the abdominal cavity, which can require a long incision. The location and length of the cut depends on the organ being operated on.

Keyhole surgery – the way ahead?

An increasing number of operations are now performed by keyhole (laparoscopic) surgery rather than standard open surgery involving a large incision to reveal the operating site. There are several advantages of laparoscopic surgery, but it is not suitable in every case and for every procedure. The main advantage is that only two or three very small incisions are needed – usually no more than 1–2cm (½–¾in) long. This not only reduces the risk of infection but also speeds recovery. Plus there is less scarring. But laparoscopic surgery is often a longer procedure than open surgery. Conventional open surgery is more appropriate in emergency situations where the surgeon has to have rapid and clear access to the operating site.

HERNIA REPAIR

One of the most commonly performed operations on the digestive system is the repair of a hernia. There are several types of hernia, and treatment varies depending on the type and position. The most common is in the groin (an inguinal or femoral hernia), which is caused by a weakness or defect in the abdominal wall that allows the intestines to protrude through. If a small bend of intestine gets stuck in the defect, the blood supply to the bowel may be blocked. This results in 'strangulation' of that section of the intestine, which is extremely painful and needs immediate surgery so that the intestine can be freed and circulation restored. If the trapped intestine is damaged beyond repair, the affected part has to be cut out and the healthy portions joined together.

In the UK, the majority of hernia repair operations are carried out on a day-case basis under local or general anaesthesia. A 2.5–5cm (1–2in) incision is made over the site of the hernia and through the layers of muscle. The hernia is then pushed back through the defect in the abdominal wall and the weak spot is repaired, sometimes using a mesh made of polypropylene or Gore-Tex that is stitched in place.

On average, the procedure takes 45–60 minutes; although if the procedure is done by 'keyhole' surgery it takes longer. Painkillers are given after the operation to deal with pain around the site of the operation. Although a patient may resume normal activities within a week or two, heavy lifting must be avoided for three months to avoid straining the abdominal wall.

Some hernia operations are now performed by keyhole (laparoscopic) surgery, which allows a swifter recovery and less postoperative pain (see pages 128–129 for a step-by-step procedure of laparoscopic hernia repair).

An inguinal hernia

a This contrast X-ray of an inguinal hernia shows barium pooled in the herniated part of the intestine (bottom left).

b A large hernia protrudes from the groin – it will need surgery to push the displaced intestine back inside the abdominal wall.

c After cutting through the tissue layers, surgeons locate the herniated section and repair the rupture.

Laparoscopic hernia repair

A relatively recent technique that was first used in 1982 but not widely introduced until 1990, laparoscopic hernia repair uses tiny incisions and delicate endoscopic instruments. Only certain surgeons choose to learn this technique, but patients can benefit considerably, with a quicker return to normal activity and less pain.

Hernia repair is one of the most commonly performed operations in the Western world – about 120,000 hernia repair operations are carried out each year in the UK alone. Until the 1990s, all these operations were performed by open surgery, which involves making a comparatively large – 5cm (2in) – opening in the abdominal wall. In contrast, laparoscopic hernia repair requires only tiny incisions through which the endoscopic instruments are passed. The technique, which is also known as minimally invasive or keyhole surgery, minimises damage to the abdominal wall, so the patient heals more quickly with smaller scars and suffers less pain after the operation.

While open surgery remains the standard by which other techniques are judged, laparoscopic hernia repair has become increasingly common in the last few years. Nevertheless, the procedure may not be offered by every hospital and clinic, for a number of reasons. Laparoscopic hernia repair requires extensive, specialised training, and its use is mainly restricted to the repair of inguinal and femoral hernias. Even for these conditions, there is still considerable debate over whether the new techniques are preferable to the standard ones (see page 127). The general consensus is that laparoscopic procedures are most suitable for treating recurrent hernias, while open surgery is often still best for treating first-time hernias. As research and expertise develop, however, the newer techniques may become more widely practised.

How is it done?

This diagrammatic cross-section of a patient's abdomen shows the two main stages of surgery.

a Carbon dioxide is pumped into the abdominal space through a cannula (hollow tube), making space for the surgeon to work. Using forceps and viewing the procedure through an endoscopic camera, the surgeon grips the hernia (basically a loop of intestines in a membranous sac) and pulls it back through the hole in the abdominal wall.

b Once the hernia has been pulled back, the hole in the abdominal wall is patched up with a mesh patch, which is stapled to the inside of the wall.

The procedure – step by step

1 Once the patient is fully anaesthetised, and his abdomen swabbed with iodine, the surgeon makes three or four 1cm (½in) incisions in the abdomen. In this case there are three – a central one near the belly button and one on either side.

2 Next, cannulae (hollow tubes down which instruments can be passed) are inserted through the incisions. Into one of these, the surgeon inserts a laparoscope, a telescopic video camera that allows him to see inside the abdominal cavity. Carbon dioxide is pumped through another cannula to make space to work in between the abdominal wall and the peritoneum (the membranous sac that contains the internal organs).

3 While an assistant steadies the cannulae, the surgeon passes endoscopic forceps and scissors down them, carefully watching the video screen to guide his movements. Using these instruments, he clears away connective tissue so that he can get a clear picture of what's going on. Once this is done, he grips the neck of the hernial sac with the forceps and pulls it back through the hole in the abdominal wall.

4 Now the hole needs to be patched. A piece of synthetic mesh is trimmed into shape, and then rolled up like a cigarette and fed down the central cannula. Once inside the patient, forceps inserted through cannulae on either side are used to unroll it and move it into position. A stapling device is introduced down one of the cannulae and the patch is stapled in place – surgeons use up to 30 staples. The abdominal space is deflated, and as the peritoneum returns to its normal position it squeezes up against the abdominal wall, helping to secure the patch in place.

5 The instruments and then the cannulae are removed and the tiny cuts are sewn up.

6 With the operation complete, the tiny wounds are dressed and the patient is taken to the recovery room. There is only minor scarring and the patient is often allowed to leave the hospital, in the company of a friend or relative, within six hours.

RELIEVING A GUT OBSTRUCTION

An obstruction can occur anywhere along the digestive tract, from the oesophagus to the rectum, bringing the digestive machinery to a standstill. The most common causes of obstruction are:

- strangulated hernias;
- adhesions following previous abdominal surgery;
- narrowing of the bowel due to inflammation, radiotherapy or infection;
- tumours.

Without surgery, the part of the gut nearest the obstruction stretches and becomes swollen and distended as it fills up with air and fluid. The gut beyond the obstruction remains collapsed. The muscular wall of the gut increases its contractions in an attempt to overcome the blockage. This causes colicky pain – intermittent, sharp, severe pain that occurs in waves – and constipation. Surgery is vital to remove the blockage and restore function to the gut.

Treatment for an obstructed oesophagus

In some cases of inoperable cancer of the oesophagus, the narrowed area can be stretched with a tiny balloon. Alternatively, a flexible metallic tube called a stent can be placed through the narrowed area to hold it open, allowing the individual to swallow. This may be enough to relieve symptoms. Where possible an operation may be performed to remove the tumour. After oesophageal surgery patients are usually fed via a nasogastric tube.

Tumour removal

A tumour is a common cause of obstruction, but it may not become apparent until it blocks the tract completely or causes perforation. When surgeons remove a tumour, they aim to cut out a certain amount of healthy tissue around it to ensure that no cancerous tissue is left. The cut ends are joined together, if possible, to re-establish continuity of the gastrointestinal tract.

RE-ROUTING PARTS OF THE INTESTINE

The intestine may have to be re-routed surgically to bypass an obstruction or to rejoin two sections of the digestive tract after a diseased part has been removed. Ideally, the cut ends of the intestine are rejoined end to end, but if this not possible the intestine is brought up to the skin where it is formed into a spout (made from the intestine itself) to empty into a plastic bag on the surface of the abdomen. Faeces are then collected in the bag. The opening is called a stoma and may be permanent or temporary. The precise name of the operation depends on which part of intestine is brought to the skin. If it is the ileum (the last part of the small intestine) it is called an ileostomy, or colostomy if it's made from the colon. Both operations require a prolonged recovery period.

The procedure takes two to three hours, and involves a week's stay in hospital. As well as the physical recovery, time is needed to learn about day-to-day stoma care and hygiene, and to adjust psychologically to having a stoma (see page 155).

Formation of an ileostomy

An ileostomy is usually formed on the right lower part of the abdomen. There are two types of ileostomy: end ileostomy, which is permanent; and loop ileostomy – a

> *The average adult's small intestine is roughly four times longer than the person is tall.*

Obstruction due to inflammatory bowel disease
This barium X-ray shows constriction and obstruction of a portion of the intestine due to Crohn's disease (lower right). It may require surgery to remove the affected region and relieve the obstruction.

Step-by-step colostomy

1 The patient's abdomen is shaved, wiped with iodine and covered in a clinging plastic wrap, which helps to guard against contamination. Surgeons cut directly through the wrap and the layers of skin, fat and muscle that make up the abdominal wall.

2 Clamps are used to pull back and hold in position the layers of the abdominal wall, exposing the intestines. The diseased part of the colon is then cut out.

3 The upper cut end of the colon is brought to the surface through a small incision above and to the side of the belly button, separate from the main incision, so that a cuff of colon is left protruding. The lower cut end is sealed off with sutures.

4 The main incision is closed by suturing together the layers of the abdominal wall and the skin. The cuff of colon protruding from the smaller incision is folded back, and its outer edge is sewn to the skin to form the stoma.

5 The abdomen is cleaned and the main incision is dressed. A colostomy bag is fitted over the stoma immediately after the surgery. It is either attached to a moulded flange that adheres to the skin around the stoma, or, as shown here, attached directly via a sticky patch with a hole in the centre, in the back of the bag.

Diversions in effect

This illustration shows the new route food will take on its journey through the digestive system after a colostomy operation. The colon is cut and brought to the surface to form a stoma (1), which will be connected to a colostomy bag. The damaged part of the colon (2) is bypassed.

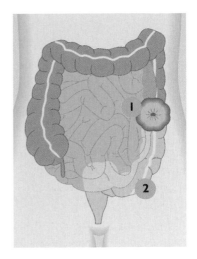

temporary, reversible procedure. An end ileostomy is usually formed if both colon and rectum have been removed, as may be necessary in cases of severe ulcerative colitis. The patient is taught how to empty, change and dispose of the stoma bag, which needs to be worn at all times. Without proper care, the contents of the stoma bag may leak causing skin irritation.

A loop ileostomy is formed to divert digested material away from the large intestine further along. A loop of ileum is brought up through the skin and opened in the middle at one side only. A spout is formed by turning the ileum inside out, allowing liquid faeces to drain into a stoma bag attached to the skin. Faeces that issue from an ileostomy are especially fluid, so care must be taken to avoid dehydration. A loop ileostomy can be reversed after several weeks by suturing or stapling the ends together.

Formation of a colostomy

A colostomy is the surgical creation of an opening of the colon onto the skin, similar to an ileostomy. A permanent end colostomy may be done when a tumour is removed and the two ends of the large intestine cannot be safely joined together. The end of the colon nearest the stomach is then brought through the abdominal wall. The end of the colon usually lies flush with the skin after the operation. The faeces produced are fairly runny as the colon is the part of the intestine that normally absorbs water from intestinal contents as they pass through.

A temporary loop colostomy is done to divert the intestinal contents away from the rest of the colon. A loop of colon is brought through the abdominal wall and kept in place with a glass or plastic rod. An opening is made in the loop of bowel to allow drainage into a colostomy bag. This can be reversed at a later date.

REMOVING PARTS OF THE INTESTINE

Several conditions can necessitate the removal of parts of the small or large intestine, including severe forms of inflammatory bowel disease (Crohn's disease and ulcerative colitis), and tumours of the intestine.

Crohn's disease often affects the small intestine, but it can affect the large intestine too. In many cases, different areas of the intestine are affected simultaneously, with varying degrees of severity. Surgical removal of the diseased intestine is done as a last resort when a person's symptoms do not respond to drugs. Without surgery, persistent inflammation can cause severe narrowing of the intestine and lead to obstruction. In such cases, the narrowed part has to be removed. Crohn's disease can appear in any other part of the gut, so surgeons usually remove only the smallest possible part of the intestine. Between 30 and 50 per cent of individuals with Crohn's disease have a recurrence of the problem after surgery.

In someone suffering from Crohn's colitis (Crohn's disease that specifically affects the colon), the colon can be 'rested' by creating a temporary ileostomy or colostomy. In very severe cases, the whole of the colon may be removed and the person has a permanent stoma.

Banding haemorrhoids

a *First, the doctor places a short viewing device (proctoscope) inside the rectum. Then, the banding instrument is inserted through the proctoscope to grasp the haemorrhoid.* **b** *A rubber band is positioned around the swollen vein, which eventually shrinks and falls off.*

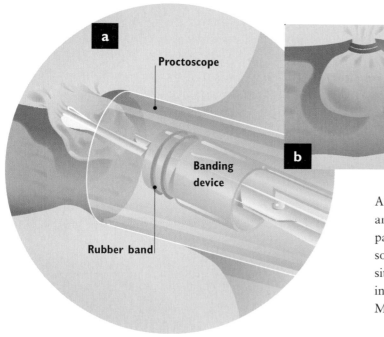

Proctoscope

Banding device

Rubber band

Colectomy – removing the colon

Removal of part or the whole of the colon is most often performed in individuals with ulcerative colitis. Long-standing ulcerative colitis can lead to changes in the lining of the colon and eventually may become cancerous. The risk of cancerous changes increases with severity and duration of the disease. Surgery is usually performed when the inflammation is severe and prolonged, resulting in a condition called toxic megacolon.

The colon is removed at least up to the rectum. When only part of the colon is removed, the end of the small intestine (the ileum) is brought out through the skin to form an ileostomy. In severe cases, the rectum is also removed. After this operation, the individual may have a permanent ileostomy. In some cases, however, a natural pouch may be formed from the ileum and attached to the anus so that faeces can be passed normally. Patients tend to pass watery motions several times a day, but this gradually settles down as the intestine recuperates.

TREATMENT OF HAEMORRHOIDS

Haemorrhoids (piles) are swollen veins in the anus. They usually cause bleeding from the back passage, an anal lump and discomfort. In many cases haemorrhoids improve with a change of diet to relieve constipation and creams and suppositories to relieve inflammation and discomfort (see page 123). More severe haemorrhoids may need more radical treatment. One of the most common procedures for treating protruding haemorrhoids is band ligation (see left). Haemorrhoids that don't protrude from the anus can be treated by an injection of a chemical that seals the veins. In the most severe cases, piles can be removed surgically under general anaesthesia.

REPAIR OF AN ANORECTAL ABSCESS

Anorectal abscesses – a collection of pus in or around the anus – are very common. Abscesses are removed and pus drained under general anaesthesia. The cavity left behind is cleaned out and packed with gauze so that it heals from the inside. In some cases, an internal connection is found between the site of the abscess and the rectum, and through which an infection is perpetuated. This is called an anal fistula. Most fistulas are easily treated by surgery.

A TO Z

OF DISEASES AND DISORDERS

This section gives information on the main illnesses and medical conditions that can affect the digestive system. Liver and gallbladder disorders are covered in detail in another volume in the series.

This index is divided into two sections: Symptoms, and Diseases and disorders. The entries are arranged alphabetically and each is structured in a similar way:

What are the causes?

What are the symptoms?

How is it diagnosed?

What are the treatment options?

What is the outlook?

How can it be prevented or minimised?

SYMPTOMS

APPETITE LOSS
A common general symptom of illness rather than an indicator of a specific problem.

A loss of appetite may be related to nausea or abdominal pain in gastrointestinal disease, but in general it just represents the fact that an individual is unwell. Loss of appetite should be distinguished from difficulty swallowing (dysphagia) and painful swallowing (odynophagia).

What are the causes?
Nausea, vomiting, abdominal bloating or pain often result in a marked loss of appetite. In general, most illnesses will also, as mentioned above, result in loss of appetite. This is most marked in the presence of malignant tumours, which can cause weight loss and muscle wasting.

What are the treatment options?
Treatment depends on the cause of the appetite loss. Generally speaking, anything that makes the patient feel better also improves appetite.

CHANGES IN BOWEL HABIT
Any variation from normal in stool consistency and frequency of bowel motions.

A change in the frequency and consistency of stools gives important clues about what is going on within the bowel. The presence of blood or mucus in stools is a strong indicator of abnormality.

What are the causes?
Basically, there are two changes: constipation or diarrhoea. Constipation, characterised by a failure of the bowels to open, is often associated with hard stools. It can be brought on by a number of factors.
- **Diet** Lack of fibre in the diet and not drinking enough water are the most common causes of constipation.
- **Age** Declining muscle tone along the gut can mean that stools take longer to pass through the system. Age is also often linked to a low-fibre diet.
- **Medication** Several drugs can cause constipation, such as codeine or aluminium-based antacids.
- **Medical conditions** Underactivity of the thyroid gland and depression can cause constipation.

- **An obstruction** If the colon is narrowed or has tumours, these will impede the passage of stool.
- **Anal pain** Haemorrhoids or anal fissures can make passing stools painful and lead to a reluctance to open the bowels, eventually resulting in constipation.

Diarrhoea involves increased frequency and volume of stools, which may be soft or watery. Mucus or blood may be present. Most causes fall into one of four main groups.
- **Diet or infection** Most short episodes of diarrhoea are due to food, drink or a combination of the two that disagrees with the system, or to gastroenteritis.
- **Medication** Diarrhoea is a side effect of several types of drug, including antibiotics, ulcer-healing drugs and senna.
- **Medical conditions** Overactivity of the thyroid gland (hyperthyroidism), diabetes mellitus, anxiety and inflammatory bowel disease can all result in diarrhoea. Coeliac disease often results in loose, pale, bulky stools.
- **Tumours** Diarrhoea, especially with bleeding or increased mucus in the stools, can be due to bowel tumours.

How is it diagnosed?
Doctors have strict definitions of what constitutes diarrhoea or constipation, which may differ from a patient's own understanding of the terms. Nevertheless, patients reporting a persistent change in bowel habit, or

Monitoring bowel habit

A change in bowel habit can be an important symptom of several digestive problems. When taking your medical history, your doctor will want to know about the normal pattern of your bowel habits, and about any changes to those patterns. Be prepared to answer the following questions as clearly as possible.

- *Before the onset of the symptoms that caused you to see the doctor, what was the normal frequency of your stools?*

- *Has the frequency, size or hardness of your stools changed?*

- *Is there any blood in your stools? If so, how much and what colour is it?*

Blood in the stools is a sign that you should visit your doctor immediately.

with rectal blood or mucus, need careful investigation to rule out a tumour. Initial investigations will include:

- examination of a stool sample for evidence of infection (p. 100);
- examination of the bowel itself, either with a barium enema (p. 108) or by sigmoidoscopy (p. 114) or colonoscopy (p. 115);
- small bowel barium follow-through (p. 107), if there is associated pain or a suspicion of coeliac disease;
- endoscopic biopsy (p. 112) of the duodenum if coeliac disease is suspected.

What are the treatment options?

Apart from treating underlying causes, specific short-term measures can help to reduce the severity of bowel habit symptoms. Drinking more water and using bulking agents that act as replacement dietary fibre can help with constipation. Drugs that increase secretion of fluid by the gut, such as senna, are also useful, but must be taken only under medical supervision. Diarrhoea can also be treated with drugs that slow down the muscle activity of the bowel wall, for example loperamide or codeine.

DIFFICULTY IN SWALLOWING
The sensation of food sticking in the throat or being difficult to swallow is also known as dysphagia.

Difficulty in swallowing is a worrying symptom for any patient. The difficulty may occur only when eating certain foods, for example bread or potato, or it may be so extreme that a person cannot swallow any solids or liquids. Dysphagia always requires careful investigation.

What are the causes?

Dysphagia may be due to a nerve or muscle problem in the oesophagus that results in the failure of the swallow reflex; it is often seen after a stroke. The danger is that the food will 'go down the wrong way' and end up in the lungs.

If food can be swallowed but then sticks, the cause is almost certainly in the oesophagus. Irritation of the oesophagus by stomach acid (oesophagitis) is a common cause of mild symptoms, as are oesophageal infections, such as *Candida*, for patients with weak immune systems. Severe symptoms indicate an obstruction – a physical blockage such as a tumour of the oesophageal wall or pressure from swelling outside the oesophagus.

Sudden-onset dysphagia may result from swallowing a solid object, such as a boiled sweet or a coin, or from a problem with the sphincter between the oesophagus and the stomach, a condition known as achalasia.

How is it diagnosed?

The oesophagus is examined with an endoscope, which gives a direct view of the wall of the oesophagus and allows biopsies to be taken from it (p. 112). Sometimes a barium swallow is carried out to look for specific diseases such as achalasia.

What are the treatment options?

Patients with an obstruction of the oesophagus may need to soften or liquidise food before eating. Narrowing of the oesophagus can be treated by stretching with an endoscopic balloon or insertion of a stent (p. 124). Tumours can be treated with laser or conventional surgery, or radiotherapy.

FATIGUE
A feeling of perpetual tiredness.

Fatigue is a symptom that many people report to their doctors and often represents the results of a 'modern lifestyle' with the stresses of work and home life. Unless it is accompanied by other more specific symptoms, however, it can be difficult to work out the underlying problem. It is important to differentiate between tiredness due to overwork or lack of sleep and that due to an underlying illness. It is also vital to be clear about the meaning of fatigue. Fatigue is often characterised by a perpetual feeling of tiredness, lethargy and apathy; but falling asleep without warning points to sleep-associated problems and represents an entirely different symptom.

Beyond the digestive system, fatigue can be caused by an underactive thyroid gland (hypothyroidism).

What are the causes?

Almost any illness will induce a sensation of tiredness, although a few specifics are important to consider.

- **Anaemia** Low haemoglobin levels result in fatigue associated with shortness of breath, notably on mild exertion, and possibly ankle swelling. Other illnesses can produce similar symptoms, especially heart disease.
- **Inflammation of the bowel wall** Patients with Crohn's disease or ulcerative colitis frequently suffer fatigue, often in combination with diarrhoea and abdominal pain.

- **Irritable bowel syndrome** Chronic fatigue is often associated with irritable bowel syndrome.
- **Malabsorption** If key nutrients are not absorbed from the gut, as in coeliac disease, fatigue results, often in combination with anaemia.
- **Tumours in the bowel** As with any cancer, bowel tumours may cause tiredness, along with weight loss and change in bowel habit.

How is it diagnosed?

The doctor's job is to find out if an underlying illness is causing the fatigue, and in taking a medical history (p. 96) will try to identify appropriate next steps. A physical examination can help to diagnose hypothyroidism.

What are the treatment options?

Treatment depends on the causative illness. Fatigue associated with illness should resolve as the illness is treated and the patient's health improves.

How can it be prevented or minimised?

The fatigue of everyday life is common. To avoid becoming fatigued, follow these common-sense measures:
- make time to eat properly;
- find time to relax and exercise;
- don't drink too much alcohol;
- get enough sleep – most of us know how much sleep we can survive on and how much we need to feel good the next day; aim for the latter not the former.

JAUNDICE
Yellow discoloration of the skin and whites of the eyes.

Haemoglobin, the oxygen-carrying pigment in red blood cells, is broken down into a substance called bilirubin. The liver processes bilirubin into the bile salts that are excreted into the small intestine as bile, which helps in fat digestion and gives stools their brown colour. A problem at any of the breakdown stages results in a build-up of bile salts, which are orange–yellow in colour, in the tissues of the body – notably in the skin and the whites of the eyes.

What are the causes?

Three main problems result in jaundice.
- **Increased breakdown of red blood cells (haemolytic anaemia)** In this condition, there is too much bilirubin for the liver to process, the overflow causing the yellow 'staining'.

- **Problems with the liver's ability to process bilirubin** Any illness involving the liver, such as hepatitis, alcohol abuse, inherited liver deficiencies or liver tumours, will result in a backlog of bilirubin waiting to be processed.
- **Blocked bile duct** Gallstones, tumours of the pancreas or rare tumours of the bile ducts can block the flow of bile from the liver to the small intestine. The processed bile salts spill back into the blood, causing jaundice. The failure of bile to reach the bowel results in pale waxy stools that look rather like putty.

How is it diagnosed?

After taking a careful history (p. 96), the doctor will probably use some other tests to narrow the diagnosis.
- **Blood tests** A sample of blood will be taken. A full blood count indicates whether there is any breakdown of red blood cells and reveals other abnormalities in the way the liver is functioning (p. 99). Blood analysis is also used to diagnose viral hepatitis and the causes of liver damage.
- **An ultrasound scan** The most common next step is a scan of the liver, gallbladder and pancreas (p. 103); this test looks at the structure of the liver and reveals obstructions to the flow of bile or masses in the body of the liver.

Further tests will depend on what has been found.
- **ERCP** If an obstruction is suspected an endoscopic retrograde cholangiopancreatogram (ERCP) is carried out (p. 111), often allowing an obstruction to be relieved.
- **CT scanning** Computer tomography (CT) scanning is used to identify lesions within or obstructing masses outside the liver.
- **Biopsy** A liver biopsy, taken using a needle passed through the skin, can help pinpoint the cause of jaundice.

What are the treatment options?

Jaundice will disappear once the underlying cause is treated. Sometimes, drugs to alleviate associated symptoms, such as itchiness, may be prescribed.

NAUSEA AND VOMITING
Nausea is the sensation of needing to vomit. Vomiting is the forceful expulsion of the stomach contents through the mouth. Both are common symptoms.

Nausea and vomiting have very similar causes. The sensation of nausea and the physical action of vomiting are controlled by the 'chemoreceptor trigger zone' (the CTZ, also known as the vomiting centre), an area of the brain that receives information from the eye, inner ear, digestive tract and bloodstream. Conflicting data from the eyes and inner ear can activate the CTZ, as happens with travel sickness and vertigo. The gut also has a strong sensory network of nerves that detect problems within the bowel and induce vomiting.

- **Gastroenteritis** This is possibly the most common cause of vomiting in adults. Infections can increase secretion of fluid in the digestive tract, and at the same time slow muscle activity. The muscular walls of the gut are stretched, producing a feeling of bloatedness. Vomiting is the body's way of relieving this discomfort.
- **Physical stimuli** Retching due to an object in the back of the throat or vomiting when the stomach becomes stretched, either due to overeating or failure of the stomach to empty, are both examples.
- **Toxins** Chemicals in your blood (such as poisons and chemotherapy agents) stimulate the CTZ directly, causing vomiting (often severe in the case of chemotherapy).
- **Emotion** Nausea and vomiting may be a response to unpleasant stimuli such as pain, fear or anxiety, or the sight, sound or smell of someone else being sick.

What are the treatment options?
Dealing with the cause of the vomiting is the best way of reducing nausea and vomiting. Drugs that reduce the symptoms (p. 116) act by blocking the initiation of vomiting or by helping the bowel to push food and fluid through the system, so that it cannot be regurgitated.

PAIN
Probably the most distressing of all symptoms, pain arises from anything that causes damage to the body, either due to a direct injury or due to inflammation.

Pain is detected by special pain receptors on specific types of nerves. The signal is then transmitted to the brain, which interprets the type and site of the pain. Although unpleasant, pain is a vital protection mechanism. In the digestive tract, pain causes a reduction in the amount of food eaten and encourages resting – both of which are important in allowing the gut to rest and repair itself.

What are the causes?
Pain can be caused by damage to the digestive system due to physical injury or trauma. It can also result from inflammation (as in appendicitis) or an obstruction of the

bowel (as in Crohn's disease), which leads to stretching of the bowel wall. Strong contractions of the bowel (as in colic caused by gastroenteritis) are also painful.

What are the treatment options?
The primary goal is to treat the underlying disease or cause of the pain, but painkillers are important for relieving the symptoms. Simple analgesics, such as paracetamol, are useful for abdominal pain due to gastroenteritis. Strong opioid painkillers, such as codeine, are more effective, but have a sedative effect and also cause constipation.

WEIGHT LOSS
Rapid loss of weight is often a warning of something more severe.

Rapid weight loss is one of the most worrying symptoms seen in a doctor's clinic. A patient with other symptoms whose weight is steady is usually unlikely to have a serious underlying illness.

What are the causes?
Pain or difficulty in eating may be due to dental problems, such as ill-fitting dentures, ulcers or abscesses. Pain or difficulty in swallowing usually stems from diseases of the oesophagus, such as tumours, inflammation, infections (most commonly *Candida*) or a motility problem (such as achalasia).

Pernicious anaemia damages cells in the stomach, resulting in severe B_{12} deficiency.

If there is no obvious cause at the 'top end' then function is probably affected somewhere along the digestive tract. Failure to absorb nutrients from food (malabsorption), usually in association with bowel inflammation, is one cause of weight loss. Another is failure of the glands that play a role in digestion, as in chronic pancreatitis. Finally, weight loss may indicate a severe underlying illness, such as a tumour either within or outside the bowel.

How is it diagnosed?
Reaching a diagnosis involves careful assessment of all the patient's symptoms followed by investigations targeted towards suggested diagnoses.

What are the treatment options?
Treatment depends on the underlying cause of the weight loss, but ensuring an adequate calorie intake is the most important immediate treatment.

DISEASES AND DISORDERS

ACHALASIA
A problem with the sphincter at the end of the oesophagus, which causes swallowing problems.

Achalasia occurs in about 1 in 200,000 adults. At present, around 250 people in the UK are affected.

In achalasia, the sphincter between the stomach and the oesophagus will not relax, so food cannot pass into the stomach as normal. The underlying cause is not known.

What are the symptoms?
Achalasia causes rapid onset of difficulty in swallowing. It can occur at any age. Food that is unable to pass into the stomach may regurgitate back up into the mouth.

How is it diagnosed?
A barium swallow (pp. 106–7) will show a baggy dilated oesophagus, with a narrow channel through the sphincter. Manometry (p. 102), to measure the pressure in the oesophagus, or upper gastrointestinal endoscopy (p. 110) can help to confirm the diagnosis.

What are the treatment options?
Three different treatments are available:
- a balloon passed in via an endoscope can be inflated to stretch the sphincter, often producing a rapid improvement in symptoms;
- injections of small doses of botulinum toxin via an endoscope, to relax the muscle in the sphincter;
- cutting the outer layers of muscle around the sphincter in order to allow it to open.

What is the outlook?
Although the treatments are effective, only surgery is permanent – the others may have to be repeated.

AIDS, HIV AND THE GUT
Gastrointestinal illnesses that develop as a result of infection with the human immunodeficiency virus (HIV).

Infection with the human immunodeficiency virus (HIV) weakens the immune system, making it more vulnerable to infection. It can also lead to acquired immunodeficiency syndrome (AIDS), a combination of illnesses that include regular and persistent gastrointestinal conditions.

What are the symptoms?
Most of the symptoms are due to rare infections, known as opportunistic infections, which only tend to affect people with a compromised immune system; some arise because of rare cancers.
- **Difficulty chewing and swallowing due to pain** Fungal infections of the mouth and oesophagus, particularly *Candida*, can cause painful inflammation in the mucus lining of the upper gut. Viruses such as herpes simplex and cytomegalovirus may also cause ulcers to develop.
- **Chronic diarrhoea** Persistent and distressing diarrhoea may occur due to a wide range of infectious organisms, including parasites such as *Cryptosporidium*, bacteria such as *Salmonella* and *Campylobacter* and some viruses.
- **Bowel tumours** Certain types of otherwise rare bowel cancers are seen in people suffering from AIDS. These include Kaposi's sarcoma and lymphoma. Such cancers can cause bleeding from the rectum, and motility problems if they obstruct the bowel.
- **Jaundice** This 'yellowing' of the skin may arise due to sclerosing cholangitis – a narrowing of the bile ducts between the liver and the bowel.

As well as specific conditions, many of the drugs used to treat people infected with HIV cause gastrointestinal symptoms such as nausea or diarrhoea.

How is it diagnosed?
The diagnostic tools used depend entirely on the symptoms. If diarrhoea is a problem, doctors will analyse a stool specimen for parasites and bacteria. If a person is experiencing pain and difficulty swallowing, upper gastrointestinal endoscopy (p. 110) is usually carried out. Direct viewing of the bowel using a sigmoidoscopy (p. 114) or colonoscopy (p. 115) enables doctors to detect inflammation or ulceration. Many people with these symptoms have already been diagnosed as HIV positive. Occasionally, however, gastrointestinal symptoms due to an unusual infection may be the first indication of a suppressed immune system. In these cases, doctors will advise the person to undergo HIV testing.

What are the treatment options?
The aim of treatment is twofold – to treat the particular condition causing the symptoms and, in addition, to use drug therapy to prevent replication of the virus and improve immunity. Most infections can be effectively treated with appropriate antibiotics. If a cancer is causing the symptoms, chemotherapy is considered.

What is the outlook?

Advanced drug therapies now available to combat HIV infection mean that AIDS patients are much less likely to suffer from repeated gastrointestinal infections.

APPENDICITIS
Inflammation of the appendix.

The appendix is a short, blind-ended tube that opens into the caecum. Inflammation and infection of this tube is known as acute appendicitis.

What are the causes?

Acute appendicitis is the most common surgical emergency in the Western world.

In many cases of appendicitis the root cause is unclear, but in some cases inflammation arises because the appendix becomes blocked, usually by a faecolith – a small, hard ball of faeces – which becomes lodged inside the central space. As a result, there is a build-up of secretions in the appendix and, if it is not removed, it becomes gangrenous and at risk of bursting and emptying its contents into the abdominal cavity. This can lead, in turn, to peritonitis.

What are the symptoms?

The exact location of the appendix varies from person to person so the pain and symptoms associated with appendicitis are not always consistent. The classical symptoms, however, are fairly constant, and include:
- pain that starts in the centre of the abdomen, around the umbilicus (belly button) and then moves to the right lower quarter of the abdomen;
- nausea and vomiting accompanying the pain;
- mild fever;
- diarrhoea.

How is it diagnosed?

The most helpful procedure in diagnosing appendicitis is a physical examination (p. 98). The doctor examines the abdomen to localise the painful area and will test for 'rebound tenderness' – increased pain after removing pressure – in McBurney's point, a spot about halfway between the umbilicus and the lower right corner of the abdomen. A rectal examination is done to try to pinpoint the source of pain, and then a sample of blood is taken to check the number of white blood cells. The presence of inflammation is confirmed if the levels are elevated.

What are the treatment options?

The only appropriate therapy for an acutely inflamed appendix is surgical removal (p. 126). Early surgery is advised in order to reduce the risk of peritonitis. The appendix is usually removed through a small incision in the lower abdomen or, less commonly, via a laparoscope passed through a tiny puncture site in the abdominal wall.

What is the outlook?

Most people recover rapidly from surgery for appendicitis, often being discharged about two days later. The scar heals quickly and full recovery is the rule. If the appendix has ruptured it can take longer to recover from the operation, as the bowel often stops functioning for a couple of days.

CANCER
See Tumours, p. 155.

COELIAC DISEASE
An inflammatory reaction to gluten, a dietary protein.

Gluten, a component of cereal crops, can cause an inflammatory reaction in the small intestine. This condition, known as coeliac disease, results in the inability of the bowel to absorb certain nutrients, causing anaemia, weight loss, abdominal discomfort and diarrhoea.

What is the cause?

Coeliac disease is a direct result of hypersensitivity to gluten, which is found in wheat, rye and barley. Eating foods containing gluten results in damage to the wall of the small intestine. The usual lining of finger-like projections, called villi, disappears and the surface becomes flat. This loss of the villi reduces the surface area of the intestine so that it is unable to absorb nutrients from food. The underlying cause of the hypersensitivity is unknown.

What are the symptoms?

The symptoms of coeliac disease can develop at any age but often first appear in people in their twenties and thirties. They include:
- fatigue and generally feeling unwell;
- diarrhoea and abdominal discomfort;
- mouth ulcers;
- muscle spasms or weakness;
- a blistering rash on the arms and legs.

How is it diagnosed?

Experts use two types of test to make a diagnosis of coeliac disease. A person with the condition will have specific types of antibodies in the blood and so a sample of blood is taken for laboratory testing. In addition, an upper gastrointestinal endoscopy (p. 110) is used to take a small sample of tissue from the duodenum, the first part of the small intestine. When the tissue is examined under a microscope, the flattened appearance of the bowel due to the loss of villi can be clearly seen.

Coeliac disease tends to run in families, and mainly affects people from Northern Europe.

What are the treatment options?

Complete exclusion of gluten from the diet is the only way to allow the small intestine to repair itself. A single slice of bread is enough to cause a recurrence of the symptoms, so people with the condition are advised to adhere strictly to a gluten-free diet. The doctor or a nutritionist will give advice and guidelines on gluten-free foods.

What is the outlook?

At present there is no complete cure for coeliac disease, although a gluten-free diet will enable the wall of the intestine to return to normal, allowing proper absorption of nutrients. Most people recover completely as long as they adhere strictly to a gluten-free diet.

CROHN'S DISEASE

See Inflammatory bowel disease, p. 148.

CYSTIC FIBROSIS

An inherited disease affecting the function of the pancreas, bowel and lungs.

Cystic fibrosis is a serious condition that results in recurrent chest infections and the failure of the pancreas to release enzymes that are vital for the breakdown and absorption of nutrients from food. Until recently, people with cystic fibrosis died in their teens but advances in medical treatment mean this is no longer always the case.

What is the cause?

Cystic fibrosis is a genetically inherited condition – approximately 1 in 2000 of the British population carries the gene abnormality, which is located on chromosome 7.

It is a 'recessive' disease, which means that a child with cystic fibrosis must have inherited a defective gene from both parents; if the gene is inherited from one parent only, the child has no symptoms but is a 'carrier' of the disease and could pass it on to the next generation. Two parents who are cystic fibrosis carriers have a 1 in 4 chance of conceiving a child who suffers from the disease.

What are the symptoms?

The gene abnormality results in problems with secretion of mucus in the lungs, pancreas and bowel, and it is this that causes the symptoms of the illness. These may include:

- diarrhoea and weight loss due to loss of pancreatic function – the pancreas cannot produce the enzymes essential for digestion of food;
- in babies, obstruction of the bowel by a very thick greenish bowel secretion (meconium);
- recurrent chest infections with a persistent cough and breathlessness.

How is it diagnosed?

A family history of the disease is often a useful indication that cystic fibrosis is the underlying diagnosis. Initially the doctor will take a blood test (p. 99) to look for the specific gene abnormalities that are present in cystic fibrosis. A 'sweat test' may also be carried out. Children with cystic fibrosis have high levels of salt in their sweat – a sweat test is able to measure these levels.

Parents who are known to be carriers of the cystic fibrosis gene may be offered genetic counselling and fetal genetic screening when they are planning a family.

What are the treatment options?

There is a range of therapies offered to people suffering from cystic fibrosis and individual treatment depends on the organs affected by the disease.

- **Pancreas** Artificial pancreatic supplements in the form of capsules can be given to replace the natural enzymes that are no longer being produced. The supplements are taken with meals to replace the patient's own pancreatic function and allow the normal digestion of food, relieving the diarrhoea and malabsorption.
- **Gastrointestinal tract** Blockage of the bowel by meconium, in babies, requires surgical intervention to relieve the obstruction.
- **Lungs** The most important part of treating cystic fibrosis is therapy to keep the lungs as healthy as possible. It is advances in this field that have led to the great

Gene therapy for cystic fibrosis

Attempts are being made to use gene therapy in the treatment of cystic fibrosis. The aim is to replace the abnormal gene with a functioning copy. Harmless viruses are manipulated to carry the gene. The viruses are inhaled by the patient so that the gene enters cells in the lungs allowing them to produce normal mucus. This can help patients to avoid chest infections and reduce the damage to their lungs. As yet, the treatment is experimental and not entirely effective, but it is hoped that gene manipulation could one day offer real help to patients with diseases due to gene abnormalities.

improvements in life expectancy. Early treatment with antibiotics for any sign of infection in the chest, coupled with regular, intensive physiotherapy to keep the airways clear of mucus is vital in order to avoid breathing problems.

What is the outlook?

Until ten years ago, children with cystic fibrosis died in their early teens because of overwhelming lung damage. Modern physiotherapy and careful use of antibiotics has led to a dramatic improvement, with many sufferers now reaching adulthood with an improved quality of life.

DIVERTICULAR DISEASE

Pockets of bowel that protrude out from the intestinal wall, which may bleed or become inflamed.

The small pouches of intestinal lining (diverticula) that protrude out from the gut wall in diverticular disease are common. Their exact cause is unclear, but it seems to be related to a Western diet that is low in fibre and high in protein. The condition is very common in Western countries, but quite rare in the developing world where vegetables form the staple diet.

What are the symptoms?

In themselves, diverticula are harmless and 90 per cent of affected people are completely unaware that they have diverticular disease. A proportion will suffer from mild diarrhoea or constipation and mild pain in the lower left abdomen, which is relieved by passing wind or opening the bowels. However, complications can develop that cause the following symptoms.

- Constipation, a change in bowel habit and rectal bleeding can occur in severe diverticular disease where strictures (narrowings) form in the part of the bowel most badly affected – usually the sigmoid colon.
- Severe abdominal pain, constipation and fever can be a sign that a diverticulum has become inflamed – a condition known as diverticulitis. In severe attacks, abscesses may form and if these rupture it can lead to peritonitis or obstruction of the bowel.
- Haemorrhage from blood vessels in the bowel wall adjacent to a diverticulum. The vessels may bleed profusely and cause shock from acute blood loss, although mild bleeding usually stops spontaneously.

How is it diagnosed?

In an otherwise healthy patient with only mild symptoms, the doctor may arrange a barium enema (p. 108) or a colonoscopy (p. 115). Diverticular disease gives the intestines a very distinctive appearance, and is easily recognisable in both these tests. In people with severe diverticulitis, the diagnosis is made from the symptoms.

What are the treatment options?

In people with a mild form of diverticular disease, a high-fibre diet can help to avoid the development of complications, although treatment for constipation may be required in some cases. For diverticulitis and abscess formation, the doctor will prescribe antibiotics, intravenous fluids and a period of fasting to allow the bowel to rest. Severe complications sometimes require emergency surgery to remove the affected part of the gut.

DYSPEPSIA

Pain or discomfort in the upper part of the abdomen, commonly known as indigestion.

Dyspepsia (from the Greek for 'faulty digestion') is a broad term used to describe symptoms in the oesophagus, stomach and duodenum. These symptoms can be indicative of a serious problem such as peptic ulcers or *Helicobacter pylori* infection, which is now known to be a major cause of stomach ulcers. In most cases, however, there is no particular reason for the symptoms.

What are the symptoms?

Dyspepsia covers a wide range of symptoms that include the following:

- heartburn and acidity;
- belching;
- nausea;
- pain and abdominal distension;
- an early feeling of fullness when eating.

Non-ulcer dyspepsia is a syndrome analogous to irritable bowel syndrome (p. 149). It is often stress-related and usually brought on by eating or drinking.

How is it diagnosed?

Upper intestinal endoscopy (p. 110) may be carried out to check for ulcers or a malignancy. When the symptoms are present but the stomach appears normal, non-ulcer dyspepsia is diagnosed.

What are the treatment options?

Most dyspepsia does not have a specific cause, so treatment involves medication to reduce discomfort, such as antispasmodics, antacids and anti-wind agents. Non-ulcer dyspepsia sufferers should keep an eye on their diet and lifestyle to try to identify and avoid foods and behaviours, such as drinking and smoking, that cause problems.

FOOD ALLERGY

An abnormal immune response triggered by a particular food.

There are three different mechanisms that can give rise to gastrointestinal symptoms, all of which are often referred to as 'food allergy':

- the normal response to irritants and toxins in food;
- an abnormal response to food due to an existing problem such as lactose intolerance;
- a true allergic reaction to a specific food such as peanuts or shellfish. A true food allergy occurs when the immune system is triggered by a particular food. This response involves the release of histamine, a chemical that makes the body react in an abnormal and sometimes life-threatening way.

What are the symptoms?

True food allergy will result in symptoms starting within an hour of the food being ingested. They include:

- swelling of the lips and tongue;
- vomiting;
- wheezing and breathlessness;
- eczema;
- migraine;
- in severe cases, hypotension, tachycardia and shock.

If the symptoms have delayed onset, making a direct connection with particular trigger foods is more complex. Abdominal discomfort with bloating and diarrhoea are often blamed on food allergy but usually prove difficult to link with a single food item.

How is it diagnosed?

There are inherent difficulties in all allergy testing techniques, but the following may be used to help pinpoint the exact food that is causing the problem.

- **Skin patch testing** This involves placing a selection of possible allergens on the skin then measuring any allergic response by the extent of redness or rash that develops. Often results do not match the foods the patient suspects.
- **Dietary exclusion** This involves systematically excluding particular foodstuffs from the diet to see whether symptoms improve. It can take a long time and often does not reveal useful results.
- **Dietary challenge** This technique involves feeding the patient a suspect food, on its own, to see whether it causes symptoms. Proper dietary challenge usually requires admission to hospital and medical supervision.

HELP YOUR DOCTOR TO HELP YOU

Keeping a food diary

Food allergies that produce delayed reactions can be extremely hard to diagnose, because there is often no clear link between eating a trigger food and developing symptoms. One way to help your doctor identify your problem food is to keep a food diary – a record of food and drink, together with a list of your symptoms.

- *Make careful notes on what and when you eat and drink.*
- *Be sure to list all the ingredients of every meal – minor ingredients such as food additives are often allergic triggers.*
- *Record the timing, duration and severity of your symptoms – use a scale to rate them.*

- **Food diary** This involves keeping a record of symptoms and foods, and trying to correlate the two (see box, p. 142). Some doctors do not consider food diaries to be scientifically valid, but many patients find them helpful.

What are the treatment options?

Simple exclusion of any trigger food is the most straightforward and effective way of treating true food allergy. Most patients have a good idea as to what causes their symptoms, particularly if they have kept a detailed food diary, and are able to exclude the culprits from their diet.

The treatment of a life-threatening allergic response (anaphylaxis) is a medical emergency and requires injection of adrenaline, antihistamines and steroids to halt the anaphylaxis and prevent severe breathing difficulties.

FOOD POISONING

See Gastroenteritis.

GASTRITIS

An inflammation of the wall of the stomach, resulting in mild symptoms.

Gastritis simply means inflammation of the mucus lining of the stomach. It is a common condition that ranges in severity from being completely asymptomatic to causing extreme discomfort. When it does cause symptoms, gastritis results in upper abdominal pain that is sometimes made worse by eating, nausea and a sensation of being full after only a small amount of food. Bloating, wind and heartburn can also be associated with gastritis.

Helicobacter pylori is often contracted during childhood, but may not cause symptoms for many years.

What are the causes?

There are many causes of gastritis, including viral infection and alcohol abuse. Here, we look at the two main ones.

- **Non-steroidal anti-inflammatory drugs (NSAIDs)** This group of drugs, which includes aspirin, is used to treat a range of common conditions from angina to arthritis. As a result, a large proportion of the population take these drugs regularly. They can damage the protective lining of the stomach, resulting in inflammation.
- *Helicobacter pylori* This bacterium has been proven to be responsible for peptic ulcers and gastritis. It is responsible for most episodes of gastritis seen today.

How is it diagnosed?

Although the doctor may suspect gastritis from the symptoms (especially if a person has been taking an NSAID), the only way to obtain a definitive diagnosis is by performing an upper gastrointestinal endoscopy (p. 110), which allows the doctor to inspect the stomach lining directly. Blood tests, breath tests and tissue sampling of the stomach lining may be performed, and will confirm whether *Helicobacter pylori* is present.

What are the treatment options?

If a drug is the cause of the symptom, stopping it and changing to another type of medication is the only way of curing the gastritis. If the patient needs to stay on the medication, the doctor may prescribe a powerful drug called a proton pump inhibitor (p. 119) that turns off the acid production in the stomach. These drugs can reduce the risk of developing gastritis caused by taking NSAIDs. Infection with *Helicobacter pylori* is treated with a one-week course of two antibiotics plus a proton pump inhibitor, which successfully eradicates the infection in over 90 per cent of patients.

GASTROENTERITIS

Inflammation of the gastrointestinal tract.

Of all gastrointestinal illness, gastroenteritis is the one that most of us will probably have suffered at least once. The condition is extremely common and is usually due to a virus or bacterium in food that has not been destroyed during the cleaning or cooking process.

What are the causes?

A huge range of organisms can cause food poisoning. Many are viruses, such as rotavirus or astrovirus, which are especially common in children, or the Norwalk virus in older children and adults. Bacteria such as *Escherichia coli* (*E. coli*), *Salmonella*, *Campylobacter* or *Shigella* are other major causes, as are parasitic micro-organisms such as *Giardia*, amoebae and *Cryptosporidium*.

What are the symptoms?

The familiar symptoms include nausea, vomiting, abdominal pain and diarrhoea. Sometimes, a person with gastroenteritis develops a high temperature. Severe infections with certain organisms, such as those that cause dysentery, can lead to bloody diarrhoea. A very serious

Why do I get diarrhoea on holiday?

Travellers' diarrhoea is a very common complaint, affecting many people each year. As holidays take in more exotic locations, the number of attacks of gastroenteritis increases. The cause is often *E. coli*, sometimes *Shigella*, *Salmonella* or a virus. It lasts for two to four days, with diarrhoea and cramping abdominal pains. Good hygiene and careful selection of food at mealtimes provide the best way of avoiding an attack, as the infection is often due to poor food preparation and the use of reheated food. If an attack jeopardises a short holiday or business trip, a single dose of antibiotics (usually ciprofloxacin) can reduce the length and severity of the illness, otherwise drinking plenty of fluids is the key to recovery.

ASK THE EXPERT

form of gastroenteritis is cholera, a bacterial infection that is now rare in developed countries, which causes torrential diarrhoea and severe illness. Most attacks of gastroenteritis last for about two to four days and clear up without treatment. Affected people rarely visit the doctor so the causative organism is not identified. If the illness persists, however, a visit to the doctor is essential, and a stool test can be arranged to identify the bacterium or parasite responsible for the infection.

What are the treatment options?
The most important part of treatment is maintaining good hydration by drinking plenty of fluids. Usually, plain water is enough, but in hot climates and in people with other illnesses, such as diabetes mellitus, maintaining the salt and water balance of the body's fluids with oral rehydration salts is recommended. These can be bought as sachets, or made up using boiled water and orange juice with salt and sugar added. If a person has severe gastroenteritis and diarrhoea and vomiting are persistent, the doctor may need to give intravenous fluids. In some cases, antibiotics are given to shorten the length of the attack.

How can it be prevented or minimised?
Basic food hygiene is the key to avoiding gastroenteritis (pp. 43–45). Keeping cooked and raw meat separate, using different knives and chopping boards for meat and salads and, above all, thoroughly washing hands and work surfaces before, during and after food preparation are vital in order to avoid infections.

GASTROINTESTINAL HAEMORRHAGE
Bleeding from the bowel, which varies in severity.

Any bleeding from the bowel is abnormal. However, it is not always serious and in many cases is due to a minor ailment such as haemorrhoids. Despite this, the bleeding should always be checked out by a doctor as, in some cases, it may be the first sign of a more serious condition. If bleeding is heavy, it can lead to anaemia. If sudden and profuse blood loss is not treated promptly, shock can develop, which can be fatal.

What are the causes?
There are numerous causes for bleeding in the gut, of which peptic ulcers are the most common. In people with long-standing liver disease, the increased resistance of the liver to the flow of blood from the bowel results in dilated veins in the abdomen. In the oesophagus, these veins are called varices and because they are under high pressure they blow up into balloon-like structures that bleed easily.

A condition known as angiodysplasia can cause bleeding from abnormal blood vessels in the wall of the lower bowel. Benign outgrowths from the bowel wall called polyps, diverticula and haemorrhoids can all cause gastrointestinal haemorrhage although the bleeding associated with these conditions is not usually heavy. When faced with bleeding from the lower gut, a doctor's main concern will be to exclude cancer of the bowel. Malignancies usually bleed slowly, however, causing anaemia rather than severe haemorrhage.

What are the symptoms?
The symptoms of bleeding will depend on where in the bowel the bleeding is originating. Blood loss from low down in the bowel tends to be bright red in colour, whereas if bleeding occurs in the stomach or upper gut, the blood has gone through a digestive process and stools appear tarry and black.

Commonly experienced symptoms include:
- vomiting either of bright red blood or of partially digested blood (which resembles coffee grounds) due to blood loss in the oesophagus or stomach;
- smelly black stools known as melaena;

- abdominal pain (notably when associated with an ulcer in the stomach);
- nausea.

Often the gastrointestinal symptoms are accompanied by general symptoms of blood loss – dizziness, fainting and shortness of breath.

How is it diagnosed?

The doctor will often be guided in making a diagnosis by the symptoms and type of bleeding. If the bleeding is causing vomiting or melaena, then an upper gastrointestinal endoscopy (p. 110) is carried out so that the doctor can directly examine the oesophagus and stomach for a bleeding point. Bleeding from the lower bowel is investigated using a colonoscopy (p. 115). If the site of blood loss remains unclear, an angiogram will be arranged. In this procedure, radio-opaque dye is injected into the blood vessels of the gut so that any bleeding into the bowel shows up on an X-ray. For people who have slow blood loss resulting in anaemia, where doctors suspect that the bleeding is originating in the gastrointestinal tract, these same investigations will be carried out.

What are the treatment options?

With advances in technology, it is often possible to treat the source of bleeding during an endoscopic procedure (p. 125). Oesophageal varices can be injected with a substance to seal them up, or a small rubber band can be placed around them to stop the flow of blood. Peptic ulcers can be injected with adrenaline or a sealant, or cauterised with a laser or heating device to stop them bleeding. Bleeding in the intestine is treated in similar ways to lesions in the stomach.

With advances in endoscopic equipment, surgery is reserved for profuse bleeding that is not responding to any other treatment. Bleeding cancers, however, especially those in the colon or rectum, usually require the removal of the affected part of the colon (p. 132).

What is the outlook?

Although in many cases treatment is effective at stopping haemorrhage, bleeding from the upper part of the gut can be an extremely serious, life-threatening condition. Recent data suggests that bleeding requiring emergency endoscopy may be fatal in 15 per cent of patients; those at greatest risk are the elderly and patients with other serious medical problems. For others, it is the ailment causing the bleeding that determines its outcome.

GASTRO-OESOPHAGEAL REFLUX
The movement of the contents of the stomach back up into the oesophagus.

Gastro-oesophageal reflux disorder (GORD) is extremely common. In fact, reflux is a normal occurrence and it is only when symptoms appear that it is labelled a medical condition. These symptoms are caused by stomach acid leaking back up from the stomach into the oesophagus, irritating the more sensitive lining of the oesophagus and causing pain. In the majority of cases the valve or sphincter at the entrance to the stomach appears normal, although some patients will have an anatomical abnormality, such as a hiatus hernia, that disrupts the function of the valve.

What are the symptoms?

In the majority of people, the main symptom is heartburn – a burning pain running up and down the centre of the chest. The pain is often brought on by particular activities, such as bending over when gardening, or by certain foods or alcohol. Some people experience stomach acid or bile entering the back of the mouth causing a bitter taste. In addition to these symptoms, there are three main complications of GORD.

Some 75 per cent of the population suffer from heartburn at some time in their lives.

- **Oesophagitis** Acid damage can cause inflammation and even ulcers in the lining of the oesophagus.
- **Strictures** In severe, long-term GORD, the oesophagus can become narrowed.
- **Barrett's oesophagus** This occurs when the cells in the lining of the oesophagus undergo a change and resemble those in the stomach or small intestine. The cause of this change is not clear, although it is almost certainly a protective response to the stomach fluids attacking the oesophagus. Barrett's oesophagus can increase the risk of developing cancer so a programme of regular endoscopy may be recommended to pick up early signs of tumours.

How is it diagnosed?

The doctor usually makes a diagnosis of GORD based on the classic symptoms. For a young person with no other symptoms, the doctor is likely to advise lifestyle changes and medication. In people over the age of 45 and those who have other symptoms, upper gastrointestinal endoscopy (p. 110) is carried out in order to eliminate other conditions, such as a hiatus hernia, and to determine the extent of damage to the oesophagus. Studies to measure the acidity in the oesophagus may be done (p. 102).

Helping with heartburn

Heartburn is a very common problem. One in every 20 patients seen by a GP is there because of heartburn or indigestion. It is the doctor's job to rule out any other, more serious causes for the symptoms, and this involves looking for signs of a significant problem in the oesophagus. The doctor will want to know if you are experiencing any of the following:

- *weight loss;*

- *difficulty or pain in swallowing;*

- *vomiting, especially if there is blood in the vomit.*

If these symptoms are absent it is less likely that there is a serious disease causing the problem.

What are the treatment options?

Treatment focuses on reducing the amount of acid in the stomach and preventing it reaching the oesophagus. Certain changes in lifestyle, such as reducing alcohol intake and eating fewer rich foods, can help to relieve symptoms. In severe cases, some people may benefit by raising the head of the bed so that they do not lie flat at night.

Neutralising the refluxing acid during an attack should resolve the symptoms quickly. Effective antacids are available over the counter and should be taken early on during an attack either as chewable tablets or as a liquid. Doctors may also prescribe preventive medicines, such as ranitidine and omeprazole, which act by reducing the production of acid in the stomach (p. 119).

In severe cases, hiatus hernias may be repaired surgically. Keyhole surgery can improve the efficiency of the valve between the oesophagus and the stomach.

What is the outlook?

GORD responds very well to antacid drug treatment. Strictures are rare these days, but even if they do develop the narrowed area can be dilated during endoscopy. Where surgery is necessary the outcome is generally excellent, although after the operation some people suffer from the sensation of food sticking in the gullet.

How can it be prevented or minimised?

Lifestyle changes can reduce both the severity and the frequency of symptoms – rich foods, alcohol and smoking all contribute to GORD, as does being overweight. Even minimal weight loss can help to prevent the reflux of stomach acid into the oesophagus.

HAEMORRHOIDS

Dilated veins in the rectum that cause soreness and bleeding.

Haemorrhoids, commonly known as piles, are dilated veins just inside the rectum. They are associated with the presence of small tags of skin around the anus and often protrude through the anus, causing irritation. Haemorrhoids frequently develop in association with constipation and having to strain in order to pass stools; they may also occur in pregnancy. If haemorrhoids are long-standing, the blood inside them clots, making them hard and sometimes painful.

What are the symptoms?

Not everyone with haemorrhoids has symptoms, but for those who do the main complaint is itching. The presence of small amounts of bright red blood on the surface of stools or on the paper after wiping is another common sign. If the haemorrhoids become large enough to protrude through the anus – a complication associated with straining to open the bowels – they can become extremely painful.

How are they diagnosed?

Diagnosis is usually made with proctoscopy, in which a short, hollow viewing instrument is inserted through the anus and slowly withdrawn. Any haemorrhoids are clearly visible as the tube is pulled out. If the doctor is concerned about bleeding from the rectum, an examination using a flexible endoscope (p. 114) may be carried out. This is because bleeding from the lower bowel can arise from several more serious diseases, including cancer.

What are the treatment options?

Basic changes in lifestyle, such as increasing dietary fibre and fluid intake to avoid constipation and straining, will help to reduce the symptoms. If the haemorrhoids are large or painful, the doctor may inject them with a sclerosing agent that causes them to shrivel up. In some cases, surgery is required to remove the veins completely (p. 132).

HEARTBURN
See Gastro-oesophageal reflux, p. 145.

HERNIA
An abnormal protrusion of intestine through a gap in a layer of tissue.

Hernias occur when the pressure within the abdomen pushes a part of the intestine through a weakened area in the muscle wall so that it protrudes and can be felt as a lump. A hernia can occur in the groin or scrotum (inguinal), where the leg joins the abdomen (femoral) or through the bellybutton (umbilical). Hiatus hernias affect the stomach and oesophagus (see below).

What are the symptoms?
The soft mass of intestine is often clearly visible as an uncomfortable or painful swelling. In severe situations, the part of intestine in the hernia can twist, cutting off its blood supply and causing acute pain. If this condition, known as a strangulated hernia, remains untreated the affected tissue can die due to the lack of blood supply. Strangulated hernias are most commonly seen in the femoral area and require urgent surgery.

How is it diagnosed?
A hernia can be easily diagnosed from the physical symptoms it causes, including the appearance of a lump and a dragging or aching sensation.

What are the treatment options?
Surgeons usually advise that hernias are repaired to avoid strangulation. Surgical repair, which can be done either by open surgery (p. 127) or laparoscopic surgery (p. 128), involves pushing the intestine back into the abdomen and then reinforcing the weak area in the abdominal wall. Although the surgery is straightforward, hernias sometimes recur. If there is a delay before surgery, a truss can be worn to support the weak area.

HIATUS HERNIA
Part of the stomach protrudes into the chest cavity.

The gap in the diaphragm where the oesophagus passes through on its way to the stomach is called the hiatus. If the diaphragm becomes weakened, most commonly due to age, pressure from the abdomen can force part of the stomach through this gap forming a hiatus hernia. Normally the hiatus acts like a sphincter, helping to control the opening between the stomach and the oesophagus and preventing stomach acid from spilling into the oesophagus. In a hiatus hernia, the sphincter can no longer function properly and stomach acid can leak back (reflux).

What are the symptoms?
Acid reflux produces the symptoms of gastro-oesophageal reflux (heartburn) (p. 145), especially when lying flat. The hernia itself can interfere with swallowing, giving the sensation of food sticking in the throat.

How is it diagnosed?
Hiatus hernia is diagnosed with an upper gastrointestinal endoscopy (p. 110) or a barium swallow (pp. 106–7).

What are the treatment options?
Symptoms of heartburn can generally be controlled with antacids and other medication, or with lifestyle measures such as a healthy diet, losing weight, giving up smoking and raising the head of the bed at night. In severe cases, surgery can repair the hernia, but many recur.

EXPERIENCING AN INGUINAL HERNIA

I first noticed the bump just after doing some work in the garden. It was about 5cm (2in) across, in my groin just above my testicle. It didn't hurt, and would come and go.

Gradually it got bigger, although I could easily push it back in. Eventually the testicle became enlarged, and I'd get a dragging sensation in it, so I went to see my doctor who diagnosed an inguinal hernia and suggested I wear a truss to ease the discomfort. He referred me to a surgeon in the local hospital, who put me on the waiting list to have it repaired.

After the operation, I was a little sore. I was allowed home the next day on strict orders not to do any gardening or lift anything for six weeks. Now I feel as good as new, and the only sign of my hernia is a 10cm (4in) scar, hidden in the crease of my groin.

HIRSCHSPRUNG'S DISEASE
A congenital disease that appears in early childhood, causing constipation and a dilated colon.

Hirschsprung's disease is a rare congenital condition that affects about 1 in 5000 babies. The symptoms are due to a malformation of the nerves that control the movement of the gut. In a healthy person, waves of contractions (peristalsis) run along the intestinal walls, pushing food through the gut, rather like pushing toothpaste out of a tube. The signals that propagate the muscle contractions are transmitted via the nerves of the intestinal wall. In a child with Hirschsprung's disease, part of the nerve system is missing, so peristalsis stops at that point and the bowel becomes obstructed.

Hirschsprung's disease is four times more common in boys than in girls.

What are the symptoms?
The doctor will suspect Hirschsprung's disease if a child has severe constipation or an obstructed bowel in the first couple of years or life, although if the abnormality is minor the condition may not cause problems until adulthood. An affected child will have the following symptoms:
- difficulty emptying the bowels;
- colicky pain;
- a distended abdomen;
- poor appetite;
- vomiting, in severe cases.

How is it diagnosed?
Usually, the first investigation is a barium enema (p. 108). In a child with Hirschsprung's disease the colon will be much wider than normal. The diagnosis is confirmed by measuring the pressure of the sphincter at the anus, which fails to relax, or by taking a biopsy (a tissue sample). This can be done during surgery or during a proctoscopy procedure (p. 114). Microscopic examination of the biopsy tissue will show whether nerves are absent from the affected part of the large intestine.

What are the treatment options?
Surgery to remove the part of the bowel that has no nerve supply, and rejoin the unaffected areas, is usually curative, with no long-term complications. A temporary colostomy may be necessary before the main surgery, if the child is seriously underweight and needs urgent restoration of at least partial gut function.

INDIGESTION
See Dyspepsia, p. 141.

INFLAMMATORY BOWEL DISEASE
A term that describes two key diseases in which the bowel becomes inflamed – Crohn's disease and ulcerative colitis.

The two conditions Crohn's disease and ulcerative colitis overlap considerably in their signs and symptoms, and doctors categorise them both under the title of inflammatory bowel disease. One difference, however, is that Crohn's disease can affect any part of the bowel, while ulcerative colitis is confined to the colon and rectum.

What are the causes?
There are many theories as to the cause of these diseases, but none have been fully proven. Certain infections (the measles virus, live vaccines and mycobacteria) have all been proposed as being responsible, but the evidence is not strong enough to pin the blame on any of these with certainty. In both diseases the body's immune system seems to become abnormally stimulated and this becomes self-perpetuating, resulting in inflammation and ulceration of the wall of the intestine. It is this inflammation that causes damage to the lining of the gut and the resulting symptoms.

What are the symptoms?
Although the symptoms of these two conditions are often so similar that doctors find it difficult to tell them apart, there are a few distinguishing features.
- **Ulcerative colitis** Diarrhoea is the main symptom, with bowel motions occurring up to 15 to 20 times a day when an attack is underway, often with blood and mucus in the stool. The loss of blood may result in anaemia. In a very severe attack, the colon may become dilated, a dangerous complication that results in fever, feeling very unwell and abdominal pain with the diarrhoea.
- **Crohn's disease** Because it can involve the whole of the digestive tract, from mouth to anus, Crohn's disease can cause a huge array of symptoms. Mouth ulcers are often a problem. In the small intestine, inflammation results in pain, narrowing and even obstruction of the bowel, leading to vomiting. The ileum (the final part of the small intestine) is commonly affected, causing pain, obstruction and sometimes problems absorbing vitamin B_{12}. Crohn's disease in the colon can be similar to ulcerative colitis,

with the passage of bloody diarrhoea due to inflammation, and formation of ulcers. Passages, called fistulae, can form between the bowel and the skin.

How is it diagnosed?
The doctor will probably suspect inflammatory bowel disease from the symptoms; blood tests will be done to look for indications of inflammation and also to check for anaemia (p. 99). The diagnosis is then confirmed by taking a small sample of tissue – a biopsy – from the intestinal wall during colonoscopy (p. 115). If the doctor suspects that Crohn's disease has affected the small intestine, a barium follow-through (pp. 106–7) usually highlights any areas of inflammation or narrowing.

What are the treatment options?
There are four main treatment options.
- **Anti-inflammatory drugs** These drugs, for example mesalazine, are used to reduce the inflammation in the bowel wall. It is important not to confuse these with anti-inflammatories of the aspirin family, as these can make the symptoms worse.
- **Immunosuppressant drugs** These are used to reduce the immune response in the bowel. Steroids can be useful, but side effects may limit the dose. Drugs such as azathioprine help to reduce the level of steroids needed.
- **Surgery** Generally doctors prefer to avoid surgery, but in patients with severe symptoms that are not responding to medication, the affected part of the bowel may need to be surgically removed.

AT THE LEADING EDGE
Antibody therapy in Crohn's disease
Recently a new type of treatment for Crohn's has become available. The inflammation in Crohn's disease is at least partially due to a chemical the body produces, called tissue necrosis factor (TNF). TNF attaches to cells in the intestine at a specific part of the cell wall (a receptor) and in doing so triggers the inflammation. Antibody therapy aims to prevent the attachment of TNF to the cell wall, by binding to TNF, breaking the cycle of inflammation. The antibodies are administered as a drug, infliximab, which has been shown to be helpful in certain types of Crohn's disease, stopping attacks that did not respond to other treatments.

- **Diet** A low-fibre, high-vitamin diet may help to alleviate symptoms, and some patients also claim that avoiding certain 'trigger' foods produces improvements.

What is the outlook?
Both Crohn's and ulcerative colitis are 'relapsing and remitting' diseases. In other words, they flare up from time to time, often without warning. Although medication can reduce the frequency and severity of attacks, it does not cure them altogether. As ulcerative colitis affects only the colon, removal of the colon effectively cures the disease, but may leave the patient with a stoma, or bag, and is usually reserved for severe cases (p. 131). Crohn's can affect any part of the digestive tract, so surgery to remove one portion may not cure the disease. In fact, repeated surgery can result in a marked reduction in the length of the bowel and consequent difficulty absorbing nutrients.

IRRITABLE BOWEL SYNDROME
A collection of gastrointestinal symptoms that are thought to be stress related.

Irritable bowel syndrome (IBS), also known as functional bowel disorder, is extremely common and affects women more than men. The syndrome is a collection of symptoms that arise in the gut. In its mildest form, it develops at times of stress, such as before exams or interviews, and causes diarrhoea. In some people, however, the condition becomes continuous and leads to more upsetting symptoms.

What are the causes?
As yet we do not know why some people suffer severe symptoms and some do not. Stress can bring on attacks or make them worse for some people, while for others certain foods are the trigger – fruit and the artificial sweetener sorbitol are common culprits. The anatomy of the intestines appears completely normal in people with IBS, although recently abnormalities in some of the chemicals in the intestinal wall have been found in some sufferers.

What are the symptoms?
The symptoms of irritable bowel syndrome are numerous and vary between individuals. A person with the syndrome may have one or more of the following:
- indigestion (dyspepsia) and burping;
- gastro-oesophageal reflux (heartburn);
- nausea and fatigue;

EXPERIENCING IRRITABLE BOWEL SYNDROME

My first 'attack' was in my late 20s. It seemed I'd inherited the 'sensitive tummy' of my family; my dad and two aunts suffered terribly with digestive complaints.

I thought it was food poisoning at first, but the diarrhoea would come and go, and the pain was intense. Then I considered a food intolerance and kept a food diary for months, but I never identified a culprit. After another severe attack I went to see the doctor again.

My GP asked about my lifestyle and my job, which was going through a stressful patch, and suggested that I had irritable bowel syndrome. The abdominal pain was due to rapid contractions of my intestines, so she prescribed an antispasmodic drug. Since then I've learned to handle stress better and generally the IBS is under control, but I still suffer symptoms on the odd occasion.

- pain in the upper abdomen or, if the colon is the main site, colicky abdominal pain;
- constipation, diarrhoea and bloating.

The sensation of needing to open the bowels again immediately after going to the toilet is common, along with attacks of diarrhoea in the morning, which then settle for the rest of the day.

How is it diagnosed?
Before making a diagnosis of IBS it is important to rule out other gastrointestinal conditions that cause discomfort and a change in bowel habit. If there is any doubt about the diagnosis, a colonoscopy (p. 115) or barium enema (p. 108) is often carried out.

What are the treatment options?
Identifying and avoiding trigger factors and adopting a healthy lifestyle are the most important general measures, but no single treatment will work for everybody with IBS and there is no apparent cure for all the symptoms. Several medications may be tried until individual symptoms are relieved. The following treatments may help:
- peppermint oil capsules or dimethicone can help bloating and burping;

- antispasmodics, such as buscopan, spasmonal or mebeverine (colofac), may relieve abdominal pain;
- antidiarrhoeals, such as loperamide, are sometimes used to treat severe diarrhoea;
- high-fibre diets often improve symptoms in those with marked constipation, but can exacerbate bloating;
- in a few people, drugs are used to modify the way the disturbances in the bowel are perceived. This involves the use of drugs that were originally designed as anti-depressants, such as prothiaden. Although not everyone with IBS is depressed, evidence suggests that these drugs can markedly improve symptoms, especially if pain is a major symptom.

Hypnotherapy and psychotherapy have been shown to be helpful in many patients with IBS, sessions being targeted at improving gut symptoms. Such approaches are becoming more widespread and more easily available.

ISCHAEMIC BOWEL DISEASE
Loss of the blood supply to the intestines, resulting in a range of symptoms.

Bowel ischaemia can be described as a 'heart attack of the gut'. Just as a heart attack is caused by blockage of the blood vessels supplying blood to heart muscle, so bowel ischaemia is due to blockage of the arteries in the bowel.

What are the causes?
Atherosclerosis, in which patches of hard cholesterol form in the walls of the arteries, is the main cause of bowel ischaemia. These 'plaques' gradually build up until the artery becomes narrowed or blocked, reducing the supply of oxygenated blood to the bowel. Sometimes, a blood clot travels from another part of the body and blocks the artery. Smoking, high blood pressure, diabetes and high cholesterol all increase the risk of bowel ischaemia.

What are the symptoms?
The symptoms of gut ischaemia vary depending on the extent of the blockage. Mild ischaemia results in griping, sometimes severe, abdominal pain, notably after eating, when the blood flow requirements of the gut increase but the narrowed arteries cannot supply the demand.

If the main artery to the bowel, the mesenteric artery, becomes blocked, the gastrointestinal equivalent of a heart attack occurs. The affected bowel becomes starved of blood and oxygen and without immediate treatment the affected part can be severely damaged, or even die off, leading to perforation and peritonitis. If this occurs, the patient suffers severe abdominal pain and vomiting. Bloody diarrhoea occurs as the attack progresses.

How is it diagnosed?

If the doctor suspects a gradual narrowing of the arteries, an angiogram will probably be arranged. In this procedure, radio-opaque dye is injected into the main artery of the bowel, via a catheter in the groin, and a series of X-rays is taken that will show up any narrowed areas. Acute bowel ischaemia usually causes symptoms severe enough to require emergency exploratory surgery. The appearance of the bowel during the operation confirms the diagnosis.

What are the treatment options?

Narrowing of the arteries can be treated by threading a catheter into the affected vessel and inflating a tiny balloon in the narrowed segment. In some cases, drugs help to improve the flow of blood in the bowel.

Complete obstruction of the blood flow to the bowel is treated by surgically removing the dying section of bowel. The outlook for surgical patients is good, especially if treatment is prompt and the bowel has not perforated. Often, however, nutritional problems will result following the removal of a large section of gut.

LACTOSE INTOLERANCE
Gastrointestinal symptoms related to the consumption of dairy products.

Some people are unable to consume dairy products without experiencing abdominal discomfort and bloating along with nausea and diarrhoea two to three hours afterwards. These people are described as having lactose intolerance – a situation in which the gut is unable to break down the sugar in cow's milk, known as lactose.

What are the causes?

In order for lactose to be digested and absorbed from the gut, it must be broken down into its two constituent sugars, glucose and galactose. The enzyme responsible for this breakdown process is lactase, which is found in the cells lining the small intestine.

For adults in the majority of the world's ethnic groups, lactose intolerance is the norm. The ability to produce lactase is lost at weaning, but this does not generally cause

problems because dairy products are largely absent from the diet in such cultures. In the Western world, however, where dairy products feature heavily in the normal diet and populations tend to have mixed ethnic backgrounds, the picture is more complicated. Ethnic groups such as Native Americans, Afro-Caribbeans and Asians often retain their racial tendency to be lactose intolerant. Ethnic groups such as the Caucasians normally retain the ability to produce lactase after weaning, but even within this group many people develop lactose intolerance for one of two reasons.

- Some babies are born with a complete absence of lactase in the gut – a congenital condition called alactasia.
- In others, who initially produce lactase normally, the levels drop with increasing age. A diet rich in dairy products or a significantly reduced level of lactase can give rise to symptoms in such cases.

What are the symptoms?

Babies with alactasia develop the following symptoms immediately they are fed with cow's milk products:

- vomiting;
- colic;
- failure to gain weight.

People who develop lactose intolerance later in life will notice bloating, discomfort and diarrhoea occurring as the undigested lactose is broken down by the gut bacteria.

How is it diagnosed?

Lactose tolerance testing used to be the standard method used to diagnose the condition, but is rarely performed now. The patient fasts for eight hours and is then given a dose of lactose. Blood samples are then taken at regular intervals to measure blood glucose (sugar) levels. If levels do not rise, this indicates that the lactose is not being broken down. Alternatively, the patient may be administered a modified version of this test, using a dose of lactose labelled with hydrogen. In lactose intolerance, the hydrogen can then be detected on the patient's breath.

Up to 90 per cent of Asians and Afro-Caribbeans are lactose intolerant, compared with about 12 per cent of Caucasians.

What are the treatment options?

The simplest solution is to exclude dairy products from the diet. Young children with alactasia require total exclusion, but adults can usually tolerate small amounts of lactose. Discovering exactly how much can be tolerated involves a process of trial and error, and the amount is likely to be different for each affected individual.

OBSTRUCTION OF THE BOWEL
Any blockage that prevents the normal passage of food through the gastrointestinal tract.

A wide variety of conditions can lead to obstruction of the bowel. Generally, the site of the blockage determines the symptoms. Obstruction of the bowel can have serious consequences, from acute pain to malnutrition.

What are the causes?
There are numerous causes of bowel obstruction, which fall into two groups: abnormal functioning of the bowel and structural problems. Functional problems can result from:
- a chemical imbalance in the body, usually of calcium, which can paralyse the muscle within the intestinal wall;
- handling the bowel during surgery, which often results in the muscle tissue 'going on strike', a condition known as paralytic ileus;
- Hirschsprung's disease, where the nerves that stimulate peristalsis do not function properly (p. 148).

Without muscle activity there is no peristalsis to keep chyme – the mixture of food and gut secretions – moving forwards, and the contents of the intestines stagnate. The intestinal lining responds by secreting fluid, which combines with gas produced by bacteria to distend the gut, resulting in bloating and vomiting.

Structural problems cause actual physical blockage or interfere with gut movements. Structural bowel obstruction can be caused by many different conditions, including:
- a hernia, where a loop of intestine may become trapped and twisted outside the abdominal wall, preventing the intestinal contents from passing through.
- tumours of the colon, which may completely block it;
- strictures due to inflammation in Crohn's disease;
- twists in the intestine causing a volvulus, a kink that obstructs the passage of bowel contents;
- intussusception, a condition that affects newborns, where the intestine telescopes inside itself so that the outer layer squeezes the inner layer, blocking it;
- bands of fibrous tissue, called adhesions, that form either following surgery on the bowel or as a result of inflammation in the bowel, for example after peritonitis. Adhesions act as a belt, squeezing around the bowel and effectively blocking it;
- atresia, where a portion of the bowel fails to develop properly, resulting in a blind end. This most commonly occurs in the duodenum or anus and is usually found in babies who are unable to feed due to the obstruction.

What are the symptoms?
Preventing the passage of food through the bowel results in four main symptoms, all of which come on suddenly:
- abdominal pain;
- bloating;
- vomiting;
- total constipation.

Depending on the site of the obstruction, the patient may not even be able to pass wind.

How is it diagnosed?
The symptoms immediately indicate to a doctor that the bowel is obstructed. If a person is experiencing intermittent rather than continuous symptoms, which may happen with Crohn's strictures or with adhesions, then a barium meal and follow through (pp. 106–7), or a CT scan (p. 104), may confirm the diagnosis.

What are the treatment options?
Most cases of acute obstruction require an urgent operation (p. 130). Surgeons can remove tumours, relieve a volvulus or intussusception and repair atresias. The success of surgery for these conditions depends on the cause. If tumours have spread before surgery is carried out, the outlook is poor. In contrast, volvulus rarely recurs because the colon is stitched to hold it in place.

Intermittent bowel obstructions due to adhesions are usually treated by laparoscopic (keyhole) surgery in order to avoid handling the bowel, as this in itself may cause further adhesions to form. Whatever the treatment, however, adhesions often recur.

PARASITIC INFECTIONS
Intestinal infections caused by parasitic worms.

Parasitic worms are now rare in developed countries but are commonly present in the intestines of people in under-developed countries with unprocessed drinking water. The worms latch onto the intestinal wall and feed on blood from the host or on the contents of the digestive tract.

What are the causes?
There are several types of parasitic worm that colonise human intestines. Tapeworms are found in countries where beef and pork are consumed, especially if the meat is not thoroughly cooked. Threadworm infection usually affects children in temperate or cold climates, such as in Northern

Europe, although it is comparatively rare. Hookworm, ascaris and strongyloides are found mainly in underdeveloped countries with poor sanitation.

What are the symptoms?
Worm infections sometimes produce no symptoms at all, but they may cause:
- abdominal pain;
- diarrhoea or constipation;
- weight loss and malabsorption (in severe infections);
- anaemia due to infection with hookworm;
- severe night-time itching around the anus, where the threadworm lays its eggs.

How is it diagnosed?
The most effective way to diagnose parasitic infections of the gastrointestinal tract is to examine the contents of the bowel (p. 100). The eggs of the infecting worm can often be identified in a stool sample; sometimes the worms themselves are visible. Blood tests may show evidence of infection and/or anaemia (p. 99). An increase in the number of a specific type of white blood cell (eosinophils) may also be seen. In some cases, the doctor will carry out an endoscopic procedure such as colonoscopy (p. 115) or upper gastrointestinal endoscopy (p. 110) and is able to see the worms in the stomach or intestine.

Tapeworms grow inside the intestine and can reach lengths of up to 10 metres (33 feet).

The only effective treatment is with specific antibiotics that destroy the infecting worm. In cases of threadworm, the whole family will need treating. Improved food hygiene and good sanitation should avoid further infections.

PERITONITIS
Inflammation of the membrane that lines the abdominal cavity and covers the abdominal organs.

Peritonitis is a very serious condition that occurs when the delicate membrane that surrounds and protects the abdominal organs becomes infected or inflamed. Infection can occur, for example, if an inflamed appendix perforates, releasing bacteria into the abdominal cavity. Peritonitis also develops if the gut perforates, for instance due to a peptic ulcer or inflammatory bowel disease, allowing acidic stomach or intestinal contents to leak through the perforation into the abdominal cavity. Rarer causes of peritonitis include tuberculosis and abdominal tumours.

What are the symptoms?
If peritonitis is due to perforation, the symptoms are sudden and, if untreated, may be life-threatening. They include acute severe abdominal pain and nausea, often with vomiting and loss of appetite. A universal symptom of peritonitis is 'guarding', where the muscles of the abdomen contract in order to keep the contents still. Symptoms may settle on their own, but infection resulting from the leak of intestinal contents or bacteria into the abdominal cavity or bloodstream can result in septicaemia and shock.

How is it diagnosed?
A person with peritonitis will be in shock, with low blood pressure and a rapid heart rate. The abdomen is rigid and very tender. The cause of the peritonitis may be diagnosed from the patient's medical history – for instance known peptic ulcers or abdominal pain suggestive of appendicitis.

What are the treatment options?
Peritonitis almost always requires surgery to repair the perforation and wash out the abdominal cavity, in order to reduce the inflammation and infection. A drain may be left in the abdomen to allow any new fluid to be drained off.

What is the outlook?
Peritonitis can be life-threatening. The onset of infection around the bowel in the abdomen usually results in septicaemia – spread of infection into the bloodstream – which requires intensive care. Once the septicaemia is treated, however, the patient should make a full recovery.

PEPTIC ULCER DISEASE
Inflamed ulcers in the lining of the stomach or the duodenum (the first part of the small intestine).

Peptic ulcers can occur either in the stomach or in the duodenum. Duodenal ulcers are about twice as common as gastric (stomach) ulcers; on average, about 15 per cent of the population will suffer from a duodenal ulcer at some time in their lives. It was long thought that stress and anxiety contributed to the formation of peptic ulcers, but experts are now confident that this is not the case.

What are the causes?
The primary cause of peptic ulcers is the bacterium *Helicobacter pylori*, but certain drugs can also cause peptic ulcers. These include non-steroidal anti-inflammatories,

such as aspirin, and steroids. This is because these drugs prevent the formation of the protective layer of mucus in the stomach or intestines, allowing acid produced in the stomach to damage the lining. Tumours of the stomach can also lead to ulceration of the lining, as can excess production of stomach acid.

What are the symptoms?
It is not usually possible to determine the location of an ulcer from its symptoms, since both gastric and duodenal ulcers can cause the following problems:
• dyspepsia, commonly called indigestion;
• abdominal pain after eating;
• nausea or loss of appetite.
In some people, peptic ulcers are completely asymptomatic. At the other end of the scale, an ulcer may form close to a blood vessel in the stomach or duodenal wall and cause a severe gastrointestinal haemorrhage.

How is it diagnosed?
Peptic ulcers are almost always diagnosed by upper gastrointestinal endoscopy (p. 110), during which the doctor is able to directly view the stomach lining. Ulcers sometimes show up on barium meal X-rays (p. 106), although this test is rarely carried out these days. Small samples of tissue – biopsies – can be taken from the ulcer to check for *Helicobacter pylori* infection and to ensure that it is not malignant.

At least 95 per cent of all duodenal ulcers and 60–70 per cent of all stomach ulcers are due to infection by Helicobacter pylori.

What are the treatment options?
If doctors diagnose infection with *Helicobacter pylori*, a week-long course of two types of antibiotic (pp. 122–23), plus a third medication to reduce acid production in the stomach (p. 119) eliminates the bacteria in 90 per cent of cases. This treatment cures most peptic ulcers.

If the ulcer is caused by a drug, stopping the culprit, and prescribing an alternative if necessary, allows the ulcer to heal. If it is not possible to stop the drug, the doctor will probably prescribe a strong acid inhibitor (pp. 118–19) to help the ulcer heal and to prevent it recurring. A cancerous ulcer usually requires surgical treatment.

What is the outlook?
Once treatment has allowed a peptic ulcer to heal and the factors that triggered its formation have been removed, the chance of a recurrence is about 1 in 100.

PYLORIC STENOSIS
Narrowing of the pylorus (the sphincter that separates the stomach from the duodenum). If the pylorus becomes too narrow, food cannot leave the stomach.

Pyloric stenosis in adults is usually the result of duodenal ulcer disease, where scarring due to the disease narrows and stiffens the pylorus. Cancers of the stomach can sometimes cause the same symptoms. In babies it is a congenital abnormality that is seen more commonly in boys than girls. The muscle that forms the sphincter is thickened, narrowing the pyloric channel.

What are the symptoms?
Pyloric stenosis in babies results in 'projectile' vomiting, usually starting in the second week of life. In adults, it causes bloating, nausea and projectile vomiting of large volumes of food and fluid. It is rare to suffer abdominal pain due to the stenosis itself, although there may be pain due to the ulcers that caused the stenosis.

How is it diagnosed?
Doctors usually diagnose this condition using gastroscopy (upper gastrointestinal endoscopy, p. 110) or one of the many barium investigations (pp. 106–8).

What are the treatment options?
In babies, a small operation is carried out to cut through the thickened muscle; this is very effective at relieving the symptoms. In adults, the pylorus can be stretched using a balloon passed down inside an endoscope and inflated in the narrowed area (p. 124). If this is not successful then surgery to open up the pylorus is carried out.

If a cancer is the cause of the obstruction then surgeons can remove the affected part – a gastrectomy, for example, is the removal of the stomach – and rejoin the cut ends, which can help to relieve symptoms, although this obviously has severe implications for the patient's digestion.

What is the outlook?
In babies, surgery can permanently cure the problem. In adults, balloon stretching may not completely resolve the problem and symptoms may return, requiring surgery.

TUMOURS

In Britain, tumours of the gastrointestinal tract are the most common type of cancer.

The three main types of digestive cancers are: oesophageal (which affects the passage leading from the throat to the stomach); gastric (which affects the stomach); colorectal, affecting the large intestine.

What are the causes?

Smoking is a major risk factor for all types of tumour, as are poor diet and a family history of gastrointestinal cancer. More specific risk factors include: long-term gastro-oesophageal reflux for oesophageal cancer, infection with the bacterium *Helicobacter pylori*, pernicious anaemia and previous operations on the stomach for gastric cancer.

What are the symptoms?

Symptoms vary according to the type of cancer.
- Oesophageal cancer causes pain and difficulty in swallowing. Initially only solid foods cause problems, but as the tumour grows, swallowing liquids also results in regurgitation. Weight loss almost always occurs.
- Tumours arising in the stomach are often very advanced before causing symptoms. Pain, feeling full after small meals, nausea, vomiting and vomiting blood can all be due to stomach cancer, often associated with weight loss.
- Colorectal cancers cause bowel habit changes, anaemia, rectal bleeding, pain, weight loss and bowel obstruction.

How is it diagnosed?

There are two main methods of diagnosis.
- **Endoscopy** Doctors examine the upper or lower digestive tract, depending on the site of the cancer (pp. 110–15).
- **Barium studies** The type of study depends on the type of suspected cancer: barium swallow for oesophageal cancer (pp. 106–7), barium meal for gastric cancer (pp. 106–7) and barium enema for colorectal cancer (p. 108).

What are the treatment options?

Surgery is the main treatment option – if the cancer has not spread it may be possible to remove it entirely by cutting out a section of the digestive tract. In patients with gastric cancer, for instance, doctors might surgically remove the stomach (a gastrectomy). Chemotherapy and radiotherapy may be used to reduce the risk of cancer returning, and also if the cancer has spread beyond the gut. Some cancers need special procedures – for example, inoperable oesophageal cancer may require insertion of a stent, a hollow tube that keeps the oesophagus open, to allow the patient to eat (p. 124). Colorectal cancer patients may need a permanent colostomy (p. 131).

What is the outlook?

Chances of full recovery tend to be poor, because most cases are not diagnosed until they are well advanced. However, the outlook for colon cancer is improving as treatment improves. If the tumour is completely removed and has not spread, then a cure is likely. Colonoscopy (p. 115) is used as a screening tool for colorectal cancer.

ULCERATIVE COLITIS

See Inflammatory bowel disease, p. 148.

LIVING WITH A COLOSTOMY

I have suffered from ulcerative colitis for many years, and after a particularly severe attack a few years ago my specialist recommended that I have a colostomy.

I was very reluctant, because I knew it would mean having a colostomy bag and I was frightened of how it would make me feel about my body. Would people be able to see it? Or worse still, smell it? Would I still be able to go swimming? And what about things like sex? Eventually, the pain of my condition forced me to reconsider and although it has taken me some time to get used to it, living with 'the bag' has not been as bad as I'd imagined – few people even know I wear one.

A specialist stoma nurse, taught me how to change the bag, which I have to do after every bowel motion. After the operation these were frequent, but the nurse assured me they would settle down after a few weeks and they did – now they're like clockwork. I have to watch what I eat, because some foods create a lot of gas, which can blow the bag up! Also, my skin sometimes gets irritated by the adhesive used to attach the bags. I did have to give up swimming, but my family and especially my husband have been very supportive, and my life is pretty well back to normal – better, because I'm not in pain.

Index

Acknowledgments

Carroll & Brown Limited would also like to thank:

Editorial assistant
Charlotte Beech

Picture researchers
Richard Soar, Sandra Schneider

Production manager
Karol Davies

Production controller
Nigel Reed

Computer management
Elisa Merino, Paul Stradling

Indexer
Kathy Croom

3-D anatomy
Mirashade/Matt Gould, Lee Harding

Illustrators
Andy Baker, Jacey, Debbie Maizels, Mikki Rain, Nick Veasey, Philip Wilson, John Woodcock

Photographers
Jules Selmes, David Murray

Photographic sources
1 SPL
6 *(left)* Biophoto Associates
  (right) Prof S Cinti/CNRI/SPL
7 Howard Sochurek/MII/Medipics
8 *(top)* Images Colour Library
  (top left) BSIP Dr Pichard T/SPL
9 *(top)* Telegraph Colour Library
  (bottom) Alfred Pasieka/SPL
10 *(top left)* GettyOne Stone
  (bottom) Scott Camazine/SPL
10/11 GettyOne Stone
  (background) Images Colour Library
11 *(top)* BSIP Dr Pichard T/SPL
  (bottom left) GettyOne Stone
12 *(top)* Biophoto Associates/SPL
13 TEK Image/SPL
14 *(left)* Dan McCoy/Rainbow/SPL
  (right) GettyOne Stone
15 Scott Camazine/SPL
16 *(bottom left)* Scott Camazine/SPL
19 *(top)* GettyOne Stone
20 *(bottom left)* Telegraph Colour Library
  (bottom right) Biophoto Associates/SPL
21 *(top)* Wellcome Medical Library, Medical Arts Service, Munich
  (bottom) British Technical Films/SPL
22 CNRI/SPL
24 *(right)* Telegraph Colour Library
25 *(right)* Prof PM Motta/Dept of Anatomy/University 'La Sapienza', Rome/SPL
26 *(top)* Quest/SPL
  (bottom) Biophoto Associates
28/9 Profs PM Motta and T Naguro/SPL
30 GettyOne Stone
32 Scott Camazine/SPL
33 Dan McCoy/Rainbow/Medipics
34 GettyOne Stone
35 *(top)* GettyOne Stone
  (second from top) Pictor
38 *(top right)* Telegraph Colour Library
40 Nick Veasey/Untitled
41 Telegraph Colour Library
42 *(bottom)* GettyOne Stone
43 CNRI/SPL
45 *(top right)* Telegraph Colour Library
49 Prof S Cinti/CNRI/SPL
51 *(right, second from bottom)* Carl Schmidt-Luchs/SPL
  (right, bottom) Telegraph Colour Library
53 Image Bank
54 *(left)* GettyOne Stone
58 Carl Schmidt-Luchs/SPL
59 GettyOne Stone
60 Telegraph Colour Library
62 *(left)* Science Pictures/Oxford Scientific Films
67 *(top)* Image Bank
  (bottom centre) The Stock Market
70 Dr Kari Lounatmaa/SPL
71 *(left)* Secchi-Lecaque/Roussel-UCLAF/CNRI/SPL
76 Nick Veasey/Untitled
83 *(left)* The Stock Market
88 *(top)* The Stock Market
89 *(top)* GettyOne Stone
90 *(left)* BSIP VEM/SPL
  (right) Alfred Pasieka/SPL
91 Mehau Kulyk/SPL
94 *(bottom)* David Scharf/SPL
97 GettyOne Stone
100 *(bottom)* Profs P M Motta and F M Magliocca/SPL
101 *(left)* Jim Varney/SPL
102 *(top)* P Hawtin, University of Southampton/SPL
  (bottom) John Greim/SPL
103 BSIP Dr Pichard T/SPL
104 *(left)* BSIP Gems/Europe/SPL
  (right) BSIP VEM/SPL
105 Simon Fraser/RVI, Newcastle Upon Tyne/SPL
106/7 Chris Priest/SPL
107 *(top)* Salisbury District Hospital
  (bottom) SPL
108 SPL
109 *(top left, bottom right)* Kevin Harrison/Medipics
110 Dr Klaus Schiller/SPL
111 Dr V S Wong
112 *(left)* KeyMed
  (right) Kevin Harrison/Medipics
113 Kevin Harrison/Medipics
115 *(top right)* BSIP VEM/SPL
  (bottom) CNRI/SPL
117 *(top)* Prof P Motta/Dept of Anatomy/University 'La Sapienza', Rome/SPL
  (bottom) Profs P M Motta, K R Porter and P M Andrews/SPL
119 *(left)* Prof J James/SPL
  (right) Manfred Kage/SPL
120 *(top)* Dr Kari Lounatmaa/SPL
122 *(top)* Profs P M Motta and F M Magliocca/SPL
  (bottom) Howard Sochurek/MII/Medipics
123 *(top)* BSIP VEM/SPL
  (bottom) Alfred Pasieka/SPL
124 *(left)* Kevin Harrison/Medipics
  (right) Volker Steger/SPL
125 *(left)* BSIP Laurent/H American/SPL
  (right) Dr V S Wong
126 Antonia Reeve/SPL
127 *(left)* Mehau Kulyk/SPL
  (centre) Biophoto Associates/SPL
  (right) Mig/Medipics
128/9 Kevin Harrison/Medipics
130 SPL
131 Robert Harris/Medipics

Back cover *(right)* Prof J James/SPL